Manufactured in the United States of America
First Printing 2000

MONEY MAGAZINE

MANAGING EDITOR Robert Safian **EXECUTIVE EDITOR** Eric Gelman, Denise B. Martin **ASSISTANT MANAGING EDITORS** Glenn Coleman, Craig Matters (website), Sheryl Hilliard Tucker **EDITORS-AT-LARGE** Jean Sherman Chatzky, Michael Sivy **SENIOR EDITORS** Marion Asnes, Jim Frederick, Jon Gertner, William Green, Alexander Haris, Ellen Stark, Teresa Tritch, Walter Updegrave **SENIOR WRITER/COLUMNIST** Jason Zweig **ASSOCIATE EDITOR** Scott Medintz **SENIOR WRITERS** Peter Carbonara, Jerry Edgerton, Amy Feldman, Pablo Galarza, John Helyar, Amy Dockser Marcus, Pat Regnier, Penelope Wang, Suzanne Woolley **STAFF WRITERS** Joan Caplin, Lisa Reilly Cullen, David Futrelle, Lisa Gibbs, Leslie Haggin, Laura Lallos, Jeanne Lee, Eric Moskowitz, Nick Pachetti, Rob Turner, Carolyn Whelan **WRITER-REPORTERS** Adrienne Carter, Brian L. Clark, Jeff Nash, Michael J. Powe, Laura Washington **CONTRIBUTING WRITERS** Paul Lukas, Bethany McLean, Joseph Nocera, Andrew Serwer, Rob Walker **ART DIRECTOR** Syndi C. Becker **DEPUTY ART DIRECTOR** Scott A. Davis **SENIOR ASSOCIATE ART DIRECTOR** MaryAnn Salvato **ASSOCIATE ART DIRECTORS** Marci Papineau, Michael Scowden **DESIGNERS** Semi Kang, Steven Oh **INFORMATION GRAPHICS DESIGNER** Myra Klockenbrink **ART PRODUCTION COORDINATOR** Tommy McCall **PICTURE EDITOR** Jane Clark **DEPUTY PICTURE EDITOR** Cathy Mather **FEATURES PICTURE EDITOR** Betsy Keating **ASSISTANT PICTURE EDITOR** Shawn Vale **CHIEF OF REPORTERS** Katharine B. Drake **SENIOR STAFF** Judy Feldman, Roberta Kirwan **STAFF** Andrea Bennett, Erica Garcia, Grace Jidoun, Patrice D. Johnson, Daphne D. Mosher (mail), Brian P. Murphy, Natasha Rafi **EDITORIAL PRODUCTION MANAGER** Allegra-Jo Lagani **COPY CHIEF** Patricia A. Feimster **OPERATIONS CHIEF** Lionel P. Vargas **SENIOR COORDINATOR** Sukey Rosenbaum **STAFF** Sally Boggan, Martha E. Bula Torres, John D'Antonio, Judith Ferbel, Emily Harrow, Eve Sennett, Libby Stephens **PUBLIC RELATIONS DIRECTOR** Patrick Taylor **ASSISTANT TO THE MANAGING EDITOR** Lysa Price **ADMINISTRATIVE COORDINATOR, DESIGN** Llubia Reyes **STAFF** Merrily Brooks, Amy Wilson **CONTRIBUTING CORRESPONDENTS** Linda Berlin, Barbara Hordern, Ann S. Knol, Stephen Marsh, Melanie J. Mavrides, Laura Mecoy, Marcia R. Pledger, Elizabeth S. Roberts, Carol F. Shepley, Nancy Stesin, Jeff Wuorio **CONTRIBUTING TAX EDITOR** Mary L. Sprouse **DIRECTOR OF IMAGING** Richard J. Sheridan **IMAGING STAFF** Janet Miller (manager), Michael D. Brennan, Edward G. Carnesi, Jeffrey Chan, Janet Gonzalez, Marco Lau, Angel A. Mass, Kent Michaud, Stanley E. Moyse, Claudio M. Muller, Lorri O. Stenton, Paul Tupay **DIRECTOR OF TECHNOLOGY** Jeffrey W. Fulton **TECHNOLOGY STAFF** Al Criscuolo, Kevin Kersey (technology managers), Lawrence J. Shine (database administrator), John Deer, Frank B. Cuffe (systems administrators), Paul Nocera, Joe Z. Peng, Andrew M. Ross, Michael Sheehan **WEBSITE DESIGN DIRECTOR** Caldwell Toll **PRODUCTION DIRECTOR** Mark Thomas **PRODUCTION MANAGER** Tim Ungs **PRODUCER** Waits May **PROGRAMMER** German Todorov **ASSOCIATE PRODUCER** Borzou Daragahi **PRODUCTION ASSISTANT** Eric Mortensen **ADMINISTRATIVE ASSISTANT** Savy Mangru

TIME INC. HOME ENTERTAINMENT

PRESIDENT Stuart Hotchkiss **EXECUTIVE DIRECTOR, BRANDED BUSINESSES** David Arfine **EXECUTIVE DIRECTOR, NON BRANDED BUSINESSES** Alicia Longobardo **EXECUTIVE DIRECTOR, TIME INC. BRAND LICENSING** Risa Turken **DIRECTOR, LICENSING** Scott Rosenzweig **EXECUTIVE DIRECTOR, MARKETING SERVICES** Carol Pittard **DIRECTOR, RETAIL & SPECIAL SALES** Tom Mifsud **DIRECTOR, BRANDED BUSINESSES** Maarten Terry **ASSOCIATE DIRECTORS** Roberta Harris, Kenneth Maehlum **PRODUCT MANAGERS** Dana Gregory, Andre Okolowitz Ann Marie Ross, Niki Viswanathan, Daria Raehse **ASSOCIATE PRODUCT MANAGERS** Victoria Alfonso, Jennifer Dowell, Dennis Sheehan, Meredith Shelley, Lauren Zaslansky **ASSISTANT PRODUCT MANAGERS** Ann Gillespie, Meredith Peters, Virginia Valdes **TELEMARKETING MANAGER** Marina Weinstein **ASSOCIATE MANAGER, E-COMMERCE** Dima Masrizada **LICENSING MANAGER** Joanna West **ASSOCIATE LICENSING MANAGER** Regina Feiler **LICENSING COORDINATOR** Laury Shapiro **ASSOCIATE MANAGER, RETAIL & NEW MARKETS** Bozena Szwagulinski **COORDINATOR, RETAIL MARKETING** Gina Di Meglio **EDITORIAL OPERATIONS DIRECTOR** John Calvano **ASSISTANT EDITORIAL OPERATIONS DIRECTOR** Emily Rabin **BOOK PRODUCTION MANAGER** Jessica McGrath **ASSOCIATE BOOK PRODUCTION MANAGER** Jonathan Polsky **ASSISTANT BOOK PRODUCTION MANAGER** Suzanne DeBenedetto **FULFILLMENT MANAGER** Richard Perez **ASSISTANT FULFILLMENT MANAGER** Tara Schimmimg **FINANCIAL DIRECTOR** Tricia Griffin **FINANCIAL MANAGER** Robert Dente **ASSOCIATE FINANCIAL MANAGER** Steven Sandonato **ASSISTANT FINANCIAL MANAGER** Tamara Whittier **EXECUTIVE ASSISTANT** Mary Jane Rigoroso

Library of Congress Catalogue Card Number: 00-103197

MONEY BOOK SERIES
DESIGNER Laura Ierardi, LCI Design

HARDCOVER ISBN: 1-929049-09-9

Profitable Investing in the New Century

■ Andrew Feinberg
and the Editors of MONEY

MONEY BOOKS

Time Inc. Home Entertainment / 1271 Avenue of the Americas / New York, NY 10020

Contents

Introduction

*T*his is an extraordinarily exciting time to be an investor. The U.S. market has just enjoyed the greatest 18-year run in its history. In 1999, the Nasdaq Composite rose 85.6%, posting the largest single-year advance for any index—ever. Ground-breaking new companies are emerging almost every day; many of them insist they will make our lives better and help us live longer. (Forget the stocks, where can we get our hands on the *products?*)

Never has investing assumed such a central role in our culture. Friends who seldom used to talk about the market now give stock tips. Friends who used to discuss stocks occasionally now hardly speak of anything else. Utter strangers feel free to buttonhole you, eager to share the next great—really great—investment idea. Why is it always something you've never heard of?

It's exhilarating—but it can also be unnerving and downright scary at times. Are the rapid gains of recent years, coupled with so much public fixation on the market, really a sign of impending doom?

Well, doom's cousin actually arrived in March 2000 and, as far as tech stocks were concerned, didn't depart until May. And what a visit. The Nasdaq Composite fell 40% in two months, a decline most textbooks would call a crash. TheStreet.com Internet Sector index fell over 50% from March 9 to April 14, a more devastating plunge than the Dow suffered in the 1929 Crash.

As we write this, things have improved—but what the heck does that mean? We're not precisely sure, but there are things we feel pretty certain about, and that's what we've tried to put in *Profitable Investing in the New Century.*

We still believe that stocks are the essential component of a long-term investment plan, but, because virtually every American capable of speech seems to know that already, we are convinced that stock and mutual fund selection must be done with more care than ever. We believe in equities, but with pockets of the market overvalued, we don't believe in *all* equities.

Some of the equities we like are part of the "New Economy." We think millions of investors should have Internet and biotech stocks—or funds—in their portfolios. But these packets of boundless promise should be consumed like alcohol—in moderation.

It's no surprise that believers in moderation should consider diversification to be an essential element of investment strategy, even though it has become a repugnant concept for many investors. "Got any other tools that will lower my returns?" we've heard some people ask. (No, not that we know of.) We even discuss bonds at length, despite the fact that, these days, the word "bond" is rarely mentioned in polite conversation.

Facing the New Century with Confidence

The goal of this book is to help you face the new century with confidence, and with all the necessary investment tools at your command. We tell you which 100 stocks to focus on in any market environment, and indicate when each might be a good buy. Our section on mutual funds lists 100 funds to buy right now; it is an ideal place to look for funds that could fill in a gap in your portfolio, or simply spruce it up. We also address the most confounding, annoying and sometimes excruciating decision in the investment universe: when to bid farewell to some of your stocks and funds.

The book's chapter on online investment tools may not make you a software expert, but it will greatly enhance your knowledge of where to go for the best information, the best analytic tools and the top brokers on the Web. Two of our favorite chapters are "Tax-Smart Investing" and "Avoiding the Biggest Investing Mistakes." Both will probably save you a lot of money in ways you never imagined.

We also include essential information about understanding risk (we want to improve your returns *and* keep you safe), handling stock options (you wouldn't believe how many people bungle theirs), five steps to a great retirement, managing your

401(k) and the important new tools that will help you save for college. There's a lot of great advice and we'd be dumbfounded if much of it doesn't prove helpful to you.

The new century will bring fantastic investment opportunities, some of them unimaginable today. We hope you participate in many of them. Early retirement isn't in the book's title, but we hope it might be in your future. Enjoy.

CHAPTER 1

Today's Wild Market and the New Economy

*I*f the stock market's performance throughout 2000 feels unusual, that's because it is. Stocks haven't been this volatile since the Depression. And it's not just the ups and downs that are driving investors batty, it's the way different sectors go in and out of fashion, seemingly overnight. As for consistency, there doesn't seem to be any. On a given day, the Dow can plunge while the Nasdaq soars, or vice versa. No wonder the Old Economy vs. New Economy debates continue.

The market moves are fantastic. In less than a year, the Nasdaq Composite rose by more than 100%, only to dive 40% in just two months. Imagine how those who arrived late to the party must have felt? That kind of volatility is unnerving to say the least, especially considering the extent to which we've staked our future on the stock market. Not only our retirement planning and college tuition savings, but our whole economy is tied to the performance of stocks like never before. The rapid twists and turns and the seemingly random nature of it all are enough to make an investor despair of ever understanding the market.

What about valuation? Judged by almost every measure, the overall market seems expensive historically. Nonetheless, there are hundreds of stocks that are cheap by standard measures of value. We would buy many of them at current prices. On the other hand, some of the most adored companies on the Street are trading at 100, 200, 500 or 1000 times earnings—if they have any earnings. We consider many of them overvalued, but accept the premise that some will become pillars of the New Economy. To ignore their promise would be foolish. Our advice: Buy some of them on dips—very *big* dips.

More Trades, Bigger Moves

As investors struggle to find the right value for stocks in an era of unprecedented demand for equities and relentless technological change, volatility and volume have surged.

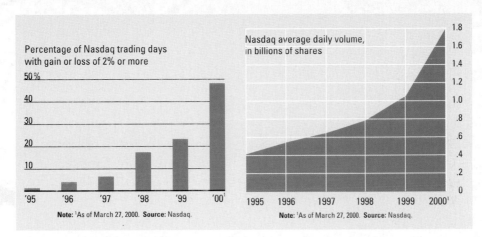

Percentage of Nasdaq trading days with gain or loss of 2% or more

Note: ¹As of March 27, 2000. **Source:** Nasdaq.

Nasdaq average daily volume, in billions of shares

Note: ¹As of March 27, 2000. **Source:** Nasdaq.

What kind of market is this? It is quite possible that what is happening to stocks really does make no sense—that we are in the grip of a national (or perhaps global) speculative frenzy. Perhaps it will end badly for all of us who are invested, and stockbrokers will begin jumping from windows again on Wall Street. It is certainly possible. But it seems to us that the market gyrations are not signs of madness. Far from it. We would argue that what looks like irrational exuberance or profound depression when viewed day by day seems much more sensible when you take a step back and look at the very real factors underpinning the market's astonishing behavior.

The three-tiered market. You often read that we have had a two-tier market as we did in the early 1970s: For years investors have been throwing money at a handful of "must own" names while neglecting everything else, especially value stocks. And indeed, in 1999 just nine stocks accounted for half of the return of the S&P 500 index, led by richly-valued tech giants Cisco Systems and Oracle. A recent variation on this theory says that we are actually experiencing a three-tier market, with the third tier being a fringe of gee-whiz stocks with great stories and scant—or non-existent—earnings.

These descriptions are credible and intriguing—but ultimately, we think, misleading. The implication is that a tiered market is inherently unstable; that as investors concentrate on fewer and fewer stocks, the market becomes increasingly vulnerable to a collapse. If these favored few should stumble, the argument goes, investors will flee all equities for more secure havens like bonds or cash. That, after all, is what happened in the 1970s with the collapse of the Nifty Fifty.

Yet if the history of this record-breaking bull market has shown us anything, it is that a meltdown in one sector—whether speculative or blue chip—does not send investors scurrying for shelter outside of equities. On the contrary, investors have stubbornly stuck with stocks, simply shifting from one corner of the market to another. Not so long ago, you'll recall, consumer blue chips were the can't-miss core of our bull market—Coca-Cola and Gillette and their ilk were powering our portfolios. But between July 1998 and March 2000, Coke lost half its value, wiping out a huge $100 billion in investors' wealth. What has this collapse of a Nifty Fifty kind of stock done to cool our ardor for equities? Nothing.

The rotational bull market. Indeed, in a market often described as moving relentlessly upward, investors have had to absorb more pain—more crushing losses—than the pundits generally recognize. Small-cap stocks—which had led the charge from 1991 to 1993, pushing the top mutual funds of the day to triple-digit returns—lagged the S&P 500 by 116 percentage points over the next six years.

Yet no amount of pain seems enough to end our love affair with stocks. From March to May of 2000, hundreds of technology stocks suffered horrific declines. Many experts had predicted that such an event would kill off the bull market, but that didn't happen.

The truth is, this bull market has been defined by a series of interlocking mini-bull and mini-bear markets, where various sectors zoomed as others sank or stagnated. That's why we think what we have today is not a tiered market but a rotational market. When bad news hits a stock or sector, investors may be quick to abandon it—but they don't flee the market. That raises an obvious question: Why?

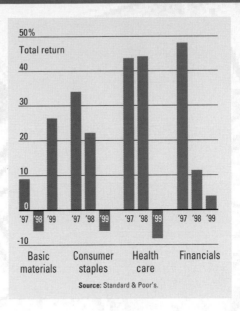

While the major stock indexes have moved steadily upward for years, different sectors of the market have taken turns leading the charge and falling behind. Among the groups that have had rapid reversals of fortune lately are basic materials, consumer staples, financial and health-care stocks.

Only stocks will substantially grow your money.
There are a host of fundamental economic reasons why stocks have thrived during the past 18 years. But one crucial factor is that as a nation we seem to have decided that we absolutely have to own stocks—that we cannot afford not to.

This is clearly something new. With the gradual elimination of traditional corporate pensions, growing doubts about the future of Social Security and longer life expectancies, we have come to recognize that we must be prepared to fund our own retirements. And if we hope to have any security and comfort during those years, we've learned, we need to make our money grow. We've also seen that after accounting for the withering effects of taxes and inflation, passbook savings accounts and bonds simply will not get the job done. Nor can we count on real estate. We need growth. As a result, we are pouring more and more money into stocks. During the past decade, some $1.3 trillion has flowed into equity mutual funds alone.

And if we all need to buy stocks, it makes perfect sense that their price has risen. After all, under every economic model, when a commodity is highly prized—when it is something that buyers

We're Addicted to Stocks

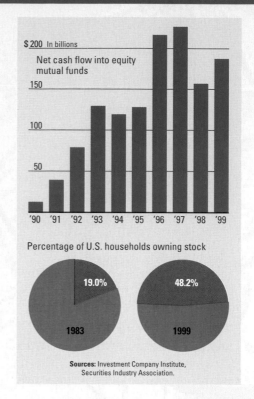

$200 In billions

Net cash flow into equity mutual funds

150

100

50

'90 '91 '92 '93 '94 '95 '96 '97 '98 '99

Percentage of U.S. households owning stock

19.0%

1983

48.2%

1999

Sources: Investment Company Institute, Securities Industry Association.

We know we need stocks to fund our retirement. Since 1990 we've poured more than $1.3 trillion into equity mutual funds. And the percentage of households owning stocks has soared.

simply can't do without—its cost will naturally go up. If you think back to the 1970s, very few people thought, "I must own stocks or stock mutual funds to be able to retire." Now nearly everyone does. That paradigm shift helps explain why historical valuation measures no longer seem to apply.

Where the volatility comes in. This does not mean, of course, that all extreme stock valuations make sense. On the contrary, there are many pockets of excess. And when investors decide that an investment isn't going to justify their lofty expectations—as happened with small-caps in the mid-1990s or Coca-Cola during the past two years—they quickly knock it down to earth. Investments that have attained the most radical valuations, like the e-tailers, get hammered hardest and fastest.

The market has been described as a giant mechanism for processing information. In that sense, the recent volatility simply reflects the struggle of investors to find the right valuations for stocks at a time when demand for them is at unprecedented levels—and when new technologies are constantly appearing, offering the tantalizing prospect of vast profits.

The new volatility also reflects the flood of information that inundates investors throughout the day. It has gotten easier and cheaper to act on this information as well, via the vast network of discount brokerages online and offline. Since 1994, when Ameritrade became the first company to offer Internet trading, the number of online brokerage accounts has climbed to 7 million.

Chasing profits; searching for safety. More recently, another factor has exacerbated market rotations: our own impatience. Buoyed by years of fantastic returns, we've become a lot less tolerant of stocks that don't deliver big profits right away. Instead of giving diversification time to work, we flit from one sector to another, chasing performance. When e-tailers disappoint, the hot money shifts to business-to-business plays, or to biotech, or to wireless.

Now another question emerges: How can you protect yourself from rapid market rotations? The difficult truth is that you probably can't. This is simply the modern version of the volatility that has always been a part of stock market investing. It has never been prudent to try to predict short-term swings—no one has found a way to do it consistently—and we wouldn't suggest you start trying. After all, the long-term argument for equities remains solidly in place—for now.

Looking at the big picture. So far, we've focused mainly on internal market dynamics—investment flows, volatility and our commitment to stocks. But there is obviously more underpinning the bull market than that. Over the long term, we believe, stock prices reflect the strength of the U.S. economy and the conditions of the world we live in. And that big picture is unquestionably good.

What could change investors' sunny outlook? As we've seen, a series of sharp selloffs in various market sectors through the years has not been enough to shake investors' faith in stocks. It would require more than a transient crisis—it would have to be something that would fundamentally alter the conditions that have supported our prosperity. Events such as soaring oil prices, a civil war in China or an unexpected disaster at home such as an earthquake, terrorist attack or nuclear accident would certainly change our reality for the worse. But even if you could predict the future, how would you know the right place to safely stow your assets in the event of such a catastrophe? U.S. bonds? The bank? Your mattress?

So where does that leave you as an investor? You could decide that stock market valuations are well ahead of themselves and that before long something will happen to make people rush out of stocks. You could go to cash or some other asset class as a safety measure. But over the past few years that has proved to be the riskiest course for investors—especially those who really need growth—as they've been summarily left behind. The alternative is to recognize the reality of the market climate we're in. That dictates a three-part strategy:

1. Accept the fact that eventually some of your equity holdings will dramatically and precipitously decline. Serious pain is endemic to this market. If you're going to be in it, you'd better get used to it.

2. Pare back on some of your biggest winners that will probably take the most serious hits. Pain is even more likely within the priciest segments of the market—the frothy tech names, including the highly profitable giants.

3. Commit new capital to solid companies in areas of the market that investors have temporarily shunned. Look at Warren Buffett's Berkshire Hathaway, which fell dramatically out of favor during 1999, making it well positioned for a comeback. Or look at what happened to Disney, which late in 1999 was being widely derided but then snapped back smartly.

In other words, our strategy can be summed up in that old saw: "Buy low, sell high." It sounds trite. But all the volatility we've seen has masked the simple truth that nothing has really changed when it comes to the fundamentals: Buy good companies and hold them; diversify; and be prepared to take some hits.

It isn't sexy, but it works.

Investing in the Post-PC Era

But what, exactly, works when you're trying to invest in the fastest-growing and most promising segments of the economy? That's what the rest of this chapter will try to address.

You can say that you believe in technology stocks, but the question must be asked: *which* technology stocks? Will the companies that have been stalwarts of so many portfolios—Microsoft, Intel, Dell, Gateway and Compaq—continue to perform well in the post-PC era? Who will profit most from the great upheavals that are sure to come?

As we see it, there are five distinct ways to invest in the New Economy:

1. You can buy, or continue to hold, the household tech titans that dominated the 1990s. Some will continue to make enormous progress in the 2000s; some will not.

2. You can pick up some of the new blue-chip stocks. These include the powers in networking, semiconductors and wireless that seem poised for many years of stellar growth.

3. You can live life closer to the edge, investing in Internet and biotech companies—or funds—that may deliver almost unimaginably large returns—or huge losses that will, at least, reduce your tax bill.

4. You can try to win at the IPO game. This doesn't require special access to new offerings; what you need instead is the willingness to buy new issues in the aftermarket once the initial buying fever has run its course.

5. Or, of course, you can entrust your money to one of the fine technology fund managers in the MONEY 100 (see Chapter 3), which is by no means a bad idea.

Threats to the Tech Titans

PC sales growth is slowing and experts see an enormous surge in the sales of competing Internet Appliances (IAs). Indeed, market research firm IDC figures that Internet appliances, including mobile phones, interactive TVs, PDAs and video-game consoles, will outsell home PCs by 2002. People who just want access to the Internet don't need a PC, which will drive IA sales for many years and scare the heck out of most PC makers.

Who has the most to lose in the post-PC era? The instinctive response may be the Wintel duopoly, since

Microsoft's software and Intel's chips have dominated the definition of the PC—their gear is on an estimated 90% of the world's PCs. "The whole world is about to change," says Michael Murphy, author of *California Technology Stock Letter*, "and the No. 1 guy is usually the most threatened."

Threatened, yes. In mortal danger? Probably not. Let's see how some of the largest old-guard gorillas measure up in today's world.

■ **Microsoft.** Microsoft has undoubtedly been the biggest beneficiary of the PC era. Ever since it rolled out MS-DOS back in 1981, Microsoft's bread and butter has been selling the world's most popular operating system, the core software program that manages the computer's look, feel and functionality. But now comes the prospect of a new era, in which more people will use IAs to get online and access Net-based applications once they get there. As a result, for the first time since perhaps Netscape's IPO in 1995, people are discussing a computing world where Microsoft is not dominant.

Yet Microsoft's strengths remain enormous, whether the court-ordered break-up of the company is ever carried out or not. Microsoft's $18 billion cash hoard plus its canny partnerships with 150 or so companies have bought it plenty of time to survey the changing landscape. It remains well positioned to capitalize on the future of the Net, whatever that future might look like. Christopher W. Mortenson of Deutsche Bank Alex. Brown expects Microsoft's Net operations to grow 50% this year, to $1.2 billion, and to reach $2 billion in 2001.

■ **Intel.** CEO Craig Barrett has pushed Intel to abandon its single-minded focus on PC processors and refashion itself into a semiconductor maker that can accommodate the more diverse chip needs of the Internet age.

The company recently unveiled a line of chips designed to speed data traffic through the Internet's pipes. It purchased DSP Communications for $1.6 billion, a strong player in wireless digital phone technology. And it presented a line of high-end servers that will populate the server farms the company is building for its entry into Internet services and Web hosting.

On sale as well: Intel-branded Internet appliances like phones, e-mail machines and TV set-top boxes that allow users to surf the Web. But that may not be enough. And Intel has been rocked by consumers' quickly changing PC tastes, which have slowed profit growth to an anemic compounded 8% over the past two years. "Intel Inside" no longer has the same cachet now that many consumers are perfectly happy working on sub-$1,000 computers loaded with budget chips from AMD or other rivals.

■ **Gateway.** The company should profit dramatically from the rapid growth of IAs and the Internet. Gateway not only makes IA hardware, but it also delivers services through its own fast-growing ISP. Gateway began 2000 with about 400,000 paying subscribers, according to Credit Suisse First Boston analyst Mike Kwatinetz. By the end of 2000, he expects that number to jump to 2.5 million. Two years ago, 100% of the company's profits came from selling PCs. Last year, the first under new CEO Jeffrey Weitzen, it earned 20% from non-PC related businesses like ISPs. In 2000, the goal is to reach 30%.

■ **Dell.** For a dissenting opinion on the significance of Internet appliances, look to Dell, which has no plans to join the first round of the Internet appliance wars. Why? In Dell's view, says senior vice president Carl Everett, "The PC will remain the center of the home."

Frankly, missing this battle probably will not hurt the world's most profitable PC maker. Unlike Gateway or Compaq, Dell has never made consumer markets one of its first priorities anyway. Dell sells nearly 70% of its systems to the government and large businesses, and much of its current growth is coming from the server market, laptops and foreign sales.

Still, Dell has misjudged consumer trends before, to the detriment of its business and its stock price. In 1997, for instance, Dell was insisting that the sub-$1,000 PC was a niche market it could safely ignore. When that market in fact exploded, Dell was a late arrival. For that transgression, as well as for allowing its revenue growth rate to slip below its historically breakneck pace, Dell's stock has had an uncharacteristically bumpy ride in recent years.

■ **AOL and Yahoo!.** For AOL and Yahoo!, the proliferation of new, cheaper Internet access devices should be a boon rather than a threat. The IA revolution may cause profits to roar at AOL and Yahoo! in ways that many investors have not yet imagined.

When you turn on your computer, the first thing that you probably see is either the Windows start bar at the bottom of your screen or the Apple menu bar at the top. Now imagine your computer with a connection to the Internet that is always up and running. What will the screen look like? Who will provide the interface, if the Macintosh and Windows desktops are either not required or perpetually pushed to the background? AOL or Yahoo!, the two most popular destinations on the Net, may well fill that role.

AOL and Yahoo! aim to be your window on everything the Net has to offer. It may turn out that the age of Net appliances will do more than drive traffic to the two portals—it will give AOL and Yahoo! a chance to challenge Microsoft's dominance of the desktop-software business. The rise of AOL and Yahoo! as dominant computing platforms would provide exactly the kind of long-term growth that investors in these stocks are betting on. The big question for investors, however, is whether this move into, effectively, the software business—which is, as yet, no more than a tantalizing possibility—would provide an extra measure of growth beyond what is already priced into the stocks.

AOL (which is merging with Time Warner, corporate parent of MONEY magazine) is the best positioned and most financially sound pure-play Internet company. But it has a triple-digit multiple. Yahoo!, though, has a P/E multiple almost twice as high; it makes AOL look like a bargain.

The New Blue Chips

The clear winners in the new world of technology are companies that construct the infrastructure of the Internet; semiconductor companies that sell to the Internet infrastructure companies and makers of wireless devices; and the companies that own the wireless phone networks and manufacture the best wireless phones. Among these elite companies are Cisco Systems, the networking king; EMC, the storage behemoth; Exodus Communications, the powerhouse in Web hosting; Oracle, the database software and B2B champ; and Sun Microsystems, whose servers are ubiquitous in the Internet world. Other potential beneficiaries include National Semiconductor, Sandisk and Smartdisk. (To learn more about them, see the table on the opposite page.)

The virtues of Cisco, EMC, Exodus, Oracle and Sun are so evident and so universally appreciated that we see little reason

Stocks to Watch in the Post-PC Era

Cisco Systems, Oracle, Sun Microsystems, EMC and Exodus Communications will benefit from increased reliance on the Internet. Unfortunately, these companies are anything but cheap. But after a sharp setback, we'd consider buying them. You also might want to consider other companies that will benefit directly from the rise of IAs, such as National Semiconductor, Sandisk and Smartdisk.

COMPANY NAME (TICKER)	SHARE PRICE	52-WEEK HIGH	52-WEEK LOW	P/E	LONG-TERM GROWTH RATE	PEG RATIO	COMMENTS
Cisco Systems (CSCO)	$67.81	$82	$28	127.9	30%	4.3	It sells essential Net hardware.
EMC (EMC)	79.25	80	26	107.1	30	3.6	The leader in network data backup
Exodus Communications (EXDS)	103.25	180	22	–	100	–	It hosts the world's websites.
Gateway (GTW)	57.56	84	28	31.4	22	1.4	Sells both Net appliances and access.
National Semiconductor (NSM)	61.19	86	21	21.1	18	1.2	Geode: chipset of choice for appliances.
Oracle (ORCL)	81.88	90	17	127.9	25	5.1	Database software is key to e-commerce.
Sandisk (SNDK)	63.81	170	18	71.7	30	2.4	Flash memory replaces hard drives.
Smartdisk (SMDK)	23.94	68	13	59.8	30	2.0	Its FireWire shuttles data faster.
Sun Microsystems (SUNW)	91.31	107	31	95.0	20	4.8	Its high-end servers help run the Web.

Note: Prices as of June 16, 2000. **Source:** Dow Jones.

to discuss them at length. All we can say to potential investors is: At these prices, be careful. Don't buy your entire stake all at once.

But a different group of new blue chips has received comparatively less attention, and we think they're very worthy of your attention. They are key players in wireless communications, which is on the cusp of blossoming into "m-commerce."

The wonderful world of wireless. Qualcomm, which licenses CDMA chipsets and system software for cell phones, rose more in 1999—2,600%—than many stocks rise in a lifetime. Nokia, Sprint PCS and several other wireless companies have also emerged as stock market darlings. These days, it seems, every company is positioning itself as the next great wireless play.

The rise of "m-commerce." In this new paradigm, "m" stands for mobile. Very soon, millions of consumers will be able to use their phones to buy and sell stocks, send and receive e-mail, purchase airline and movie tickets, order dinner, get news, weather, sports and horoscopes and browse the Internet.

Consultants at the Yankee Group predict that the wireless data market, as all this activity is called, will explode from $1.8 billion this year to $13.2 billion by 2003. (As early as 2001, nearly a third of new phones shipped in North America will have some ability to tap the Web.) The wireless data phenomenon already has done wonders for NTT DoCoMo, Japan's biggest mobile phone operator and now the most valuable company in the Nikkei index. Between February 1999 and February 2000, DoCoMo signed 4 million subscribers to a service called i-Mode that has access to 4,000 websites.

DoCoMo's quick success helps explain why British phone giant Vodafone Airtouch aggressively pursued and captured Germany's Mannesmann. The merger, the biggest ever, creates the world's largest wireless provider. "Mobile data and the internet will be the strongest driver of growth in our history," Vodafone CEO Chris Gent recently told analysts, predicting that wireless data will boost average revenue per user by 20% to 25% annually. Vodafone and companies like Nokia, analysts say, should mint profits from this trend for many years.

What's next for wireless? It all sounds grand, but what is really going to drive the growth that Gent forecasts? It has less to do with megadeals and more to do with technology: mobile networks must be upgraded to what's being called $2^{1}/_{2}$G (for "generation"—1G was analog; 2G is digital; 3G will be high-speed digital data).

Who will benefit from the upgrade? Much of the spending will flow to sellers of infrastructure, such as Canada's Nortel Networks and Sweden's Ericsson, a leading supplier of mobile network systems. Ericsson has won 50% of the $2^{1}/_{2}$G contracts so far, and with 1999's acquisition of Qualcomm's infrastructure business, it is well positioned for the coming 3G. If Ericsson can get its mobile-handset business back on track (market share fell to 12% from 15% in 1999), it should benefit big-time from wireless buzz.

Investing on the Edge

It is likely that the Internet and biotech will be two of the most successful businesses of the 21st century. But if you think the overall market is volatile, well, it's *nothing* compared to the roller coaster action in individual Internet and biotech issues, or in the sectors themselves. Which leads us to rule No. 1 of frontier investing: *Expect* volatility. Mad rises and terrifying dives come with the territory. Absent a major change in the fundamentals, hang on if you still believe in the company and its technology.

The Smart Way to Invest in the Internet

You don't need us to tell you that investing in the Internet can put a big hole in your wallet. A year ago, Beyond.com was a New Economy success story. The company had the bright idea of selling software over the Web—a perfect example of using the Internet to eliminate warehouses and lower costs. Microsoft co-founder Paul Allen loved the company and bankrolled it. Regular investors adored it too, and the stock soared from $9 to $40 in six months. But then the company failed miserably to meet analysts' revenue expectations. Today it's barely alive. The CEO has resigned; the company has laid off many of its workers. The stock languishes at $2^{1}/$_{32}$.

Beyond.com isn't alone. Everywhere you look there's carnage among Net stocks (see the table on page 20). Within a year after 1999's highs, Amazon was down 56%, Charles Schwab 33%, TheStreet.com 82%, Net.Bank 69%, eToys 93% and iVillage 89%. The papers are filled with news of embarrassing snafus in the formerly idyllic Internet world.

Clearly, Internet stocks can take stupendous dives.
But we think it's worth remembering that the Net has the potential to create wealth for a long, long time. In 1995, 5 million people were using the Web, according to market research firm International Data Corp. By the end of 2000, more than 400 million will be online. E-commerce has jumped from $2.4 billion to $20 billion in four years. By 2004, it will reach $184 billion, according to Forrester Research. Cyber bulls like Alberto Vilar, who heads Amerindo Investment Advisors, estimate that over the next five years Internet-related companies will account for $3 to $4 trillion of stock market capitalization, 10 times today's level.

E-tailers are Getting Smashed

Decline from 52-week high

eToys	−93%
iVillage	−89%
Autoweb	−86%
TheStreet.com	−82%
CDNow	−81%
Ameritrade	−72%
Amazon	−56%
AOL	−47%
Yahoo!	−44%
Charles Schwab	−33%

Note: Prices as of June 13, 2000. **Source:** Dow Jones.

How do you participate as an investor? Do you chase hot stocks willy-nilly? Do you buy overpriced market darlings like eBay or Amazon.com, which we don't believe can sustain their current extreme valuations? No.

Investors in Net stocks have an edge if they regard them not as betting slips but as real businesses—which is, after all, how they'll ultimately be valued. To do that, though, an investor has to disregard the six great myths of Internet stocks, myths that emerged and gained acceptance and cost some investors a lot of money.

■ **MYTH NO. 1.**
Profits don't matter. Eyeballs do.

Amazon.com founder Jeff Bezos likes to tell investors that he has no idea when his company will make money because he's focused on building a dominant Internet brand. Eventually, he assures them, profits will indeed come. And Yahoo!, now solidly, if unspectacularly, profitable, is held out as proof that earnings will follow once a Web business builds a massive audience.

Certainly, getting visitors to a site—and keeping them coming back—is important. But it's only half the equation. As Paul Cook, co-manager of the Munder NetNet fund, puts it, "If you have a great idea to attract users but no way to make money off of them, the traffic is worthless."

Two types of Web companies are particularly vulnerable: businesses that sell commodity products such as toys, groceries and the like; and businesses built on free services such as e-mail, electronic greeting cards, stock quotes, maps, content and what's known on the Web as "community" (message board services like iVillage). These nice freebies cost money to produce but don't bring in revenue from the end users. That means they have to depend on advertising, and ad rates are falling as the supply of Web pages soars.

Reality. The business model that's more likely to work on the Web is based on selling high-margin products, such as financial services, software or some of the business services listed in the table on page 25. If you're considering investing in such a company, ask the kinds of questions you would when researching a non-Web business. Are customers over time spending more money with the company? Does it have multiple revenue sources? If it isn't profitable, is it spending less on acquiring each new customer? Between regulatory filings and the vast amounts of free research online you should find answers to these questions.

■ **MYTH NO. 2.**

If it's a public company, it must be a real business.

Not long ago a private business had to show three years of steadily rising revenues, if not earnings, before selling stock to the public. Such a track record gave investors a sense of what the company was worth, and what they could expect down the road. Today the market has a higher tolerance for risk. Web companies have gone public with little, if any, proof that they have viable businesses. On the contrary, the IPO itself is now seen as the company's legitimizing event.

Reality. An IPO alone isn't a true sign of a solid business. A better one is backing by smart money—top venture capitalists and underwriters. Of recent IPOs, those backed by VCs have performed far better in the aftermarket.

VCs, who put up their money well before an IPO, vet scores and scores of business plans; they get to choose the most promising ideas to back. The fledgling enterprises, meanwhile, benefit from the VCs' connections with other companies, which could be potential customers or partners. You can find out who invested in a company before it went public by checking its prospectus. Among the names to keep in mind: Kleiner Perkins Caufield & Byers, an early backer of Netscape; Sequoia Capital, which funded Yahoo!; and Benchmark Capital, which, after many had passed on it, scored with eBay.

■ **MYTH NO. 3.**
In cyberspace, the early bird gets all the worms.

The digerati call this "first mover" advantage. The first company in a field to launch a Web business gets the buzz, which attracts the eyeballs, which boosts the IPO. In no time, the first mover is so strong it can't be dislodged.

The history of Amazon.com, the archetype that ostensibly "proves" the power of "first mover" advantage, suggests the problem with this myth. CDNow was wildly popular when it launched in 1994, but four years later Amazon needed only three months to overtake it as the Net's biggest music retailer.

Reality. The advantage doesn't go to the first mover. It goes to the company that customers find too expensive or inconvenient to leave. Here's another digerati term: "switching costs." CDNow has low switching costs. It sells a commodity product at a going rate. Amazon, however, was able to withstand Barnes & Noble by creating higher switching costs via its great customer service and personalized marketing. The problem for Amazon is that it has had to spend big on personnel and technology to create that loyalty.

■ **MYTH NO. 4.**
The Internet is a superior business model because costs are so low.

No stores, no salespeople, no inventory. "Old-line firms have to spend money and burn fossil fuels to sell hard goods," says Steve Harmon, an Internet analyst and venture capitalist. Net-based companies, he maintains, "never touch terra firma but still extract revenue, like eBay."

Indeed, eBay never touches the merchandise it sells. The auction site simply makes efficient use of the Web to match buyers and sellers in return for a commission.

But eBay and other Web companies have marketing and advertising costs that are many times those faced by old-line, or brick-and-mortar, companies. Online broker Ameritrade spends a whopping 27% of its revenues on advertising. By contrast,

Merrill Lynch spends 2%. "If you're online, no one's going to know you're there unless you spend large sums of money," says Derek Brown, an analyst at Prudential Volpe Technology Group.

And it's not true that virtual companies have no physical overhead. Order fulfillment is a big, real-world headache.

Reality. The cost savings of the Web are wildly overrated. What savings exist go mainly to companies that don't handle physical products and don't have very high content-creation costs. Among them: business-to-business services and, in the consumer area, auctions and financial and travel services sites.

■ **MYTH NO. 5.**
Old-line companies don't get the Web—and never will.

Manufacturers won't use the Web to deal with customers for fear of alienating their retailers. Retailers will not use it because franchisees would freak out and online sales might cannibalize existing businesses. Offline compensation systems and cultures don't mesh with online ones.

But the notion that online companies are safe behind a wall of servers and T-1 lines doesn't hold up. The Internet is still in its very early development. The biotech industry provides a parallel. In the '80s, a revolutionary method of developing drugs and treating disease promised to create huge problems for old-line drug firms. Today the major beneficiaries of biotech are old-line drug firms. They adapted, they acquired, they created partnerships. They had the cash flow to fund continued development once investor fever subsided and biotech companies couldn't raise money from the public. And the drug companies had an infrastructure that could sell and deliver goods and services for a profit.

Those same advantages exist today for many businesses that seem to be so threatened by the Web.

Reality. All business will incorporate the Internet, but few businesses will be solely Internet-based. The most viable companies will be those that develop successful strategies on and off the Web or that are helping businesses to create and execute their Web strategies. More old-line companies will mimic broker Charles Schwab's gamble. In 1996, Schwab decided that it would make a big push onto the Web, even if there was a danger of killing its existing business. Today, Schwab customers are able to do their business on the phone, on the Web or through brokers. And Schwab's assets under management have soared.

Net Returns: Modest, or Worse

That's the conclusion of our 1999 MONEY-Rosewood Capital survey, conducted by E-Poll.com. The survey asked 1,338 Web users about their finances. Two-thirds were investors. A quarter of that group held dotcom stocks. Of the Net investors, only 15% reported gains of 50% or more on their Net holdings. Over half said they had returns under 10%. Twenty-nine percent lost money. Among our other findings:

■ **Most Net-stock holders were cautious.** Thirty-two percent invested less than 10% of their portfolios. But 9% said Net stocks make up 85% or more of their holdings.

■ **Top source of investment ideas: a friend.** Top three factors in the decision to buy: review of company financials, use of the company's product or service, recent stock price move of 10% or more.

■ **Net investors apparently look at those financials quickly.** Nearly a third said they spend 30 minutes or less researching a stock. Finally, this is not a buy-and-hold crowd: 47% keep Internet stocks for six months or less; 23% dump within a month.

■ **MYTH NO. 6.**
Investors are getting rich on Net stocks.
Reality. A joint poll done in late 1999 (before the true Internet crash/correction) by MONEY and Rosewood Capital, a San Francisco venture-capital firm, found that 80% of Net investors surveyed had returns of less than 10%, including 29% who said they had lost money (see the box above for details).

So what should you buy? Even after the vicious decline of March-May 2000, valuations remain as stratospheric as Web business models remain unstable. That's why we've developed a multipronged Net investing strategy that tries to dampen risk while positioning you to gain from the Web's blazing growth.

1. Limit your exposure. You're a Web investor simply by holding an S&P index fund, which contains Cisco, MCI WorldCom, America Online and other big companies that, while not dotcoms, have a stake in the Net's growth. We would suggest that at most 3% to 5% of an equity portfolio belongs in pure Net stocks.

What, Exactly, Does a Dotcom Do?

The fever for Net stocks can blind investors to details—like a company's business. But fevers don't last—as some Net investors now know only too well. So here's our take on the prospects of today's leading Internet businesses.

■ CONSUMER-ORIENTED   ■ BUSINESS-ORIENTED

SECTOR/ LEADING COMPANIES	WHAT THE BUSINESS DOES	OUTLOOK
E-TAILERS Amazon.com, eToys, Furniture.com	**Online shopping**	Sites that bring added value, such as consistent high-quality service, have the advantage. But the Net's constant downward pressure on prices is a problem. **Prospects:** Murky
SERVICES E-Trade, Wingspan Bank, Travelocity.com	**Banks, brokerages, travel and more**	These businesses truly take advantage of Web efficiencies. **Prospects:** Good, but there's no reason to believe offline giants won't be big players online.
PORTALS Yahoo!, Lycos	**Gateways to the Web;** collect and organize sites so users can find the information they want	A handful of portals that can develop large revenue streams outside of advertising will do well, but the field is overcrowded. **Prospects:** Fair
AUCTIONS eBay, OnSale, uBid	**America's online garage sale**	Sellers will gravitate toward the few sites that have the largest number of prospective buyers, since more bids lead to the best sale price. **Prospects:** Fair
COMMUNITIES iVillage, About.com	Websites with specialized articles and **discussion boards** where people with common interests come to "talk" online	Advertisers haven't been happy with responses from community sites. Other revenue streams are developing slowly. **Prospects:** Murky
CONTENT CNet, TheStreet.com, Salon.com	**News and commentary** for general or special-interest audiences	It's been difficult for content sites to get people to pay for material. And with ad rates falling, their main source of revenue is threatened. **Prospects:** Murky
BUYING GROUPS Accompany, Mercata[1]	Websites that sign up people who want to buy a particular product, then seek a **volume discount** from vendors	Buying groups offer real economic value to the consumer, but they're untested. **Prospects:** Promising, but only if quality vendors sign on.
SOFTWARE Ariba, Healtheon	Web software **that links disparate parties**—like doctor, hospital, patient and insurer—that work together	As with software that comes in a box, the keys to success are performance and customer acceptance. **Prospects:** Good
E-MARKETERS DoubleClick, Net Perceptions	Help companies with **customer acquisition,** customer service, advertising strategies	Unlike with traditional advertising, this is a technology race; there will be only a few winners. **Prospects:** Murky
WEBSITE INFRASTRUCTURE InfoSpace.com, Exodus Communications	Provide software and services that make **building and running websites easier**	Every business these days wants to mine Internet gold. These companies make and sell the essential mining tools. **Prospects:** Good
EXCHANGES EarthWeb, Chemdex	Marketplaces for industry-specific **goods and services**	Exchanges will work in multibillion-dollar industries like chemicals and telecommunications, where supplies ebb and flow and buying is an inefficient process. **Prospects:** Good
REVERSE AUCTIONS BizBuyer[1], ImportQuote.com[1]	Sites will allow **companies that need services**—bookkeeping, computer help—to post requests for bids.	There's probably room for only one auctioneer in each business niche. The first to establish a robust marketplace will win. **Prospects:** Murky

Note: [1] Not a public company.

2. Spread out your Net investments. Start with a mutual fund, then add the stock of an "incubator," a publicly traded venture-capital company that funds Net businesses and retains significant stakes in them. Finally, if you can handle the risk, add other individual stocks.

■ **Mutual funds** Among funds that invest most of their assets in the Net, Munder NetNet's 60.2% annualized return gives it the best three-year record—there are no five-year records in Web time. Fund manager Paul Cook divides his portfolio into three "buckets": pure plays, Net-focused technology companies (including Cisco and Intel) and offline companies with good Net prospects. (The fund's number: 800-438-5789.)

■ **Incubators** At certain points, incubators CMGI and Safeguard Scientifics trade at smaller rather than larger premiums to the value of their stakes in publicly traded companies. When they're relatively cheap like this and the outlook for the sector is dicey, that's when you should you consider buying them.

■ **Other stocks** These stocks don't have to be pure Web plays, but they need to be profiting from the Web in some significant way. Charles Schwab is a great example. While not a pure Internet play, it is nonetheless one of the best growth companies in America. It could be attractive after another selloff.

■ **Business-to-business companies (B2Bs)** offer terrific opportunities—if you can buy them at lower prices. They sell the picks and shovels that prospector clients need to join the gold rush. The three companies highlighted below are well established and sell excellent products.

Inktomi sells search software that rummages through hundreds of millions of Web pages to retrieve requested information. Its 50 search customers include Yahoo!, AOL and Excite@Home, which pay a half-cent per Web page retrieved. Search is the offering that gets Inktomi in the door. Once there, it sells other services, including software that speeds up content retrieval by storing the most requested Web pages on powerful computers around the world.

VeriSign is the dominant provider of "digital certificates," the encryption technology that e-tailers use to secure transactions and that big companies employ to protect sensitive information on their computer networks. It recently acquired Network Solutions, the largest registrar of Web domain names.

Ariba's software uses the Net to connect companies and suppliers to automate the purchase of office supplies, equipment and other business essentials. It has also launched an Internet-based exchange geared to mid-size companies; buyers and sellers meet on the site, and Ariba brokers any purchases. The company estimates that it has 1 million end users and over 20,000 suppliers. Even by Net standards, though, the stock is expensive.

Investing Wisely in Biotech

Now for a true walk on the wild side, a visit to the breathtakingly volatile and (someday) gloriously profitable world of biotech.

There's a revolution going on. You may know it as cloned mice, or the Human Genome Project, or perhaps insect-resistant corn. It's a revolution with many fronts but one clear quest: unlocking the secrets of genes, the DNA strands that contain the code of life. The implications for humanity are staggering: the prevention of disease, the feeding of the world. The implications for you as an investor are less profound but still momentous: Biotechnology is America's most promising industry.

Sure, you're thinking, I've heard that before. Well, think again. It's true that in the mid-1980s, biotech burst onto the scene with promises of miracle cures and big payoffs that rarely materialized. But today, the industry is broader and healthier than ever, thanks to four key developments: huge advances in the study of genes; abundant research capital; a more sympathetic Food and Drug Administration; and the burgeoning health-care demands of an aging U.S. population. The players are no longer just scientists and dreamers in university labs and small industrial parks; they include the CEOs of the biggest drug and chemical concerns in the world.

To be sure, identifying the companies that will profit most from the coming boom is no easy task. Chasing the gene is risky business. Remember EntreMed? The small biotech drug firm shot up 600% two years ago after a *New York Times* article suggested, prematurely, that the company might have a cancer cure, only to crash when investors came to their senses. And nothing crashed harder this year than the reputed leaders of the genomics revolution: Celera Genomics plunged from 276 to $50^3/_{16}$ (82%),

Human Genome Sciences tanked from $232^3/_4$ to 50 (79%) and Millennium Pharmaceuticals cratered from 158 to $47^1/_2$ (70%).

Nonetheless, it's foolhardy not to at least consider putting a small portion of your assets into this sector. "The biotechnology revolution is in Stage 1," says William Scouten, director of the biotech center at Utah State University. Ultimately, he contends, "It will have more of an impact than the computer revolution."

The best way to invest in biotech. There are enlightened ways to tread along investing's new frontier. First, we don't think you should put more than 5% of your portfolio in the sector. And we think funds might be safer—and easier on your heart—than individual stocks. Unfortunately, there aren't any specialized biotechnology funds that we can wholeheartedly recommend. The main problem is that biotech is a relatively tiny sector—compared with, say, technology—and your choices are limited to just a handful of funds, few with anything like a long-term record. Instead, we think a diversified health-care fund is the best way for fund investors to play the industry.

Along with biotech stakes of 46.5% and 26.6% of assets, our two favorite biotech-friendly health care funds hold major pharmaceutical firms that also stand to benefit from biotech advances, either from their own research, acquisitions or licensing and marketing deals. And there's a kicker: Having tread water for some time, many big pharma stocks are trading at relatively low valuations.

Invesco Health Sciences. It is clear that John Schroer, who has run this $1.5 billion fund since 1994, has a big appetite for biotech. Amgen, Medimmune and Genentech are among his top 10 holdings. Schroer runs a diverse portfolio but isn't afraid to take positions in small aggressive names to find growth or avoid a fallout. He was there when medical device stocks rebounded and avoided health-care providers before that field faltered. As a result of such shifts, portfolio turnover in 1999 was a busy 127%. But his average annual return of 22.7% for the five years ending June 14, 2000 shows that Schroer's moves tend to pay off.

T. Rowe Price Health Sciences. Kris Jenner is an M.D. and former hedge fund manager who worked as a pharmaceutical and biotech analyst at T. Rowe Price for three years before taking over the fund in February 2000. He has made biotech stars Genentech, Medimmune and QLT top 10 holdings. "Biotech is a great industry to invest in if you have a long time horizon,"

In On the Boom

INVESCO HEALTH SCIENCES		T. ROWE PRICE HEALTH SCIENCES	
One-year return	18.7%	One-year return	43.8%
Assets in biotech	26.6%	Assets in biotech	46.5%
Annual expenses	1.22%	Annual expenses	1.16%
Phone	800-525-8085	Phone	800-638-5660

Note: Returns as of June 14, 2000. **Source:** Morningstar; fund companies.

Jenner says. "And while we're not a biotech fund, if you look at what products have the potential to change the way we practice medicine, biotech is a clear leader." About 46% of the fund's $489 million in assets is in biotech stocks, while a bevy of pharma leaders like Eli Lilly and Pfizer add diversification. Because the fund is relatively small, Jenner can pick up little-known companies—like Emisphere, a specialty chemical firm, and LJL Biosystems, which makes devices that test the effects of new drugs—that are below the radar of most large funds.

Making Money in IPOs

Few things have been more tempting in recent years than shares of a widely-hyped initial public offering (IPO). Some of the most spectacular and fastest gains ever made in the stock market are the result of initial public offerings. Notable IPOs of the late '90s, such as Amazon.com, Yahoo! and eBay, have taken companies from relative obscurity to stellar status, virtually overnight. Those who got in early got rich. Those who got in late may have bought overvalued stocks.

Many investors do well by holding on just long enough—typically, not more than six months—and then selling a now-pricey stock for many times its initial price. Others hang on and watch their promising find turn sour after the initial runup. Some grim examples: VA Linux Systems, a provider of integrated Linux-based solutions, traded as high as $320 on the day it first sold shares to the public in December 1999, but now trades at $32. Palm, the much hyped 3Com spinoff which makes handhelds, shot up as high as $165 on its first day in March but recently hovered around $27.

Assessing IPOs is tough. After all, these are incipient stocks with no trading record to go by, no market perception to use as your own gauge. These days, many IPOs don't even have earnings, or the hope for profits any time soon. Yet for those who prefer to pick stocks, IPOs are alluring rafts of profit in a choppy and uncertain investment sea. Whether you end up being richly rewarded—or dashed on the rocks of poor performance—depends on your skills in sizing up companies, their markets and investors' attitudes toward them before and immediately after they go public.

Given the media attention to IPOs, you might think they are a license to print money. Think again.

There is an axiom in the field: When you want an IPO you can't get it. But when you get it, you don't want it.

Such is the paradoxical nature of what lies on the other side of a blind hill. The IPO game is won by those who make the most educated guess about how green that grass actually is and the informed judgments about whether an IPO is worth the asking price. Not only that, you've got to be right about whether other investors will reach the same conclusion.

The first couple of IPOs you go for will have to make sense to you in a personal, concrete way. For example, you might have seen a lot of trucks on the road from a startup package delivery company, and this may prod you to do some research—always a sound substitute for relying on rumor in this hype-filled field.

Seek this essential information:

■ **What is the company's growth record?** A good benchmark is 25% a year for the past three or four years. Make sure that the growth is the result of smarts rather than luck. For example, how was our hypothetical delivery company doing several years ago, when no one was making Web purchases? This information will yield insights as to how they'll be doing when all competitors get on the Web-goods gravy train.

■ **What will the company do with the proceeds?** If the only thing keeping a company out of the desirable growth range is debt, proceeds from the IPO may be all it needs to turn the corner. Similarly, if the company is new and needs the proceeds to expand, this is a legitimate use.

A Fund Dedicated to IPOs

Kathleen Smith and her partners at Renaissance Capital opened the first mutual fund to focus on investing in initial public offerings. In 1999 her IPO Plus Aftermarket fund returned 115%. She knows, however, that even the highest fliers tend not to stay aloft for long. There's often an inevitable return to reality, which is why Smith and her co-managers do most of their buying not on opening day but during what's called the IPO aftermarket, when they decide which companies deserve to be drubbed and which seem destined for comebacks.

We decided to ask her a few questions about IPOs.

Q. Studies from the early '90s show that IPOs tend to underperform the Nasdaq for many years. Still true?

A. Those studies are based on buying every IPO offered, and it certainly wasn't true last year. If an investor bought every new-company issue in 1999 at the first-day closing price, his aftermarket return would have been 69%. But that's like buying on a dartboard basis—none of it relates at all to the research approach to investing, which is what we do. We analyze every IPO, but we don't buy every one.

Q. Tell us how you decide which ones to buy.

A. We score IPOs based on four factors: two long and two short. Short-term factors include group momentum: Is it a favorable group? For example, these days wireless is a strong area; however, the momentum is against consumer websites and financial services, so we have few holdings in these areas. Second, we look at valuation. We compare the company coming public to what we think are the most similar publicly traded comparables to give us a feel as to how this new company is going to trade. The two key long-term factors are fundamentals and management control. We want to know how much of an ownership stake top managers have, to see what kind of an incentive they have to do a good job.

Q. What's the big mistake folks make when they buy?

A. You may hear about a "hot" IPO in the pipeline and ask the broker to put in an order to buy it the minute it opens, no matter what the price. Many times that could turn out to be the highest price that stock will see for a long time.

Beware of IPOs that won't say specifically what the money's for. Too often, they're looking for a general cash infusion as a remedy for weak management. Does the company have a distinct market niche? You might find that the delivery company is benefiting from the increase in purchases from Web sites, but this doesn't mean the firm is necessarily poised to rise above the legion of delivery companies ramping up to meet this demand. Find out: Are their costs—and, hence, rates—competitive? Is their on-time record appealing to finicky Internet companies obsessed with speed?

■ **Who are the company's clients?** Their big accounts speak volumes about the quality of their product. If the delivery company handles Land's End and L.L. Bean, that's a good sign.

■ **Who are the existing shareholders?** When companies go public, they typically offer up only a fraction of their stock. The rest is owned by those who bought into the company early on, when it was a fledgling, privately-held concern. If you're looking at a Silicon Valley company and you find that its early investors include brand-name venture capitalists, and you decide the price isn't too high, then go see your broker and genuflect.

Similarly, if big chunks of stock are owned by profitable companies whose own stocks you admire, these issues are worth a closer look. Who are the managers? The toughest part of assessing IPOs is that the company has no track record. But the managers may—from previous roles as officers in publicly traded companies. If they've already been with some winners, this is a good omen. Those who've tasted success can often smell it from a distance.

The potential of the Internet and biotechnology is enormous. We think these sectors deserve some of your money, but we emphasize the word "some." Be prudent. Diversify. The early days of auto production and aviation, after all, also created investor feeding frenzies. Both proved to be very tough businesses; most entrants did not survive.

CHAPTER 2

What Smart Stock Pickers Need to Know

W all Street, of late, has been a very challenging place for the serious investor. The time between January 1999 and June 2000 constituted one of the most remarkable periods in stock market history. Beloved stocks rose sharply on the whiff of a vague rumor of the distant possibility of a deal with, well, somebody, while many stocks in the doghouse announced very good news only to find that Wall Street reacted with ... a yawn. At least the Street has been consistent in its treatment of companies that announce bad news: these offenders are taken out and shot.

What's a stock investor to do? We think the best investment strategy is to filter out the noise and concentrate on the basics that over time have usually served patient investors well. In such a volatile market, your best defense—concentrating on stocks with good fundamentals and reasonable valuations—may also turn out to be your best offense.

Focus Your Investing

The longer we watch this stock market, the more convinced we become that most investors spend their time worrying about the wrong things. They try to spot the next great Internet play, rush into the newly hot emerging market or call short-term market turns. Fact is, though, if you're an individual putting away money for the long term, much of the heavy lifting in your portfolio is going to be done by large growth stocks that you hang on to for years.

There aren't a whole lot of big-caps out there that have what it takes to do the job. Out of nearly 10,000 publicly traded companies, the real giants number only 450 or so. Eliminate those with tepid growth or mediocre financials, and you're down to fewer than 200. If you want to stick with companies that are tops in their industries, you really don't need to follow more than 100. (See page 38 for a list of the 100 stocks to follow.) And the number of stocks you must own to diversify properly is quite small—between eight and 15.

The detailed arguments for this kind of investing are presented with admirable clarity in the first few chapters of Robert G. Hagstrom's book, *The Warren Buffett Portfolio.* "When you reduce the number of stocks in a portfolio, you increase the probability of returns that are higher than the market's," argues Hagstrom, a fund manager with Legg Mason. But he warns that you also increase your chances of underperforming, "which is what makes stock selection so critical."

In fact, the data Hagstrom has amassed show that your opportunity is a bit greater than your risk. The reason: the most you can lose on a stock is 100%, but a winner can climb far more than that. A focused portfolio with one or two big winners benefits from this slight asymmetry, which gets quickly averaged away if you own more than 15 stocks. To put together such a portfolio, you need to follow a two-part strategy.

First, try to maximize your expected return. You can do this by buying stocks with the highest projected earnings growth at the lowest price. The best growth comes from companies that dominate an industry that is expanding faster than the overall economy. To make sure you're not overpaying, avoid stocks trading at P/Es that are more than double their projected earnings growth rates. The best values today have P/Es no more than 60% above their growth rates. That is, their price/earnings-to-growth ratio, or PEG, is 1.6 or less. (To review the key measures used to evaluate stocks, see the "Stock Valuation Measures" box on page 42.)

Second, you want to minimize risk. Consider only the financially strongest stocks and combine them in a way that gets you the greatest diversification. The way to do that is not to own simply the fastest-growing stocks but to combine companies that have different levels of earnings growth and P/Es. That will ensure that you own stocks in multiple industries—we'd recommend at least eight. And it will protect you from changes in market leadership—shifts between growth and value stocks. (For more on types of stocks, see box on page 36.)

Different Types of Stocks

Few stocks perform like Cisco Systems, which has doubled, on average, every 12 months since 1990. Nor are all investors beating the bushes to find the next Cisco. Why not? For every stock that delivers turbocharged returns, there are hundreds or thousands that simply dry up and blow away. So rather than risk plowing all their money into the next high-tech train wreck, most people fill their portfolios with a variety of stocks that have different profiles of performance. Here are five of the major types:

■ **Growth stocks.** Cisco—the stock of investors' dreams—is a classic growth stock, but any stock with rapidly rising profits fits the bill. Typically, growth stocks trade at price/earnings ratios that are equal to if not greater than their expected growth rates. While growth investing can be highly profitable, it can also be risky because the same investors who love a stock when its earnings are expanding smartly may bail out in a hurry if the growth rate slows. That, in turn, can drive the stock's price through the floor.

■ **Momentum stocks.** Think extreme growth investing. Momentum investors buy stocks in companies with earnings that are growing at increasingly higher rates. Indeed, some momentum investors will buy a stock simply because its price is going up. This can be a very lucrative investing strategy, but it only works for limited periods of time. When the music stops, as it invariably does, anyone left holding an unloved momentum stock could see its value disintegrate.

■ **Value stocks.** These are simply issues that are undervalued compared to their real earnings potential. The market is down on them because their earnings have taken a temporary hit, their product line is in a momentary lull or some other passing event has knocked their price down. The key word here is "passing." A value

We divide the blue chips we want you to look at into three categories, which should be represented about evenly in your focused portfolio.

■ **Star Growers:** These stocks regularly turn in earnings growth of 16% a year or more. They should easily outpace the S&P 500's 10% to 12% historical average annual return, assuming they aren't overpriced when you buy them and that their P/Es don't collapse once you own them. Cisco and Oracle carry P/Es of more than double their growth rates; they'd be terrific buys after a selloff but not at today's prices. The most attractive picks investor bets that whatever ails these companies will end, and that—given enough time—their price will rise to reflect their true value.

■ **Cyclical stocks.** Some stocks, like those of steel makers or oil producers, are considered cyclical because their companies' services or products aren't in constant demand throughout all parts of the business cycle. For example, steel makers see sales rise when the economy heats up, spurring builders to put up new skyscrapers and consumers to buy new cars. But when the economy slows, their sales lag too. And steel stocks, which rode up as investors anticipated the boom, ride down on expectation of the bust.

■ **Income stocks.** Stocks that pay relatively high dividends, like utilities and real estate investment trusts (REITs). Income stocks are generally favored by conservative investors who want a steady stream of cash from their investments and count on the dividends to buoy the stock's price if the market takes a spill.

Today, most investors don't give dividends a second look. After all, many of the great stocks of our time, like Dell, Microsoft and Cisco, don't even pay dividends. And between 1990 and 1999, the aggregate dividend yield on the Standard & Poor's 500-stock index fell from 3.7% a year to as low as 1.1%. Why? The simplest explanation is that many companies just didn't have to offer dividends in order to get investors to buy their stock. What's an extra 1.1% when the market is posting double-digit gains year after year?

Well, unless our depleted ozone layer is replaced with laughing gas, the stock market won't post double-digit gains forever. And whenever that happens, dividends are likely to resume a more important role. Indeed, nearly half of the market's 11.4% average annual gain between 1926 and 1999 came from reinvested dividends.

now trade at P/Es of 30 or less, based on analysts' projections of next year's earnings.

■ **Solid Citizens:** These stocks have annual growth rates of 13% to 15%—just above the market's long-term return. In this group, balancing price and P/E against projected profits is crucial. The best values carry P/Es below 21.

■ **Overlooked Talent:** By definition, stocks with earnings growth of 12% or less can't beat the market's long-term 11.4% return unless their P/E ratios increase. But that doesn't mean you should ignore

100 Top Stocks for a Focused Portfolio

You need to follow only about 100 stocks to find the broad-shouldered blue chips that can muscle their way to market-beating returns. We assembled this list by selecting top stocks with revenues and market caps of $5 billion or more, positive revenue and earnings growth for the past five years and debt at less than 60% of capital. Ideally, you should own stocks from all three subcategories, which reflect different levels of earnings growth over the next five years.

COMPANY NAME (TICKER SYMBOL)	PRICE	P/E RATIO	5-YEAR GROWTH RATE	INDUSTRY
STAR GROWERS				
Applied Materials (AMAT)	97.94	41.4	25	Semiconductor equip.
Best Buy (BBY)	64.63	39.2	25	Electronics retailing
Cisco Systems (CSCO)	67.44	127.0	30	Computer networking
Compaq Computer (CPQ)	28.06	26.2	20	Computer hardware
Dell Computer (DELL)	50.00	54.1	30	Computer hardware
Gap (The) (GPS)	29.63	19.2	20	Apparel retailing
Gateway (GTW)	59.88	32.7	25	Computer hardware
Home Depot (HD)	48.31	38.7	24	Building supplies
Intel (INTC)	139.00	44.9	20	Semiconductors
Limited (The) (LTD)	21.63	18.0	17	Apparel retailing
Lucent Technologies (LU)	62.13	49.0	20	Communications equip.
Microsoft (MSFT)	80.69	47.7	25	Computer software
Nortel Networks (NT)	67.75	100.0	20	Communications equip.
Oracle (ORCL)	86.19	125.0	25	Computer software
Pfizer (PFE)	46.88	44.2	19	Pharmaceuticals
Safeway (SWY)	42.50	19.1	17	Food retailing
Schlumberger (SLB)	77.63	63.6	18	Oil and gas drilling
Schwab (Charles) (SCH)	34.19	50.9	20	Brokerage
Staples (SPLS)	17.69	19.9	28	Specialty retailing
Sun Microsystems (SUNW)	95.94	99.0	20	Computer hardware
Tyco International (TYC)	44.38	20.6	20	Manufacturing
UnitedHealth Group (UNH)	81.06	20.4	16	Managed health care
Viacom B (VIA.B)	66.94	92.8	20	Entertainment
Walgreen (WAG)	28.00	38.4	17	Drugstores
Warner-Lambert (WLA)	129.69	53.0	19	Health care
WorldCom (WCOM)	40.31	21.3	27	Long-distance phone
SOLID CITIZENS				
Aetna (AET)	67.44	13.7	14	Managed health care
Aflac (AFL)	47.06	19.8	15	Insurance
Albertson's (ABS)	34.38	12.9	14	Food retailing
Alcoa (AA)	28.56	13.2	15	Aluminum

COMPANY NAME (TICKER SYMBOL)	PRICE	P/E RATIO	5-YEAR GROWTH RATE	INDUSTRY
American Express (AXP)	52.63	25.6	14	Financial
American Home Prod. (AHP)	61.56	32.1	13	Health care
American Intl. Group (AIG)	115.81	31.5	14	Insurance
AT&T (T)	35.00	19.4	13	Long-distance phone
Automatic Data Proc. (AUD)	52.44	40.2	15	Data processing
Baxter International (BAX)	68.00	22.3	13	Health-care supplies
Boeing (BA)	39.81	16.2	15	Aerospace
Bristol-Myers Squibb (BMY)	54.13	23.3	13	Health care
Citigroup (C)	63.00	17.7	15	Financial
Coca-Cola (KO)	53.50	37.1	14	Beverages
Colgate-Palmolive (CL)	57.00	34.1	13	Household products
Costco Wholesale (COST)	32.38	23.9	15	Retailing
Disney (Walt) (DIS)	41.75	51.0	15	Entertainment
Enron (ENE)	74.19	52.9	17	Natural gas
Federated Depart. Stores (FD)	34.75	8.6	14	Retailing
General Electric (GE)	49.44	39.5	14	Manufacturing
Gillette (G)	31.63	25.0	13	Personal care
Halliburton (HAL)	49.75	61.6	15	Oil and gas drilling
Hewlett-Packard (HWP)	119.75	33.9	15	Computer hardware
Honeywell (HON)	36.69	11.7	15	Manufacturing
Illinois Tool Works (ITW)	55.25	16.2	13	Manufacturing
IBM (IBM)	114.50	26.1	14	Computer hardware
Johnson & Johnson (JNJ)	89.88	26.7	13	Health care
Lilly (Eli) (LLY)	86.75	32.9	15	Pharmaceuticals
Newell Rubbermaid (NWL)	23.81	11.9	15	Housewares
Nike B (NKE)	35.56	17.3	15	Footwear
SBC Communications (SBC)	48.13	21.0	13	Telephone
Schering-Plough (SGP)	48.81	29.7	15	Pharmaceuticals
Sysco (SYY)	39.50	29.9	13	Food distribution
Target (TGT)	52.44	17.7	15	Retailing
Textron (TXT)	53.94	11.5	14	Manufacturing
United Technologies (UTX)	56.88	16.3	15	Manufacturing
Wal-Mart Stores (WMT)	53.56	36.3	14	Retailing
Wells Fargo (WFC)	38.31	15.0	13	Banking
OVERLOOKED TALENT				
Abbott Labs (ABT)	41.88	23.5	12	Health care
Air Products & Chem. (APD)	31.25	13.0	11	Chemicals
Allstate (ALL)	23.94	9.2	10	Insurance

(continued)

COMPANY NAME (TICKER SYMBOL)	PRICE	P/E RATIO	5-YEAR GROWTH RATE	INDUSTRY
AMR (AMR)	27.94	6.3	8	Airlines
Anheuser-Busch (BUD)	74.75	22.5	10	Beverages
Bank of America (BAC)	47.00	8.9	12	Banking
Bank One (ONE)	27.56	10.4	11	Regional banking
Bell Atlantic (BEL)	56.81	17.2	11	Telephone
BellSouth (BLS)	44.81	20.2	11	Telephone
Burlington Northern (BNI)	22.31	8.3	10	Railroads
Chase Manhattan (CMB)	47.00	11.7	12	Banking
ConAgra (CAG)	19.88	12.0	10	Foods
Deere & Co. (DE)	39.25	19.4	10	Machinery
Delta Air Lines (DAL)	50.81	7.0	8	Airlines
Dow Chemical (DOW)	33.38	14.3	8	Chemicals
Duke Energy (DUK)	59.69	14.8	9	Electricity
Emerson Electric (EMR)	59.19	17.9	11	Electrical equipment
Exxon Mobil (XOM)	83.94	22.0	10	Oil
FedEx (FDX)	34.44	15.2	12	Air freight
Gannett (GCI)	60.94	16.3	12	Publishing
GTE (GTE)	68.88	18.2	12	Telephone
Heinz (H.J.) (HNZ)	41.81	16.3	9	Foods
Hershey Foods (HSY)	49.63	20.9	10	Foods
Kimberly-Clark (KMB)	54.69	16.5	11	Household products
McDonald's (MCD)	31.13	20.2	12	Restaurants
Merck (MRK)	72.31	25.9	12	Pharmaceuticals
Merrill Lynch (MER)	120.63	16.6	12	Investment banking
Minnesota Mining (MMM)	86.06	18.2	11	Manufacturing
Philip Morris (MO)	24.94	6.8	12	Tobacco
Procter & Gamble (PG)	54.69	18.5	12	Household products
Raytheon B (RTN.B)	22.06	14.6	10	Defense electronics
Sara Lee (SLE)	18.13	13.5	10	Foods
Southern Co. (SO)	24.88	12.2	6	Electric
Sprint (FON)	59.00	29.7	12	Long-distance phone
Texaco (TX)	57.75	13.9	8	Oil
Washington Mutual (WM)	27.88	8.1	12	Savings and loan
S&P 500	**1479.13**	**25.6**	**9**	

Notes: All prices as of June 21, 2000. P/Es based on analysts' estimates for fiscal 2000. **Source:** Baseline.

them: They're attractive because they can outpace growth stocks in periods when investors become value-conscious. What you should buy at any given time depends on what's on sale. In early 1999, it would have been commodities, oil and specialty chemicals. The best deals change over time, of course, and you can track our 100 select blue chips at www.money.com/sivy.

Searching for Blue-Chip Bargains

The strange recent behavior of the stock market may have brought some good news to bargain-hunting investors. Markets like these can offer great buying opportunities. In particular, many blue-chip growth stocks have been knocked down to discount prices.

To make smart stock-portfolio decisions today, it's vital to understand why the extraordinary divergence between beloved stocks and out-of-favor issues has occurred. Essentially, there are two forces that propel stock prices higher—rising earnings and falling interest rates. In periods of falling interest rates, most stocks move up together. But when rates are rising—as they have been since mid-1999—share prices have to fly on only one engine, growing profits. That means stocks with the fastest earnings growth continue to climb, while others stagnate or fall.

If investors were completely rational, mild divergence would develop whenever interest rates were rising. And that would be that. But investor groupthink can greatly exaggerate the trend. If shareholders become obsessed with momentum, they ignore value stocks—no matter how cheap—and flock to a small group of hot issues, exaggerating the split.

No matter where the market goes from here, it makes a lot of sense for investors to favor blue chips that have fallen substantially in the recent past. If the market environment worsens, high-flying growth stocks would likely fall the most. A stock trading at a 90 P/E could easily go to a 45 P/E, a 50% decline. But a stock at a 15 P/E might drop only to 12, a 20% loss.

Moreover, if the market races ahead again, depressed blue chips may actually offer the greatest profit opportunities. The reason is that excessive divergence misprices growth—and specifically undervalues the growth prospects of less flashy stocks. That means that the smartest investment strategy today is to look for moderate growth stocks trading at below-average P/Es.

Stock Valuation Measures

Here are some of the key fundamental tools to measure the health of your stocks. You can find measures like these at virtually any online investing site (see Chapter 7 for the best ones). Use these tools to gauge a company that you hear described as a good investment. Taken together with the latest news on a company, measures like these can give a rough idea of whether a stock is cheap, fairly priced or overpriced compared to others in its class.

■ **Price/earnings ratio.** As you know, the P/E ratio is a stock's price divided by its earnings per share. What you may not know is that it's now calculated in a new way. Traditionally, investors have looked at P/Es based on the previous 12 months' profits, known as trailing earnings. Today, though, investors commonly cite P/Es based on the consensus analysts' forecast of the next 12 months' profits, or forward earnings, convinced that it is a better reflection of a stock's future value. But take care: all projections involve guesswork.

■ **Profit margins.** Income divided by revenues. Good margins for a software company might be 25%, while 2% is considered fabulous for a grocery chain. So when gauging a company's profit margin, be sure to compare it with that of other companies in the same industry.

■ **Debt-to-equity ratio.** A company's debt divided by shareholder's equity (or the value of its assets after all liabilities have been subtracted out). This ratio is often used as a measure of a company's health: the higher it is, the more vulnerable a company's earnings may be to industry changes and swings in the economy.

■ **Return on equity.** Net income divided by shareholder's equity, or, literally, how much a company is earning on its money. This ratio can be used to show how a company's earnings measure up against those of the competition, as well as how they compare with past performance. A rising return on equity (ROE) is a good sign.

■ **Price-to-book value ratio.** A stock's price divided by its so-called book value, expressed on a per-share basis. The book value is calculated by adding up the worth of everything the company owns and then subtracting its debt and other liabilities. As with all ratios, this one is most useful when looked at in the context of a particular industry and a company's own history.

■ **PEG and PEGY ratio.** The PEG, or price/earnings/growth, ratio is calculated by taking the P/E ratio based on forward earnings and dividing by the projected growth rate. Stocks with a PEG ratio of less than one (meaning that they are trading at less than their projected growth rate) are generally said to be cheap, while a PEG ratio of 1.6 or higher indicates a stock that may be overpriced. For stocks that pay a substantial dividend, the PEGY ratio—which is the P/E divided by the projected growth rate plus the dividend yield—may be an even better measure than PEG alone.

How to tell when a cheap stock is no bargain.

There are a couple of things about value investing that people dislike. It doesn't always pay off fast. It can also be risky in the short run: Stocks that look cheap can fall further. Nonetheless, over the long term, value strategies keep pace with growth investing and are less risky, especially if you start when the market is showing extreme divergence, as it is now.

To protect yourself against volatility, it makes sense to invest in stages. Start by putting only half of your standard investment into a new stock. If it promptly tanks, you can buy on the dip and lower your average investment cost. Remember, stocks can drop, say, 35% in the six months after you've purchased them, only to soar to a 50% profit after 18 months.

The art is in distinguishing between value stocks that are likely to keep falling and those that are all the way down. There's no magic formula, but we think it helps to divide them into four groups, depending on what they need for success:

■ **Stocks at the whim of external forces.** A company that operates in a heavily regulated—or hostile—environment is unlikely to be a good investment. Such a company may no longer be able to control its own destiny, no matter how well it executes its business plan. Philip Morris is the poster child for this group. This cigarette maker and food stock was so undervalued at about $26 a share in mid-2000 that it could more than double. Or the company could be destroyed by waves of lawsuits, until all that's left is melted Velveeta. Don't ask us—consult a lawyer.

■ **Stocks that are just doing badly.** Occasionally, the price of a company's shares is low because sales are sluggish and its market share is falling. Competitors may be executing more effectively and introducing better products. Avoid such companies unless you know that the situation will soon change. Xerox has been very cheap for many months but needs to revamp its product line. Maybe the company will get that done soon—but then again, maybe it won't. Nike's another one. It's a solid brand, but earnings are still disappointing. And what if the whole running-shoe fad is over? On a statistical basis, these stocks are buys, if you diversify broadly among them and have a decade-long time horizon. But we think the next two categories are more promising.

■ **Stocks working through specific problems.** Spotting a company just before its restructuring pays off can mean big profits. But these stocks can also be pitfalls. For instance, many investors have been disappointed by several stocks recently that are working through merger-related troubles. Big mergers generally benefit companies over a 10-year period. But two recent studies found that more than 60% of all mergers hurt stock prices in the first year or two. Throughout the first half of 2000, three companies have stood out as prime examples. Compaq has yet to integrate its 1998 acquisition of Digital Equipment and find a way to compete with Dell. Lockheed's acquisitions overloaded management and delayed airplane deliveries. And Union Pacific's 1996 merger with Southern Pacific snarled rail traffic so severely that the industry has yet to recover. We believe all three of these stocks will eventually pay off, but they've all been bad calls from a timing point of view.

■ **Stocks already on the upswing.** If you buy stocks after they've reported a good quarter, you'll miss the quick blast-off, but you'll minimize your chances of sitting with dead money. As an alternative, you can closely follow daily analyst upgrades and downgrades (available free through Yahoo!) and try to catch value stocks just as they are upgraded.

In short, you should be looking for stocks whose problems have a clear end and getting in when the problems are almost solved or when the first positive results emerge. Just be prepared to wait for your profits, if you have to, and remember that it's better to make money slowly than lose money quickly.

Following the In-the-Know Crowd

Sometimes insiders can help point the way to bargains. In 1999, investors were hammering Harrah's Entertainment shares on fears that profits would plunge because the gaming industry was building too many casinos, too fast. But what Harrah's directors and CEO saw was opportunity. They started buying shares for $15 to $17 and snapped up more shares at $20, putting a total of $2.4 million into the stock. Sure enough, the company beat earnings estimates for the next three quarters and, during that time, the stock rose as high as $30.75.

The Harrah's case is an example of why many mutual fund managers and other professional investors pay attention to the trading activity of company insiders—the executives who run the business and the directors who oversee its management. Insiders know the company better than anyone else, the theory goes, so if they're buying, it's a sign that their stock is undervalued. Selling, on the other hand, could foreshadow trouble.

Does that mean you should jump on or off a stock based solely on whether insiders are buying or selling? Of course not. Insiders loaded up on Mattel and Rite Aid after those stocks stumbled, only to see them fall even harder. And there's more art in analyzing insider data than you might expect. Insiders are better at picking some kinds of stocks than others, and not all buys or sells should be given the same weight. "There are nuances," says Alan Gilston, co-manager of the Oppenheimer Discovery Fund, who uses insider data when screening for stocks to buy. "Understanding the nuances makes the difference between being successful with the technique or not."

Here's what you need to know to incorporate insider buying data into your buy-sell analysis. We'll start with the big picture, then explain how to analyze individual insider transactions.

Buying means more than selling. Though some sales are red flags, the CEO may have lots of reasons to sell stock—diversification, estate planning, cash for a new house—but he generally has only one reason to buy: He thinks it's a good investment.

Think cheap. A 1998 University of Michigan study of 1,700 stocks with heavy insider buying found that cheap stocks—those with price/earnings ratios in the bottom 20% of the market—averaged returns of 25.1% in the 12 months following the buying, compared with 15.9% for the stocks in the group with the highest P/Es.

Think small. Insider trading data are most useful when you're looking at small and midcap stocks rather than large-caps. "At a smaller company, there are more people who know everything about the company, who have a good sense of the underlying value," Gilston says.

Be patient. Executives and directors tend to buy early. Even when insiders are right, they buy as much as six months before a stock starts moving. Insider trading data are two to six weeks old when they appear publicly anyway, so this is not the kind of data that rapid-fire traders find very useful.

Check newspapers and websites to find insider data. Local newspapers carry weekly listings of insider trades for regional stocks, and similar tables for big stocks can be found in the *Wall Street Journal* and *Barron's*. If you're researching a specific company on the Web, Yahoo! Finance carries insider trades for most stocks. Also, EDGAR Online's "full search" feature allows you to display insider transaction information for a particular time period or company (www.edgar-online.com). The downside is that electronic filing of insider forms is optional, so the data are incomplete. You'll also want to have the company's proxy statement on hand for your research. Now the detective work begins.

Find out who's buying. Executives, even down to the level of vice president, are better to watch than directors. The people running the company know the most about where it's heading. Check the proxy to see how long the insider has worked for the company and what his or her industry experience is. "Three directors who just joined the board and are buying their first shares wouldn't be that significant," says John Spears, co-manager of the Tweedy Browne American Value Fund, who looks for stocks with heavy insider buying.

You can also check the insider's buying history. Yahoo! Finance's listings detail previous transactions, and you can cross-check an insider's buys with the stock's subsequent performance on a long-term price chart. A website, Insider Scores (www.insider-scores.com), even attempts to grade insiders' track records. Don't make too much of this, though. Just because an insider bet right once or twice doesn't make him Peter Lynch.

One clear rule: The more insiders buying the merrier. Don't bother analyzing purchases if there are fewer than three within a time frame of several months. And while the trades needn't be large, it's worth going to the company's proxy statement to look at insiders' existing holdings for help judging the significance of their latest purchases. "If a CFO earning $150,000 a year buys $75,000 in stock," says Spears, "that's a pound-the-table bet."

Investigate whether the buy is "a real buy." "The average investor has got to be very careful about reading positive messages into every insider buy he sees," says Bob Gabele, co-founder of First Call Insider Research Services. That's because more companies are requiring their officers and directors to own shares. For example, 11 officers and directors of car-parts retailer AutoZone bought thousands of shares in October 1999. But investors who read the proxy found that the company had just created a stock plan that included guidelines for ownership levels and provided loans for half the purchase price. That's a laudable aligning of management and shareholder interests, but not a reason to buy the stock.

Also, if the executive is exercising options and buying the stock, it's not particularly meaningful if the options were granted at rock-bottom prices.

Analyze the sell signs. Although experts say insider selling is less significant than buying, there are times when sales should make you take a closer look at a stock you hold or are considering buying. Several insiders cashing out a quarter or more of their holdings, for example, is possible cause for concern. Here again, options can make this analysis tricky. A CEO may sell a quarter of his 100,000 shares but have 1 million shares in vested options. Check the proxy statement for the insider's options.

Also consider when insiders are selling. Don't begrudge a hard-working vice president a little profit taking when a stock has soared. But if insiders are selling when the share price is falling, that's a signal they're worried. The stock may be getting cheaper for the right reasons.

The Art of Selling

Even when there are insider indicators that signal it may be time to sell your stock, deciding whether to dump your holdings is the toughest question you face as an investor. And chances are you don't get the answer right as often as you would like. Individual investors routinely "sell winners too early and ride losers too long," wrote researchers Hersh M. Shefrin and Meir Statman in a 1985 *Journal of Finance* article. They concluded that investors often succumb to fears of loss and regret when making sell decisions. People who don't want to make paper losses "real" hold on to poor performers, and those who don't want to regret a missed opportunity for profits sell winners.

It's easy to understand why. The bull market for stocks that's endured since 1982 has elevated buy-and-hold from strategy to religion. Still, there are times (even if insiders are holding tight) when the most devout buy-and-hold practitioner should consider selling: Perhaps a couple of your stocks have posted outsize gains and now represent a big chunk of your holdings. Maybe you're near a goal—college tuition, retirement, a second home— and you need to trim risk. Or you're wondering if this year's losers can rebound. Or you're just doing an annual, semiannual or monthly portfolio review.

Whatever your reason for pondering a sale, don't look at a stock's price and ask simply whether you should unload it. Instead, take time to pose questions and search for answers about the stock's prospects. Below we discuss four familiar scenarios.

I've got an enormous winner. Does it still offer me what it did a year ago? Is it too big a piece of my portfolio? This is the kind of sell dilemma we would all like to face, but it doesn't have a one-size-fits-all answer. William Nygren, manager of the Oakmark Select Fund, says you should always have in mind a target price you feel reflects the potential you saw when you bought the stock. Some managers swear by these sell targets: They hit one and get out. But that often leaves money on the table, and individuals—remember—tend to cut loose their winners too quickly. Nygren sees the target "not so much as an absolute sell signal but as a benchmark when periodically re-evaluating your investment rationale." If earnings come in better than expected, he says, "or if similar companies sell for more than expected in the private market, raise your target."

If you have a stock that's risen, say, eightfold, it probably represents more of your holdings than prudence dictates. Most benefits of asset allocation can be gained with fewer than 15 stocks, and you likely don't have time to keep tabs on many more. So you should consider setting a limit of 3% to 10%.

Or you could employ a strategy familiar to anyone who plays blackjack. Cut your position in half. That way, you lock in a profit and get to keep playing with house money.

Remember, though, that when you sell a winner, you're going to give up a big chunk of your gain in taxes (unless you're trading in a tax-deferred account). If you invest what's left in a new stock that you sell after three years, it must beat your old one by about 10% annually just to get you to where you would have been had you simply delayed the sale of the old stock.

My stock is plunging. Is it temporary? Should I buy more? Or is there a long-lasting problem? Research suggests that the biggest mistake people make is hanging on to losers. But panic is an investor's enemy, and buying on dips to average down is a time-tested investing method. What do you do? Here are a couple of strategies to consider.

Growth fund manager John McStay generally sells a stock if it declines 20%. If the market is falling, he'll cut his losers more slack, but in a strong market, even a 10% decline may prompt him to bail.

Because you, unlike most fund managers, don't have to chase short-term performance numbers, a rigid sell rule may not be a necessity. But be careful not to commit the sin of pride that McStay's dump rule is designed to avoid. That leads us to a second strategy: If a stock drops 15% or more in a flat to rising market, re-evaluate. Do you have real doubts about its long-term prospects?

My stock is going nowhere. Should I be doing something better with my money? The question of how long to wait for a stock to soar is especially relevant to investors who don't always have cash to invest in their next big idea. Many stock sales by professional money managers are prompted by their desire to buy something else.

If you conclude you don't have a better idea, consider spreading the money tied up in your going-nowhere stock among your existing best ideas, if that won't overly concentrate your portfolio. Or just sit tight. An idea will come.

My stock has done okay. But some of the fundamentals have changed. Which ones are noise, and which tell me something? Investors pay too much attention to news events that have little to do with a company's value, says Richard Howard, manager of $787 million T. Rowe Price Capital Appreciation Fund. In particular, he thinks the significance of political events and changes in company management tend to get overblown.

Likewise, Howard says, investors wrongly concentrate on price-to-earnings ratios: "Prices are not fundamentals. They reflect fundamentals."

The key is to discriminate between meaningful developments and temporary distractions. Here are two fundamental shifts that you absolutely must heed: changes in a company's core business and (remember Nike) a falloff in its market position.

If a company has changed its focus or made a major acquisition that looks questionable, it isn't really the stock you bought. Is there still a reason for you to own it? Even a well-run company can see its franchise threatened, says Tom Marsico, manager of the top-performing Marsico Focus fund and the Marsico Growth and Income fund. "When I buy stocks, I'm looking for ones that I never have to sell," he says. "But I'd be wrong to hold on just for the sake of holding on."

CHAPTER 3

Mutual Fund Strategies: Value vs. Growth

*A*h, remember those triple-digit returns dozens of fund managers delivered in 1999? Where are those gains now that we really need them?

Actually, mutual funds aren't supposed to double in a year, or a quarter. (Sorry.) But the recent explosive performance of growth funds—which over the last three years have pummeled both index and, especially, value funds—raises some crucial questions.

When constructing a portfolio, how influenced should an investor be by recent performance? In the ongoing battle between value and growth strategies, has a new winner been declared? Is indexing, which once delivered such delightful returns, now too boring for words?

Like stock pickers, fund investors also have a lot of noise to filter out. In this chapter, we want to offer you tools to evaluate your current funds, strategies for selecting new ones and some answers to the questions we raised above.

The key to success in mutual fund investing is to diversify your holdings and to stay focused. And to us, focus means two distinct things. First, it means not ditching a good fund simply because it is temporarily lagging the market averages. Second, it entails narrowing your selection process so you consider buying only the best funds around. Millions use Morningstar stars as a guide, although this system is anything but foolproof, as you will see. Our favorite approach is to select funds from the MONEY 100, a list you'll find at the end of the chapter. Happy hunting.

Escaping the Value Trap

A new kind of value fund has emerged—one that doesn't shun technology shares—and some investors must be saying,

"It's about time." For the past few years, traditional value investing has traveled a very rough road. Over the three years that ended March 31, 2000, growth funds surged an annual average of 37.1%, while the typical value fund returned a tepid 12.4%.

Whatever the next few months bring, however, the recent market turmoil is a good reminder that value still belongs in your portfolio—both as a source of diversification and (stay with us, please) strong returns over the long haul. Traditional value investing—also known as deep value—involves buying stocks that trade at below-market price/earnings ratios and waiting for investors to recognize their true worth. By contrast, classic growth investors seek out stocks with rapidly increasing earnings, which they expect to appreciate in price. At least until the recent Nasdaq nosedive, many traditional value funds, which generally avoid tech stocks, were whacked by losses. Yet from the Nasdaq peak on March 10 through the April 14 meltdown, the average value portfolio gained 1.9%. Growth funds, by comparison, racked up an extraordinary 23.2% loss.

The question, then, may not be whether value can pay off, but which type of value fund is right for you. To make the correct choice, it's important to recognize that value funds carry sharp distinctions in strategy and that some may be far more tech-heavy—and riskier—than others. (See the table on page 54.)

Value vs. growth. Over the past century, deep-value investing and growth investing have taken turns as Wall Street's favorites, typically dominating for periods of three to six years. "Value tends to underperform some 30% to 40% of the time," says Jeremy Siegel, finance professor at the University of Pennsylvania's Wharton School. "But over the long term, the evidence shows that value and growth are about evenly matched in returns."

That said, the recent value depression has been so brutal that some investors have questioned whether value as a stock-picking style can ever catch up to growth. Investors have grown increasingly impatient with underperformance. Since 1998, net cash outflows from value funds have totaled a whopping $97 billion, according to Financial Research Corp. To meet redemptions, managers have been forced to sell off stocks, thereby creating a vicious cycle of portfolio damage. Since there are few eager buyers for what these managers are unloading, the prices of many value stocks get driven down still further—prompting yet another cycle of underperformance and more shareholder redemptions.

How Tech Transforms Value

An elastic term that applies to all of the MONEY 100 funds selected below, "value investing" describes both "traditional value" and "new-style value" funds. The difference? A fund manager's willingness to buy technology stocks. As evidenced below, tech holdings dramatically boosted funds' three-year returns—and dragged down performance when the Nasdaq stumbled.

FUND NAME PHONE NUMBER (800)	% TECHNOLOGY	PORTFOLIO AVERAGE P/E	% THREE-YEAR AVERAGE RETURN[1]	% DOWN-MARKET RETURN[2]	TOP THREE STOCKS[3]
TRADITIONAL VALUE					
Clipper 776-5033	0.0	16.5	12.7	11.5	Freddie Mac, Fannie Mae, Philip Morris
Longleaf Partners 445-9469	0.0	16.5	11.5	9.3	Waste Management, FedEx, Marriott International
Tweedy Browne American Value 432-4789	3.2	17.2	13.5	9.1	American Express, MBIA, McDonald's
Vanguard Windsor II 851-4999	4.2	23.3	12.6	7.7	Chase, SBC Communications, GTE
Washington Mutual[4] 421-0180	5.2	24.2	15.7	8.7	U S West, Sprint, Bank of America
T. Rowe Price Value 638-5660	6.6	23.1	13.7	9.8	Phelps Dodge, Sprint, Stanley Works
NEW-STYLE VALUE					
Gabelli Westwood Equity 422-3554	16.1	29.2	19.2	5.7	Oracle, AMFM, GTE
Excelsior Value & Restructuring 446-1012	19.1	24.3	30.0	-6.9	Texas Instruments, Nokia, Xerox
Neuberger Berman Partners 877-9700	22.0	28.5	13.4	-0.2	Cigna, GTE, IBM
Selected American Shares 243-1575	31.1	31.7	27.2	-0.6	American Express, Texas Instruments, Hewlett-Packard
Legg Mason Value 577-8589	31.9	32.7	35.5	-0.6	AOL, Dell, Gateway
Third Avenue Value 443-1021	38.6	36.9	18.6	-4.3	AVX, Silicon Valley Group, Financial Sec. Assurance

Notes: [1]To March 31, 2000. [2]March 10 to April 14, 2000. [3] Reported as of March 31, 2000. [4]5.75% sales charge. **Source:** Morningstar.

In the face of investor flight, some fund companies have given up on deep value. According to Morningstar, some 123 value portfolios were merged or liquidated during the past three years. Even the world's most famous value investor, Warren Buffett, stumbled, with Berkshire Hathaway down a precipitous 20% over the 12 months to March 31, 2000. Says Michael Stolper, an investment adviser in San Diego: "If Buffett were a mutual fund manager today, he would have been fired."

Traditional value vs. new value. Perhaps the most stinging rebuke to deep value, however, comes from so-called new value, or relative value, managers. By adopting less orthodox value strategies—chiefly by buying tech stocks—these fund jockeys have left their deep-value rivals in the dust. This new value group includes MONEY 100 managers Chris Davis and Ken Feinberg (who is the brother of the author of this book) of Selected American Shares (three-year return as of March 31, 2000: 27.2%), David Williams of Excelsior Value & Restructuring (30%) and Bill Miller—the most successful and controversial—of Legg Mason Value (35.5%).

For new-style value managers, the notion of avoiding the nation's fastest-growing industry is a hopelessly outdated, procrustean strategy. Instead, these managers select stocks based on relative values, a technique that compares prices with industry averages or historical patterns, or with potential growth or cash flow. "The most wonderful growth companies are the best values if you can buy them at the right price," says Selected American Shares' Davis. "So why buy a struggling aluminum company, when you could buy Hewlett-Packard, which is likely to dominate the printing business for the next 10 years, at just 15 times earnings?" Davis adds, "Even if you figure that tech stocks are too expensive, it's incumbent on value managers to understand their impact, if only to make sure that your companies are not going to be roadkill."

Why don't traditional value investors just get with the program and buy tech stocks? For deep-value purists, the precept of Benjamin Graham and David Dodd, who formulated the principles of value investing in the 1930s, remains inviolable: Thou shalt not buy stocks with P/Es or price-to-book ratios above the market average.

Of course, not all value managers fit neatly into these two camps. Some otherwise deep-value managers have a rationale for tech stocks. "You want to buy stocks selling at a good value," says Marty Whitman of Third Avenue Value (three-year return: 18.6%). "But there are a lot of ways to measure value besides a low P/E based on current earnings—there's no exclusive tool." For Whitman, what counts is the quality and quantity of business assets that could be realized in a merger or restructuring. During the 1998 tech downturn, for example, he took a 40% stake in cash-rich, beaten-down semiconductor equipment makers such as Applied Materials, AVX and Electroglas, which went on to score big gains. Other new-style value managers like Legg Mason's Miller take a barbell approach, balancing daredevil positions in pricey Internet stocks with holdings in bargain-priced value fare such as Aetna and Waste Management.

How to get good value. By now you're probably wondering which value fund to buy—and perhaps which to sell. First, if you own a value fund already, how do you know what kind it is? These days, traditional value funds generally have portfolio average P/E ratios that are 50% to 60% below the S&P 500 average, and usually keep their tech holdings below 10%. New-style value funds, on the other hand, tend to have P/E ratios only slightly below the S&P 500's and invest much more heavily in technology. Which approach is better for you? That depends to a great extent on your convictions about the economy, your long-term goals and your tolerance for risk.

Traditional investors who prefer owning stocks with real earnings that trade at a big discount are the most obvious candidates for a deep-value fund, which sticks to bargain-priced equities. But even diehard New Economy believers can use one as a way of offsetting the risk of an otherwise tech-heavy portfolio.

Be warned: You may have to suffer long periods when value is out of favor. Still, these funds can really soar in the right environment—when the economy is coming out of a recession and cyclical and industrial stocks become buoyant, for example, or when falling interest rates power up financial companies. Some excellent options include Clipper, Longleaf Partners and Tweedy Browne American Value, all of which have a proven commitment to a difficult investing style and solid long-term returns.

Many investors may prefer a new-style value fund, which can keep them in tune with Wall Street's recent infatuation with high-priced growth stocks while offering more stability than a pure growth fund. But keep in mind that during periods when traditional value stocks are rebounding, these funds won't give you as much of a bounce. And if growth stocks get hammered, new value may offer only partial protection—Excelsior Value & Restructuring, for example, lost 6.9% during the Nasdaq plunge, while Clipper, a deep-value fund, picked up 11.5%. Nevertheless, over the long term, your returns may more closely mirror the overall market. And Neil Kauffman, a Philadelphia investment adviser who favors new value funds, argues, "The world is moving along, and we think investors will do best with fund managers who are open to different ways of looking at value."

Some good options: Selected American Shares, Gabelli Westwood Equity and Strong Opportunity.

Whichever fund you choose, be ready to hang on for the long term. Put simply, value investing takes guts, since you are essentially taking up residence in areas of the market that other investors are fleeing. But, as Will Browne, a fund manager at the old-line value firm Tweedy Browne, says, "Sooner or later, value is amply rewarded." Maybe this time, it will be sooner.

The Right Way to Index

Many investors last year must have felt they were tracking the wrong index. The Nasdaq Composite Index soared 85%, and the Nasdaq 100 did even better. Still, having a big chunk of your portfolio in an S&P 500 Index fund hasn't exactly been chopped liver.

Tracking that index solves a lot of problems, although investors must realize that it also creates some new ones. Yes, the returns have been excellent, the expenses are low and you don't need to make hard decisions about which stock or fund to buy. But if you think that the broad array of stocks that make up the index gives you much of the diversification you need all wrapped up tidily in one investment, you would be wrong.

Although index investing remains a powerful tool for the individual investor, buying funds based on the S&P 500 index— with its overweighting toward the giant technology stocks that have powered its extraordinary returns in recent years—exposes investors to more risk than they probably realize.

What should you do? Avoid indexing? Sell your S&P 500 fund? Hardly. We've long believed that most individuals should use indexing in building a well-diversified portfolio. And there's a place in many portfolios for an index fund that holds the stocks of the S&P 500, which does represent 80% of the U.S. market as measured by capitalization.

There's a lot more to indexing than the S&P 500.

You can, in fact, easily index most of the worldwide stock mar-

How to Split Your Money

Beginning indexers need a few thousand dollars and two funds. As your portfolio grows, you can divide the money you have allocated to stocks across different sectors.

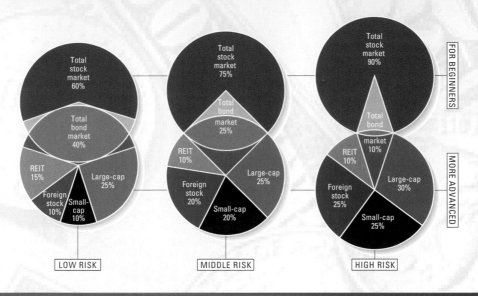

FOR BEGINNERS
MORE ADVANCED

Low Risk
- Total stock market 60%
- Total bond market 40%
- REIT 15%
- Large-cap 25%
- Foreign stock 10%
- Small-cap 10%

Middle Risk
- Total stock market 75%
- Total bond market 25%
- REIT 10%
- Large-cap 25%
- Foreign stock 20%
- Small-cap 20%

High Risk
- Total stock market 90%
- Total bond market 10%
- REIT 10%
- Large-cap 30%
- Foreign stock 25%
- Small-cap 25%

LOW RISK   MIDDLE RISK   HIGH RISK

ket and a major portion of the U.S. bond market. You can build a sensibly diversified portfolio using as few as two and as many as a half-dozen or so index funds; or you can use index investing as a base, filling in with individual stocks and actively managed mutual funds. (Active managers can be particularly valuable in the small-cap arena and in foreign markets.)

Which index funds are the right ones for you? As indexing has grown in popularity, the choices have become bewildering—there are now more than 245 index funds. We've narrowed that universe to 10 top funds (see page 60) across a variety of asset classes. And we've provided six model portfolios that vary by risk tolerance and complexity (see box above). You can create a portfolio by plugging the funds into the model that suits your temperament and needs.

Understand the benchmark that you're following. Today there are more indexes than ever. You want to make sure that the index fund you're buying holds securities that truly represent the asset class whose returns you're trying to capture.

If you aim, for example, to track the performance of the entire non-U.S. stock market, then you want the Vanguard Total International Stock Index fund, which tracks the Morgan Stanley EAFE (Europe, Australasia and the Far East) and emerging markets indexes, rather than the Schwab International Index, which sticks to the 350 largest companies in 15 developed countries.

Don't assume all index funds are low cost. You probably equate indexing with bargain-basement expenses. Yes, the average index fund carries an expense ratio of just 0.5%, vs. 1.4% for actively managed funds. But dozens of index funds are saddled with high expenses, 12b-1 fees, even sales loads.

Make the most of indexing's tax efficiency. Because index funds buy and sell stocks less frequently than the typical actively managed fund, they tend to distribute less in capital gains. So it usually makes sense to use these funds in the taxable portion of your portfolio and put actively managed funds in your non-taxable accounts. (For more on tax-efficient funds, see Chapter 6)

Indexing Strategies

For indexing beginners, or those with relatively little money to index, we recommend Strategy A below. More sophisticated investors with larger portfolios might prefer to follow Strategy B.

■ **STRATEGY A**

Consider a total stock market fund as your core index holding. Instead of plunking all your money into an S&P 500 fund, you may want to build your index portfolio around a total stock market fund that tracks the Wilshire 5,000 benchmark, which, despite its name, represents 7,000-plus U.S. stocks with readily available price data. In effect, you are indexing 99% of the domestic equity market, and you capture the performance of small stocks.

Add an intermediate-bond index fund for the fixed-income portion of your portfolio. A good starting point is Vanguard Total Bond Market (expense ratio: 0.20%). Schwab Total Bond Market Index has a lower minimum—$2,500—and a 0.35% expense ratio.

The Index Funds You Need

To create an indexed portfolio, match the funds listed below with the model portfolio on page 58 that best suits your investing style.

FUND	12-MONTH RETURN [1]	THREE-YEAR FUND RETURN[2]	EXPENSES	MINIMUM INVEST./IRA	BENCHMARK	PHONE (800)
TOTAL STOCK MARKET						
T. Rowe Price Total Equity Mkt.	16.5%	N.A.	0.40%	$2,500/$1,000	Wilshire 5,000	638-5660
Vanguard Total Stock Mkt.	17.2	19.2%	0.20	$3,000/$1,000	Wilshire 5,000	662-7447
LARGE-CAP						
Schwab 1000	16.2	19.9	0.46	$2,500/$1,000	1,000 largest publicly traded U.S.companies	435-4000
Vanguard 500	15.1	19.9	0.18	$3,000/$1,000	S&P 500	662-7447
SMALL-CAP						
Schwab Small Cap	24.7	12.1	0.49	$2,500/$1,000	Schwab index of small and mid-size U.S. cos.	435-4000
Vanguard Small Stock	21.4	11.8	0.25	$3,000/$1,000	Russell 2000	662-7447
FOREIGN						
Schwab International	19.6	11.9	0.58	$2,500/$1,000	Largest 350 stocks in developed nations	435-4000
REIT						
Vanguard REIT	4.11	1.99	0.33	$3,000/$1,000	Morgan Stanley REIT index	662-7447
FIXED INCOME						
Schwab Total Bond Mkt.	4.9	5.6	0.35	$2,500/$500	Lehman Bros. aggregate bond index	435-4000
Vanguard Total Bond Mkt.	5.2	5.9	0.20	$3,000/$500	Lehman Bros. aggregate bond index	662-7447

Notes: [1]For the period that ended June 15, 2000 [2]Annualized N.A.: Not applicable. **Sources:** Morningstar, fund companies, MONEY index.

■ **STRATEGY B**

Diversify portfolios of $15,000 or more into five or more different funds. So if you already have an S&P 500 fund, keep it as a core large-cap holding. Another sound large-cap choice is the Schwab 1000, which tracks the 1,000 largest publicly traded stocks, giving you some midcap exposure. In addition to fixed income, you'll also want, in varying percentages depending on your risk profile (see the box on page 58), money allocated to small-caps, overseas markets and REITs. There are two prime small-cap possibilities: the Vanguard Small Cap Index, which mirrors the Russell 2000, and the Schwab Small Cap Index fund, which tracks the next 1,000 stocks after the Schwab 1000. The Schwab fund is tax managed, which is ideal for taxable accounts.

When it comes to foreign investing, most index funds have a short record. Vanguard Total International Stock is a sound choice, while Schwab International Index offers a more focused play on developed countries. To add further diversification, you might look to a REIT index fund, since real estate investment trusts historically often move counter to the overall market. REITs are also an income play; the average one yielded 7.95% in mid-2000. Again, the record for index funds is short, but the most notable entry is the Vanguard REIT index.

The New Force in Funds

Now that we've told you how to index, Wall Street may be offering an even better way. Exchange-traded funds (or ETFs) are shaking up the investment world.

The first ETFs were the Spiders, introduced in 1993 to track the S&P 500 index. They perform almost exactly like a traditional mutual fund, but they can be bought and sold instantly, just like a stock. If you haven't considered buying one, you might want to do so now: Barclays Global Investors—the second largest investment shop in the world, with almost $700 billion in assets—recently launched a line of exchange-traded funds, dubbed iShares, that it hopes will be a major competitor to the traditional fund. The company offers more than 40 index portfolios that track almost every conceivable slice of the U.S. market. (Barclays Global Investors, which used to be the investment arm of Wells Fargo, essentially invented the index fund back in 1971.)

Could these new funds be the "killer app" that knocks mutual funds off their perch? Maybe. Can they make life easier for you? Definitely. Indeed, exchange-traded funds may be the best thing to happen to individual investors since Jack Bogle launched the Vanguard 500 Index fund in 1976. ETFs' most obvious selling point is that they let you trade in and out of the market or a particular sector as fast as you can point and click on your online brokerage account. (You can even short them or buy them on margin.)

If they work as advertised, they should be a boon even for dedicated buy-and-hold fund investors. Since all of the Barclays' ETFs are index-based, they have extremely low management fees. They also allow you to fine-tune your asset allocation:

Many track indexes that no mutual fund has followed before. Finally, their structure should make them extremely tax efficient.

If these new-style funds catch on, even investors who stick to traditional funds could turn out to be winners. "The mutual fund industry is ripe for reinvention," notes Don Phillips, CEO of the fund-tracking firm Morningstar. "The cost of owning stocks has plummeted, but the cost of owning funds has remained stubbornly high." Some competition may finally change that equation.

Spiders, Webs and Qubes. ETFs differ from closed-end funds in one crucial way. Closed-ends have a fixed number of shares; depending on investor demand, they can trade at a premium or a discount to the total value of the stocks in their portfolios, or net asset value (NAV). Mostly, they've traded at a discount, which is why closed-ends have been a bomb with ordinary investors.

The exchange-traded funds have gotten around that problem. Specialists at the American Stock Exchange, as well as large institutional investors known as arbitrageurs, issue shares when there are more buyers than sellers and redeem shares when there are more sellers than buyers. That should keep the price of the funds at or near their net asset value.

This system also gives the funds a tax advantage. ETF managers give the specialists stock, not cash, to meet redemptions. Thus, the fund incurs no tax liability when shares are redeemed, and investors who don't sell aren't stuck paying tax bills generated by those who have flown the coop.

The original Spiders, or SPDRs (for Standard & Poor's Depositary Receipts), were the first products to adopt this innovative exchange-traded format. Since the launch of the Spiders, many more ETFs have popped up on the Amex listings. Best known are the Internet-heavy Nasdaq 100 Trust shares (called Qubes because the ticker symbol is QQQ), and WEBS, managed by Barclays since 1996, which track individual foreign markets from Japan to Austria. Other exchange-traded products include Select Sector Spiders, which track various industry groups in the S&P 500, such as energy stocks or financial services; a Spider that tracks the S&P MidCap 400; and Diamonds, which mimic the Dow.

Thanks in part to the wild success of the Qubes, assets in ETFs have more than doubled since the summer of 1998. Such success, says Bob Turner, chairman of the Turner funds, threatens "everybody who hasn't outperformed the market after taxes and after fees—and that's a pretty big group."

But will they work? For these upstarts to take away a big piece of the traditional fund business, the new products will have to prove they can keep costs low and reliably trade at NAV. In theory, neither should be a problem. In practice, things might prove a little more complicated. Take costs. Spiders charge 0.18% a year, the same as the Vanguard 500 Index fund. (Barclays' iShare S&P 500 index fund charges about half of that, .0945% per year.) The only hitch is that you have to pay a brokerage commission every time you buy or sell shares of an ETF. Of course, that cost should be negligible for buy-and-hold investors.

What about NAV tracking? In all but some exceptional cases—notably Malaysia WEBS, after Malaysia imposed currency controls—the prices of ETFs have so far tracked closely to NAV. But Gus Sauter, manager of the Vanguard index funds (perhaps the ETFs' chief competitors), thinks that ETFs could break down during a panic. He points to what happened on 1987's Black Monday: "If you had sold S&P 500 futures during the '87 crash, they were at a 10% discount. I liken ETFs to futures because they rely upon the same arbitrage mechanism. If exchange-traded funds had been around in '87, they would have been at a 10% discount too."

Lee Kranefuss, CEO of Barclays' individual investor group, counters that Sauter is "drawing a parallel between two things that use arbitrage, but in totally different markets." The fact is, though, that any investment may not perform as intended during market panics.

A sharper knife. In the final analysis, there's a lot to like about the newcomers and not much to worry about. They stand to make fund investing more efficient than it's ever been. Of course, even efficiency has its downside. A good sharp knife is faster in the hands of a skilled cook but also makes it easier for a klutz to slice off a finger. Likewise, exchange-traded funds can make smart long-term investing easier and cheaper—but they will also let you do a lot of pretty dumb things, like day-trading funds until your brokerage costs and taxes eat away your gains. Nonetheless, these funds just may be a better way to invest.

The Star System

ETFs offer a lot of promise, but an even better way to invest would be to know ahead of time which mutual funds would beat the market. Wouldn't it be wonderful if a simple numerical system allowed us to know that?

The Morningstar ratings purport to deliver those goods. Ranging from one star (dim) to five stars (dazzling), these symbols of risk-adjusted return have become the mutual fund equivalent of two thumbs up or four chef's hats—snappy visual icons that convey what you need to know to make an informed decision. Just as you'd expect a five-star hotel to have softer towels and a better view than your average motor inn, most investors would rather buy a five-star than a lowly one-star fund.

Since they were introduced in 1985 by the fund trackers at Morningstar Inc. in Chicago, the star ratings have come to dominate the selection of mutual funds almost as sweepingly as Microsoft holds sway over software. In fact, "virtually 100%" of all new money goes into funds with Morningstar ratings of four or five stars, says fund analyst Avi Nachmany of Strategic Insight, an investment research firm in New York City.

Some recent scholarly studies on the stars are chock-full of useful insights that will help you shop more wisely. The most important revelations: It's better to buy an old fund than a new one (all else being equal), and the difference between three- and five-star funds is not as great as you may think.

Looking inside the star chamber. First, let's take a look at Morningstar astronomy. To get an overall star rating, a fund needs to be at least three years old. The firm separates all funds into four giant groups—U.S. stock, international stock, taxable bond and municipal bond—and calculates two measures for each fund. The first is a yardstick of return, the second of risk.

To get the first number, Morningstar deducts any sales charges or redemption fees from the performance of all the funds it measures. Then Morningstar calculates how often, and by how much, each fund's performance has exceeded that of a 90-day Treasury bill—the closest thing to a riskless investment—and compares it with other funds in its broad group. If the resulting number is greater than 1.0, the fund has generated a positive "Morningstar Return."

To get the second measure, Morningstar looks at how often, and by how much, a fund has performed worse than the risk-free T-bill. Again, that's compared with similar funds. The result is the "Morningstar Risk" score; here, a good score is less than 1.0.

For the final step, Morningstar subtracts each fund's risk score from its return score, then grades the results along a bell curve. The funds that score in the highest 10% get five stars; the next 22.5% get four; the middle 35% get three; the next 22.5% get two; and the bottom 10% get just a single star. The ratings are updated every month.

How old are your stars? There's one other important but little-known thing you need to understand: If a fund is only three years old, its overall star rating is based on those years alone. But if a fund has five years of history, its star rating is based on a 60-40 blend of those five years and the most recent three. Likewise, if a fund is at least 10 years old, its star rating is derived from a 50-30-20 mix of its risk and return over the past 10, five and three years, respectively.

What's the point? Back when the stars were born, Morningstar wanted to evaluate all funds over the longest possible time frame. But using just the 10-year numbers would have prevented younger funds from being rated at all. And using only the three-year numbers would have denied the funds credit for good performance in their earlier years. So Morningstar cooked up its time-weighted approach.

"There's a certain messiness to it," concedes John Rekenthaler, Morningstar's director of research. If the last three years have been more bullish than the seven years before that, then a young fund—which gets its star ratings based only on the most recent three years—is more likely to earn five stars than an older fund that is rated largely on how it performed before the recent bullish period.

Janus Olympus, for instance, was launched at the end of 1995 and has five stars—a rating based entirely on its performance from 1997 through 2000, three of the best years in stock market history. Founders Growth, whose portfolio is fairly similar to that of Janus Olympus, dates back to 1963 and earns four stars, based on its blended performance over the past 10, five and three years. That 10-year period, naturally, includes the poor returns of 1994, when the Fed jacked up interest rates, and the middling returns of 1992, when fast-growing stocks took a breather.

When you wish upon a star. So what does the new research tell us about Morningstar's stars? One study, by Mark Warshawsky of the TIAA-CREF Institute, a financial research think tank in New York City, looked at how durable the Morningstar ratings are and came up with several key findings:

■ **A single month can realign the stars.** After August 1998, when Standard & Poor's 500-stock index lost 14% of its value, 169 of the 1,897 funds that had four or five stars at the beginning of 1998 dropped to three stars or fewer.

■ **Stars can turn into meteors.** Over the course of 1998, Warshawsky found, 53.2% of all four- and five-star funds fell to three stars or fewer. In other words, the ratings are highly perishable; if you count on a five-star fund sustaining that level of brightness for long, you're probably in for a disappointment.

■ **Old stars are better than new ones.** Warshawsky discovered that funds with at least 10 years of history held onto their top star ratings better than funds with just three years under their belt. Fully 52.4% of the older funds were able to hang on to their top ratings for a full year—but only 42.1% of the younger funds avoided dropping to three stars by year-end. Thus, if you're considering two funds that both carry the same star rating, it makes sense to lean toward the fund that's been around longer (especially if its annual expenses are lower).

Another study, by Christopher Blake of Fordham University and Matt Morey of Smith College, offers more insights:

■ **Bad ratings are sticky.** Blake and Morey found that Morningstar ratings are quite good at predicting which funds will perform poorly. That is, most funds with ratings of one or two stars tend to keep them. "The stars do predict which funds will be turkeys," says Morey. If you're considering a fund with one or two stars, you'd better have a mighty good reason (perhaps it's part of a group, such as small-cap value, in which nearly all funds have done poorly, and you expect a rebound).

■ **Five stars are no better than three.** By contrast, Blake and Morey found that funds with five, four or three stars all perform about the same. "A five-star rating," says Morey, "doesn't predict future performance significantly better than you could if you just looked at the fund's past return." With a five-star fund, you're unlikely to do worse than average, but a five-star fund stands about the same chance of remaining superior as a three-star fund has of becoming superior. Even Morningstar's Rekenthaler agrees: "The odds are stacked against you if you buy a one- or two-star fund. But beyond that, I wouldn't worry a lot about whether the fund has three, four or five stars."

Add it all up, and we think it's pretty clear that a Morningstar rating is more like the two thumbs in a movie review or the chefs' hats in a restaurant critique than you may have realized. A lousy rating is usually an excellent predictor of what you'll get as a consumer. And a so-so rating is reliable too. But great reviews, because they raise great expectations, are potential heartbreakers. If you use Morningstar's system when you're investment shopping, steer toward older and cheaper funds—and always remember that the stars reflect the past far better than they predict the future.

The MONEY 100

Even using the star system, it's virtually impossible to follow all the top-rated funds. So to help you sort through the universe of stellar funds, the editors at MONEY compiled one comprehensive list to focus on. If you think there's a gap in your portfolio, look here. If you're seeking a replacement for a loser fund, the list should be able to help.

What kind of funds do we like? We prize funds with consistent performance, sound strategies, low expenses and managers who inspire trust, because these are the factors we believe are most likely to lead to success. One thing we don't try to do is predict the next hot sector or style. That's why the MONEY 100 listings represent the full spectrum of stock funds, from portfolios heavy on Cisco Systems to funds that dig up cheap names you've never heard of.

We still believe diversification is the happiest medium, given the stock market's inevitable—and inevitably unforeseen—extremes. The truth is, as the market illustrated so clearly in the first half of 2000, growth stocks don't always grow. So in addi-

Portfolio Planning Resources

■ **To bone up on the basics:** Excellent model portfolios can be found in *The New Commonsense Guide to Mutual Funds* by Mary Rowland and *Mutual Funds for Dummies* by Eric Tyson.

■ **To try online financial planning:** Check out Web tools from Fidelity (www.fidelity.com), T. Rowe Price (www.troweprice.com) and Vanguard (www.vanguard.com) to create custom combos of mutual funds.

■ **To play "what if" scenarios.** Visit the Financial Engines website (www.financialengines.com) to find formulas for assessing the potential rewards and risks of your prospective portfolio. And at www.morningstar.com, a "portfolio manager" can reveal whether your picks work well together in a truly diversified portfolio—or overlap dangerously into the same stocks and sectors.

---

tion to our growth picks, we're sticking with some value managers whose styles have been out of favor for years, such as deep-value master James Barrow of Vanguard Windsor II and dividend-loving Brian Rogers of T. Rowe Price Equity Income. Barrow and Rogers have enviable 15-year records, and the craze for all things growth shouldn't cloud that.

You'll notice that some names are tagged with our "aggressive" symbol, indicating funds with high-tech and/or high P/E strategies. The symbol often explains a fund's outperformance—and pinpoints potential dangers. Likewise, another icon identifies funds that are considered low risk within their peer groups and that have shown more predictable performance than the overall market. Remember: A healthy fund portfolio weighs risk against growth.

How to choose from 100 funds. We filled the MONEY 100 with a range of funds that can help you overhaul your portfolio or create one from scratch. If recent market madness has taught you the hard way that you have, say, too much in tech-heavy funds, then add balance with a low-tech choice like Dodge & Cox Stock. Or if you're stuck in a value slump and feel the worst of the tech wreck is over, consider jazzing up your portfolio with a fund marked by our "aggressive" symbol, such as RS MidCap Opportunities. Your first step is to figure out how much of your overall investments should be in stocks. (The resources in the box above can help.)

Large-growth Janus might nicely offset large-value **Selected American Shares**. Or consider tackling your big-cap weighting in one 50% swoop with a broad index fund like **Schwab 1000**. For your 25% in smaller-caps, **MAS Mid Cap Growth** or **MAS Small Cap Growth** could add exposure to the little names that Janus is too big to play with, while **Artisan Small Cap Value** can dig deep for bargains. **Loomis Sayles International Equity** guns for growth overseas, but if that adds up to too much tech, try **Scudder International** for more measured growth or **Hotchkis & Wiley International** for a value approach. A dash of **T. Rowe Price Emerging Markets Stock** adds the extra 5% kick.

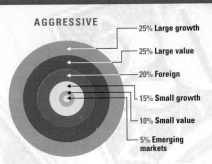

AGGRESSIVE
- 25% Large growth
- 25% Large value
- 20% Foreign
- 15% Small growth
- 10% Small value
- 5% Emerging markets

You want growth? Sure. Gonzo? No. You could choose **Harbor Capital Appreciation** or **Marsico Focus** for an aggressive 30% large-cap growth exposure, and perhaps combine it with 10% in **Fasciano** on the smaller-cap growth side (it's not so tech-rich). For a similar balance among value funds, large-cap choices like **Washington Mutual Investors** or **Neuberger Berman Partners** can be mainstream foils for the idiosyncratic, if often brilliant, small-cap plays made by **Oakmark Select** or **Third Avenue Value**. Top it all with 20% in **Acorn International** if you don't mind more small-caps, or **Putnam International Growth** for a sensibly diversified foreign stake.

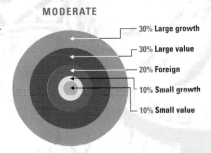

MODERATE
- 30% Large growth
- 30% Large value
- 20% Foreign
- 10% Small growth
- 10% Small value

If you don't want to make bets on an investing style or sector, stick closely to the overall market. Putting 75% of your stock assets in **Vanguard 500 Index** or **TIAA-CREF Social Choice Equity**, designed to closely mimic S&P 500 performance, could suit you well. Maybe round it out with another 15% in **Vanguard Small Cap Index** or **T. Rowe Price Small Cap Stock**. And 10% in **EuroPacific Growth** or **Fidelity Diversified International**, for smart foreign exposure. Minimalists might want a big stake in a global fund like **Capital World Growth & Income** to cover both foreign and U.S. blue chips. **Vanguard Global Asset Allocation**'s rather sizable bond stake might add ballast.

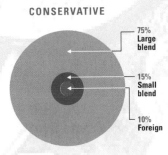

CONSERVATIVE
- 75% Large blend
- 15% Small blend
- 10% Foreign

FUND NAME	ONE YEAR	THREE YEARS	FIVE YEARS	TEN YEARS	STYLE[2]	% ANNUAL EXPENSES	MINIMUM INITIAL INVESTMENT	NET ASSETS (MILLIONS)	TELEPHONE (800)
		% TOTAL RETURN[1]							
LARGE-CAP									
Alleghany/Montag & Caldwell	10.3	27.7	28.5	—	Growth	1.1	$2,500	$1,654	992-8151
Clipper	−1.7	12.7	18.0	15.5	Value	1.1	5,000	813	776-5033
Dodge & Cox Stock	15.3	16.8	19.4	15.7	Value	0.6	2,500	4,219	621-3979
Domini Social Equity	20.3	30.2	27.9	—	Blend	1.0	1,000	1,420	762-6814
Dreyfus Appreciation	7.3	21.4	24.2	17.0	Blend	0.9	2,500	4,163	373-9387
Excelsior Value & Restructuring	42.4	31.0	28.7	—	Value	0.8	500	1,205	446-1012
Fidelity	21.3	30.4	27.0	18.7	Blend	0.6	2,500	17,027	544-8888
Gabelli Westwood Equity	18.2	19.2	23.0	16.1	Value	1.5	1,000	177	422-3554
Harbor Capital Appreciation	46.8	44.3	34.7	25.4	Growth	0.7	2,000	9,722	422-1050
Janus	45.9	40.6	32.0	22.2	Growth	0.8	2,500	49,058	525-8983
Kemper-Dreman High Return	−13.0	7.0	16.8	15.5	Value	1.2[5]	1,000	1,367	621-1048
Legg Mason Value	6.7	35.5	36.4	22.0	Value	1.7	1,000	13,332	577-8589
Marsico Focus	38.2	—	—	—	Growth	1.3	2,500	3,332	860-8686[9]
Masters' Select Equity	30.5	26.8	—	—	Blend	1.3	5,000	477	960-0188
MFS Capital Opportunities A	63.5	40.6	33.5	22.3	Blend	1.2[5]	1,000	2,483	637-2929
MFS Mass. Investors Trust A	8.3	20.3	23.2	16.9	Blend	0.9[5]	1,000	7,591	637-2929
Neuberger Berman Partners	5.9	13.5	18.4	15.2	Value	0.8	1,000	2,307	877-9700
Nicholas	6.8	17.3	19.6	15.6	Blend	0.7	500	4,900	227-5987
Oakmark	−18.1	2.5	9.9	—	Value	1.2	1,000	2,215	625-6275
Oppenheimer Main St. G & I A	18.6	23.9	22.0	23.2	Blend	0.9[5]	1,000	8,912	525-7048
Rainier Core Equity	32.1	29.0	28.5	—	Blend	1.1	2,500[7]	1,009	248-6314
Safeco Equity	5.3	18.1	20.3	17.5	Value	0.7	1,000	1,907	624-5711
Schwab 1000	20.1	27.5	26.1	—	Blend	0.5	2,500	5,278	435-4000
Selected American Shares	25.9	27.2	28.0	19.7	Value	0.9	1,000	3,798	243-1575
SSgA Growth & Income	19.6	31.7	27.7	—	Blend	1.1	1,000	443	647-7327
Stein Roe Young Investor	32.8	31.2	30.7	—	Blend	1.2	2,500[8]	1,110	338-2550
TCW Galileo Select Equities N	46.6	—	—	—	Growth	1.4	2,000	47	386-3829
TIAA-CREF Growth Equity	38.5	—	—	—	Growth	0.5	250	842	223-1200
TIAA-CREF Social Choice Equity[3]	—	—	—	—	Blend	0.3	250	—	223-1200
Torray	13.5	22.7	26.4	—	Value	1.1	10,000	1,923	443-3036
T. Rowe Price Equity Income	1.4	11.3	16.1	14.1	Value	0.8	2,500	10,261	638-5660
Vanguard 500 Index	17.9	27.4	26.7	18.7	Blend	0.2	3,000	107,365	851-4999
Vanguard Total Stock Mkt. Index	24.0	27.3	25.6	—	Blend	0.2	3,000	19,720	851-4999
Vanguard U.S. Growth	23.9	31.1	29.4	20.3	Growth	0.4	3,000	20,061	851-4999
Vanguard Windsor II	−7.8	12.6	17.9	14.3	Value	0.4	3,000	23,218	851-4999
Washington Mutual Investors	0.1	15.7	19.8	15.3	Value	0.6[5]	250	49,507	421-0180
White Oak Growth Stock	58.3	47.7	42.2	—	Growth	1.0	2,000	3,702	462-5386[9]
Standard & Poor's 500	17.9	27.4	26.8	18.8					

FUND NAME	% TOTAL RETURN[1] ONE YEAR	% TOTAL RETURN[1] THREE YEARS	% TOTAL RETURN[1] FIVE YEARS	% TOTAL RETURN[1] TEN YEARS	STYLE[2]	% ANNUAL EXPENSES	MINIMUM INITIAL INVESTMENT	NET ASSETS (MILLIONS)	TELEPHONE (800)
MIDCAP									
Brandywine	76.7	27.3	26.0	21.3	Growth	1.1	$25,000	$6,597	656-3017
First Eagle Fund of America Y	4.6	19.9	22.6	16.5	Blend	1.4	1,000	457	451-3623
Franklin California Growth A	123.8	47.4	38.9	—	Growth	1.0[5]	1,000	2,209	342-5236
Gabelli Asset	22.9	26.4	22.2	17.0	Blend	1.4	1,000	2,014	422-3554
Homestead Value	−4.5	8.5	13.7	—	Value	0.7	500	357	258-3030
Janus Special Situations	61.5	44.6	—	—	Growth	1.0	2,500	1,849	525-8983
Longleaf Partners	−9.0	11.5	14.4	15.8	Value	0.9	10,000	3,172	445-9469
Mairs & Power Growth	12.0	15.0	20.8	18.5	Blend	0.8	2,500	485	304-7404
MAS Mid Cap Growth Inst.	79.0	56.6	39.8	27.5	Growth	0.6	2,500[7]	1,842	354-8185
Nicholas-Applegate Growth	114.9	51.8	35.8	23.8	Growth	1.5[6]	1,000	450	551-8643
Oakmark Select	12.8	28.3	—	—	Value	1.2	1,000	1,502	625-6275
Oak Value	−7.7	15.2	18.4	—	Blend	1.1	2,500	309	622-2474
RS MidCap Opportunities	72.3	37.5	—	—	Growth	1.5	5,000	305	766-3863
Sound Shore	9.4	13.5	19.1	15.5	Value	1.0	10,000	1,500	551-1980
Strong Opportunity	39.6	27.9	23.9	18.7	Value	1.2	2,500	2,808	368-1030
Strong Schafer Value	−3.6	0.3	9.1	11.9	Value	1.4	2,500	448	368-1030
T. Rowe Price Mid-Cap Growth	37.2	28.1	26.2	—	Growth	0.9	2,500	6,042	638-5660
T. Rowe Price Value	5.4	13.7	19.0	—	Value	0.9	2,500	804	638-5660
Tweedy Browne American Value	1.2	13.5	18.3	—	Value	1.4	2,500	905	432-4789
Weitz Value	9.7	27.2	26.1	18.2	Value	1.2	2,500[7]	2,472	232-4161
Standard & Poor's 400	38.1	27.4	24.0	16.9					
SMALL-CAP									
Acorn	38.9	22.1	20.7	17.4	Growth	0.9	$1,000	$4,021	922-6769
Artisan Small Cap Value	22.9	—	—	—	Value	1.4	1,000	177	344-1770
CGM Focus	18.3	—	—	—	Blend	1.2	2,500	56	345-4048
Clover Small Cap Value	75.8	23.7	—	—	Value	1.4	2,500	29	226-9558
Delafield	18.7	2.6	10.8	—	Value	1.2	5,000	70	221-3079
Eclipse Small Cap Value	13.3	12.1	16.2	12.7	Value	1.2	1,000	203	872-2710
Fasciano	6.1	13.0	15.1	13.5	Growth	1.2	1,000	300	848-6050
Fremont U.S. Small Cap	129.2	—	—	—	Growth	1.5	2,000	78	548-4539
MAS Small Cap Growth	203.4	—	—	—	Growth	1.2	2,500[7]	473	354-8185
Royce Premier	30.3	12.9	14.2	—	Value	1.2	2,000	565	221-4268
Third Avenue Value	44.4	18.6	20.6	—	Value	1.1	1,000	1,639	443-1021
T. Rowe Price Small Cap Stock	37.3	17.4	19.2	14.7	Blend	1.0	2,500	1,962	638-5660
Vanguard Small-Cap Index	39.4	18.9	18.3	15.2	Blend	0.3	3,000	4,104	851-4999
Wasatch Core Growth	24.4	15.6	17.7	15.7	Blend	1.4	2,000	189	551-1700
Westport Small Cap R	51.7	—	—	—	Blend	1.5	5,000	100	593-7878[9]
RUSSELL 2000	37.4	17.9	15.6	12.7					

FUND NAME	% TOTAL RETURN[1]				STYLE[2]	% ANNUAL EXPENSES	MINIMUM INITIAL INVESTMENT	NET ASSETS (MILLIONS)	TELEPHONE (800)
	ONE YEAR	THREE YEARS	FIVE YEARS	TEN YEARS					
INTERNATIONAL									
Acorn International	98.6	31.5	25.9	—	Foreign	1.1	$1,000	$3,405	922-6769
American Century Intl. Growth	69.7	32.4	26.5	—	Foreign	1.5	2,500	5,122	345-2021
Capital World Growth & Income	29.5	21.1	21.2	—	World	0.8[5]	250	11,511	421-0180
Deutsche International Equity[4]	38.9	21.9	21.0	—	Foreign	1.5	2,500	2,567	730-1313
EuroPacific Growth	54.3	26.4	22.9	16.7	Foreign	0.8[5]	250	22,100	421-0180
Fidelity Diversified International	47.1	24.2	22.4	—	Foreign	1.2	2,500	5,945	544-8888
Hotchkis & Wiley International	22.2	10.9	13.9	—	Foreign	1.0	10,000	1,364	236-4479
Janus Worldwide	72.2	38.2	34.1	—	World	0.9	2,500	44,476	525-8983
Japan	101.2	38.5	18.2	8.9	Foreign	1.3	2,500	979	535-2726
Loomis Sayles Intl. Equity Retail	103.8	28.4	—	—	Foreign	1.3	5,000	15	633-3330
New Perspective	41.0	29.0	24.5	17.8	World	0.8[5]	250	35,806	421-0180
Putnam International Growth A	62.1	32.1	26.5	—	Foreign	1.3[5]	500	6,612	225-1581
Scudder International	51.6	25.5	21.1	13.3	Foreign	1.2	2,500	5,276	225-2470
SSgA Emerging Markets	51.4	5.1	9.5	—	Foreign	1.3	1,000	396	647-7327
Templeton Dev. Markets A	29.4	-1.5	6.0	—	Foreign	2.2[5]	1,000	2,605	342-5236
T. Rowe Price Emerg. Mkts Stock	86.7	11.1	12.1	—	Foreign	1.8	2,500	207	638-5660
T. Rowe Price Int'l Stock	33.5	17.3	16.1	11.8	Foreign	0.9	2,500	12,900	638-5660
Tweedy Browne Global Value	21.7	18.6	19.6	—	World	1.4	2,500	3,236	432-4789
Vanguard Global Asset Allocation	12.1	13.0	—	—	World	0.6	3,000	108	851-4999
Vanguard International Growth	35.4	16.8	16.7	11.5	Foreign	0.6	3,000	10,824	851-4999
MSCI EAFE	23.5	14.7	10.7	7.7					
SPECIALTY									
CGM Realty	10.6	0.0	12.3	—	Value	1.0	$2,500	$397	345-4048
Columbia Real Estate Equity	3.7	1.9	12.6	—	Value	1.0	1,000	291	547-1707
Dresdner RCM Global Tech. N	178.4	—	—	—	Growth	1.8	5,000	355	726-7240
Hancock Financial Industries A	2.0	15.0	—	—	Value	1.4[6]	1,000	574	225-5291
Invesco Health Sciences	1.0	20.9	22.1	19.7	Growth	1.2	1,000	1,615	525-8085
Longleaf Partners Realty	−7.5	−3.3	—	—	Value	1.2	10,000	578	445-9469
T. Rowe Price Science & Tech.	99.1	55.7	39.5	31.0	Growth	0.9	2,500	15,543	638-5660
Vanguard Health Care	20.5	29.4	28.8	23.3	Blend	0.4	10,000	11,810	851-4999

Notes: Data as of March 31, 2000. [1]All multiyear returns are annualized and come from fund companies. [2]Styles for stock funds: Blend—buys stocks that mix growth and value characteristics; growth—buys companies with accelerating earnings; value—buys stocks that are inexpensive relative to earnings or assets; foreign—invests at least 90% of assets abroad; world—invests more than 10% of assets in the U.S. and more than 40% abroad. [3]Fund opened April 3, 2000. [4]Previously named BT Investment International Equity. [5]Plus 5.75% maximum sales charge. [6]Plus 5% maximum sales charge. [7]If purchased through Schwab OneSource, 800-435-4000. [8]Plans for minors can have minimums as low as $100. [9]Area code 888.
Source: Morningstar, Chicago.

Money 100 Symbols

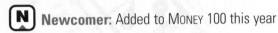 **Newcomer:** Added to Money 100 this year

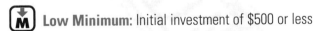 **Low Expenses:** Annual fees in the lowest 10% of funds in same category

 **Low Minimum:** Initial investment of $500 or less

 **Low Risk:** More predictable performance than the market and Morningstar risk score in lowest 10% of category

Aggressive: Consistent above-market tech weightings or P/Es

Then sit down and divvy up your stock stake. What's the proper proportion of growth funds to value? Small caps to blue chips? How do foreign stocks fit in? Sorry, there's no one-size-fits-all advice. But the three model portfolios on page 69 can be used as a guide when making your picks.

Acorn

800-922-6769   www.acornfunds.com

MANAGERS: Ralph Wanger, Chuck McQuaid

Wanger and McQuaid sniff for growth stocks selling at reasonable prices, a strategy that Wanger says has taken them "downstream from technology." Example: Getty Images, a photo and film archive that is using systems set up by gee-whiz names like Cisco and Lucent to cut costs and sell more of its services over the Internet. **Three-year return: 22.1% (as of March 31, 2000)**

Acorn International

800-922-6769   www.acornfunds.com

MANAGERS: Leah Zell, Margaret Forster

Zell and her newly named co-manager Forster are expert diggers of overseas treasures. One recent gem was Audiofina, a barely traded Belgian stock (they bought their shares straight from management) that jumped 22% on the announcement of its acquisition by U.K. media giant Pearson. **Three-year return: 31.5%**

Alleghany/Montag & Caldwell Growth

800-992-8151	www.alleghanyfunds.com

MANAGER: Ron Canakaris

Sure, Canakaris owned Cisco, EMC and Oracle over the past year. But when prices exceeded his fair-value estimates by 20%, he sold. "We've left a lot of money on the table with tech," he says. And, thankfully, a lot of risk. Canakaris now favors health-care and consumer stocks like Pfizer and Home Depot. **Three-year return: 27.7%**

American Century International Growth

800-345-2021	www.americancentury.com

MANAGERS: Henrik Strabo, Mark Kopinski

[A] Computers tag the highest-growth stocks, then Strabo and Kopinski pick the 150 they think are most likely to deliver. The typical stock is held for less than six months (Sony, Mannesmann and China Telecom were recent favorites), and it's bought without regard to country or sector. While that makes for a high-octane portfolio, it can also lead to big exposures in certain areas. **Three-year return: 32.4%**

Artisan Small Cap Value

800-344-1770	www.artisanfunds.com

MANAGER: Scott Satterwhite

Satterwhite says economic uncertainty could spell short-term trouble for his industrials and financials. But investors who can wait three years or more for their payoff can buy "a portfolio of extremely high quality—the best we've ever had." This from the man who whipped most of his peers while at Wachovia Special Values before moving to Artisan in 1997. **Three-year return: N.A.**

Brandywine

800-656-3017	www.brandywinefunds.com

MANAGERS: Foster Friess, team

[A] Knocked for going to cash during Asia's crash late in 1997, Friess and his team today feel vindicated. Thanks to this move, they insist, they rebuilt a portfolio that soared 53.5% in 1999. Not bad, considering they will invest only in small-cap and midcap stocks that have P/Es below 30 and can show three years' earnings growth. **Three-year return: 27.3%**

Capital World Growth & Income

800-421-0180   www.americanfunds.com

MANAGERS: Team

This American Funds offering is good for conservative investors who are looking to diversify abroad, since no more than 40% of assets can be parked in any one country. The managers also strive to produce a higher dividend yield than Standard & Poor's 500-stock index, which they have faithfully done since the fund's start in 1993. **Three-year return: 21.1%**

CGM Focus

800-345-4048   www.cgmfunds.com

MANAGER: Ken Heebner

While most mutual fund managers move in packs, Heebner is a lone wolf. Lately, he's been fearlessly selling short Internet stocks and plunking more than a third of the fund into steel and paper companies in emerging markets like Brazil, Indonesia and Korea. "In any given year," Heebner says dryly, "the chance that my return will resemble the S&P is pretty low." More like zero, we'd say. At his CGM Capital Development (closed, alas, to new investors), Heebner has one of the best long-term records of any fund manager ever. **Three-year return: N.A.**

CGM Realty

800-345-4048   www.cgmfunds.com

MANAGER: Ken Heebner

"You can't fall out of the basement," Heebner figures. Real estate stocks have done so poorly during the past three years—1.2% annually vs. about 27% for the S&P 500—that he thinks they offer an ideal blend of low risk and fairly high potential return. We do too. "If you think tech stocks are going to keep going up 50% to 70% a year," he adds, "you shouldn't invest here." **Three-year return: 0%**

Clipper

800-776-5033   www.clipperfund.com

MANAGERS: James Gipson, Michael Sandler, Bruce Veaco

These deep, deep value investors want only companies worth owning "even if the stock market shuts down tomorrow," says Sandler. That means no tech and, for years, lots of Fannie Mae, Freddie Mac and Philip Morris. Then there's the

25% cash and bond stake (down from as much as 40%), which at least helped hold down losses during the run on value shares in the first quarter of 2000. **Three-year return: 12.7%**

Clover Small Cap Value

800-226-9558	www.clovercap.com

MANAGERS: Lawrence Creatura, Michael Jones

(N) This little-known offering has quietly earned one of the best records in its beleaguered class. That's partly because Creatura and Jones have not shied away from technology. Last year, they snapped up software stocks slammed by Y2K concerns—and saw them bounce back mightily after Jan. 1. **Three-year return: 23.7%**

Columbia Real Estate Equity

800-547-1707	www.columbiafunds.com

MANAGER: David Jellison

Jellison is one of the best real estate managers around, but the past two years have been some of the roughest the category has seen. (Hey, when a company called Public Storage is your top holding, you know it's slim pickings out there!) Still, Jellison has minimized the fund's losses. When real estate rebounds, look for this one to bounce higher than almost all the others. **Three-year return: 1.9%**

Delafield

800-221-3079	www.delafieldfund.com

MANAGERS: J. Dennis Delafield, Vincent Sellecchia

Last year's 8.4% gain actually lands this fund in the top quarter of its small-value peers. Delafield and Sellecchia are sticking to their playbook, focusing on dirt-cheap companies that are likely to see higher share prices through buyouts or restructurings. Their turnaround bets include Unova, which makes mobile computing systems, and Delta Woodside, which manufactures textiles. **Three-year return: 2.6%**

Deutsche International Equity

800-730-1313	www.usfunds.db.com

MANAGERS: Michael Levy, Robert Reiner, Julie Wang

This trio skipped last year's rush into Japanese financial stocks (which have since tanked—again) and instead kept two-thirds of their money in Europe, where they believe a bull market is just getting started. Time will tell. Until then, know that Deutsche International (renamed last year from BT Investment International Equity) ranks in the top 15% of all foreign-stock funds during the past five years. **Three-year return: 21.9%**

Dodge & Cox Stock

800-621-3979	www.dodgeandcox.com

MANAGERS: Team

The Dodge & Cox crew avoids the higher-valued half of the S&P 500 and instead zeroes in on cheaper large-caps that seem to be moving toward some kind of earnings surprise. They're patient too, with an average holding period of four to six years. The fund rebounded last year from a rather tough 1998, thanks in part to big wagers on Alcoa, Motorola and Sony. **Three-year return: 16.8%**

Domini Social Equity Fund

800-762-6814	www.domini.com

MANAGERS: Amy Domini, team

The Domini fund legitimized socially responsible investing by producing fiscally responsible returns—helped considerably by its 42% stake in tech companies that tend to be eco- and worker-friendly. Similar funds could be cheaper, but probably not nearly as feisty: As an activist shareholder Domini badgers big shots like Arco, McDonald's and R.R. Donnelly to clean up their corporate acts. **Three-year return: 30.2%**

Dresdner RCM Global Technology

800-726-7240	www.drcmfunds.com

MANAGERS: Huachen Chen, Walter Price

The managers diversify across technology subsectors, market caps and regions, and offset the usual momentum plays with some surprising value picks. In fact, their top holding, Tyco International, is technically not a tech stock, but Chen and Price believe that the battered conglomerate's various tech and telecom divisions will soon drive its fortunes. **Three-year return: N.A.**

Dreyfus Appreciation

800-373-9387	www.dreyfus.com

MANAGERS: Fayez Sarofim, Russell Hawkins

Growth guru Sarofim is 71, but he has groomed Hawkins, 45,

for two decades. Their "foolproof" system—buying and holding profit-powered, multinational brand names—seemed almost foolish last year as Wall Street abandoned holdings like Coca-Cola and Gillette for dotcoms. "That's just not the pond we fish in,"says Hawkins. After reeling in returns that beat the S&P 500 for six of the past 10 years, these managers stick by their methods. And rightly so. **Three-year return: 21.4%**

Eclipse Small Cap Value

800-872-2710   www.eclipsefund.com

MANAGERS: Wesley McCain, Kathy O'Connor
By their balance sheets ye shall know them. McCain and O'Connor ignore corporate managers and analyst forecasts and focus strictly on financials. Highly diversified (280 stocks) and with a relatively slim 14% tech stake, the fund could be a haven in a heartless market. **Three-year return: 12.1%**

EuroPacific Growth

800-421-0180   www.americanfunds.com

MANAGERS: Team

 No sector or country guidelines here (other than no U.S. holdings). The managers, and there are seven of 'em, have the freedom to pick companies individually according to their own convictions. "It's an Athenian democracy, in a sense," says manager Mark Denning. And a lucrative one: The fund's 10-year return tops nearly 99% of its international peers. **Three-year return: 26.4%**

Excelsior Value & Restructuring

800-446-1012   www.excelsiorfunds.com

MANAGER: David Williams

Plenty of value folks try to spot companies that are reconfiguring their businesses, but few pull it off like Williams, who has whipped 99% of his peers over the past five years and has beaten the S&P 500 six of the fund's seven years. Surprisingly, nonvalue holdings like Qualcomm and Nokia helped propel the fund's 42% lift last year. In fact, Williams is 37% weighted in technology and telecommunications, although he expects that number to shrink as traditional value plays come back in vogue. **Three-year return: 31%**

Fasciano

| 800-848-6050 | www.fascianofunds.com |

MANAGER: Michael Fasciano

This tech-skeptical growth manager has found enough reasonably priced small-caps to get fully invested again. (Fasciano had a 45% cash stake not too long ago—"a once-in-a-lifetime event," he insists.) His formula—above-average earnings jumps plus below-average P/E ratios for a growth fund—still looks like a long-term winner to us. **Three-year return: 13%**

Fidelity

| 800-544-8888 | www.fidelity.com |

MANAGER: Nicholas Thakore

This fund's veteran manager, Beth Terrana, recently announced her departure. We suggest giving successor Nicholas Thakore a chance. He posted a 40.7% return with Fidelity Trend in 1999 but has spent only two years running diversified funds. Before that, Thakore ran Fidelity select portfolios. Replacement managers at Fidelity's best funds seldom turn out to be flops. The fund's largest holdings include General Electric, Microsoft, Nokia, Cisco and Citigroup. **Three-year return: 30.4%**

Fidelity Diversified International

| 800-544-8888 | www.fidelity.com |

MANAGER: Gregory Fraser

Fraser uses 27 computer models and visits with executives from hundreds of companies throughout the year to build a relatively stable portfolio of more than 400 overseas stocks, including British oil giant BP Amoco, Canadian telecom company BCE and Japanese electronics maker Kyocera. "I could easily turn up the return-generating motor,"says the head mechanic. "But I don't think my customers have the stomach for gut-wrenching volatility." **Three-year return: 24.2%**

First Eagle Fund of America

| 800-451-3623 | www.firsteaglefunds.com |

MANAGERS: David Cohen, Harold Levy

These trusted value hunters have long topped their peers by paying far more attention to cash flows than to P/E ratios. This led them to cable stocks in the mid-1990s and to tech-service names like Comdisco today. Some weak health-care buys hurt the fund last year, but Cohen and Levy's sharp eyes should help this eagle soar again. **Three-year return: 19.9%**

Franklin California Growth

800-342-5236	www.franklintempleton.com

MANAGERS: Conrad Herrmann, Canyon Chan

 California-based Franklin created this fund in 1991 to take advantage of the 1,400 public companies located in its own backyard. While heavily focused—no surprise—on Silicon Valley, Herrmann and Chan say market jitters have inspired them to buy Gap, Safeway and Wells Fargo. **Three-year return: 47.4%**

Fremont U.S. Small Cap

800-548-4539	www.fremontfunds.com

MANAGER: David Kern

This young cousin of Fremont U.S. Micro-Cap (which recently closed to new investors) has about half its assets in technology and telecommunications stocks, which helps explain how it was 82 percentage points ahead of the Russell 2000 growth index in 1999. **Three-year return: N.A.**

Gabelli Asset

800-422-3554	www.gabelli.com

MANAGER: Mario Gabelli

Gabelli likes companies going through big changes that can unlock their hidden value. That has led him to media companies and utilities and has prompted a recent investment in Ralston Purina, which Gabelli says is a prime takeover target for Swiss food conglomerate Nestlé. **Three-year return: 26.4%**

Gabelli Westwood Equity

800-422-3554	www.gabelli.com

MANAGER: Susan Byrne

Byrne considers herself a "foster parent" to underappreciated stocks that have turned around or are starting to improve their balance sheets. "We buy in the face of skepticism," says Byrne. "Then they make it, and they're adopted by growth managers." One of her latest kids: Avon. **Three-year annual return: 19.2%**

Hancock Financial Industries

800-225-5291	www.johnhancock.com

MANAGER: James Schmidt

One of the wisest financial services investors around, Schmidt blames tech stocks for "sapping attention from real earners"— like, ahem, banks—and thus for his negative return in 1999. Holdings like Merrill Lynch fared better, helping keep him on top of similar funds. Schmidt predicts a bounce for financial stocks when the Fed stops raising rates and merger activity picks up. **Three-year return: 15%**

Harbor Capital Appreciation

800-422-1050	www.harborfund.com

MANAGER: Spiros "Sig" Segalas

 Sig Segalas has thrived in recent years by owning market stars like Cisco and Intel. So what makes him special? Unlike many growth managers, he also fared well even in the value-oriented markets of the mid-1990s. Few can match his 10-year record of 25.4% annualized. And his 0.68% expense ratio puts most other active managers to shame. **Three-year return: 44.3%**

Homestead Value

800-258-3030	www.nreca.org/homestead

MANAGERS: Stuart Teach, Peter Morris

 "We've been getting a lot of angry, nasty phone calls," says Morris, as shareholders complain about Homestead's 3.2% loss in 1999. "But if sticking to investment principles means anything anymore, then that's our greatest attribute." Teach and Morris have lately been buying mid-size energy, pharmaceutical and financial services stocks. "Some of them," Morris marvels, "are cheaper than they were in [the bear market of] 1974." **Three-year return: 8.5%**

Hotchkis & Wiley International

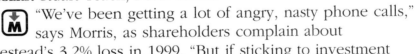

800-236-4479	www.hotchkisandwiley.com

MANAGERS: Harry Hartford, Sarah Ketterer, David Chambers

"We can't play the momentum game," says Ketterer. "It's like playing musical chairs: When the music ends, you can be left without a chair." The trio wants companies with strong cash streams that return real value to shareholders, either through dividends, stock buybacks or investments that spark further sales and profits. That's why they've recently been grabbing shares of consumer-products giant Unilever. **Three-year return: 10.9%**

Invesco Health Sciences

| 800-525-8085 | www.invesco.com |

MANAGER: John Schroer
Johnson & Johnson meets PE Biosystems. This is an impressive mix of 60 old and new health-care and biotech companies that are poised to benefit from the fossilization of baby boomers and the introduction of gene therapies that could revolutionize medicine. **Three-year return: 20.9%**

Janus

| 800-525-8983 | www.janus.com |

MANAGER: Blaine Rollins

[A] This high-testosterone fund's approach is less about P/E ratios and more about owning companies like Cisco, Sun Microsystems and others that dominate their markets and reinvest in operations to spur even more growth. **Three-year return: 40.6%**

Janus Special Situations

| 800-525-8983 | www.janus.com |

MANAGER: David Decker
Part value, part growth, this fund includes stocks that Decker thinks are poised for turnarounds, as well as overlooked companies whose increasing cash flows and rising returns on that capital suggest potential pops. Big scores by Apple, China Telecom and Station Casinos helped generate a 52.5% gain in 1999 vs. 21% for the S&P 500. **Three-year return: 44.6%**

Janus Worldwide

| 800-525-8983 | www.janus.com |

MANAGERS: Helen Young Hayes, Laurence Chang

[$] [A] Hayes and her co-manager have outshone 98% of their world-stock peers during the past five years, largely by wagering on fast growers with lots of lucre rolling in. Among them are Mannesmann (Germany), NTT DoCoMo (Japan) and Sprint (U.S.). Its tech stake (about 50%) is easily twice that of the average world stock fund's. **Three-year return: 38.2%**

Japan

800-535-2726   www.scudder.com

MANAGER: Seung Kwak

Buying undervalued companies of all sizes in almost every industry, Kwak gives you the widest imaginable slice of Japan. Last year saw an awesome 120% gain for the fund, as international investors jumped back into the world's second largest consumer market and bid up Japanese stocks. Don't expect as big a gain this year. Most experts say Japan still has a long way to go before turning around its moribund economy. **Three-year return: 38.5%**

Kemper-Dreman High Return Equity

800-621-1048   www.kemper.com

MANAGER: David Dreman

Don't dump Dreman for his lousy returns of late. The celebrated manager is doing what he told you he'd do: buying values. "And if 1998 was a terrible year for value," he notes, "there has never been anything like '99." After scoring double digits for six of the past 10 years, Dreman lost 13% in 1999, largely on health care, banks and tobacco. He's had gains in oil services and cheaper tech, like Apple, as he waits for a market turn. "If there's another year like the last," he jokes, "I'll quit." **Three-year return: 7%**

Legg Mason Value

800-577-8589   www.leggmason.com

MANAGER: William Miller III

Bill Miller has hammered the S&P 500 nine years in a row by betting big on technology. So it's news when he declares, "The simpleminded game of overweighting tech to outperform the market is over." He's scaled back the hot sector to about half his former allocation and upped his stakes in Aetna and Waste Management. His outlook for the year? Single-digit market returns. **Three-year return: 35.5%**

Longleaf Partners

800-445-9469   www.longleafpartners.com

MANAGERS: O. Mason Hawkins, G. Staley Cates, John Buford

Longleaf was up a mere 2.2% last year, thanks to its big stake in Waste Management, which lost two-thirds of its value right after Longleaf bought it. "Everybody thinks we've gone brain dead," says Cates. They won't be flatliners forever. The 20 or so stocks in Longleaf's portfolio trade at 53% of what the managers think they're worth—far below the 69% of appraised value the portfolio has averaged in the past decade—which means big potential gains ahead. **Three-year return: 11.5%**

Longleaf Partners Realty

800-445-9469	www.longleafpartners.com

MANAGERS: C.T. Fitzpatrick, O. Mason Hawkins, G. Staley Cates
They buy not just real estate investment trusts, but realty-related businesses, like hotels, timber and mortgage financing. Many of Longleaf's holdings are trading at around 40% of their true value. **Three-year return: -3.3%**

Loomis Sayles International

800-633-3330	www.loomissayles.com

MANAGERS: Eswar Menon, Alexander Muromcew, John Tribolet

N **A** A management triumvirate divvies up emerging markets (Menon), Asia (Muromcew) and Europe (Tribolet) and settles on about 120 holdings. The managers believe communications and information technology will be powering global growth, which basically explains why Nokia, Ericsson and Yahoo! Japan are in their top 10. **Three-year return: 28.4%**

Mairs & Power Growth

800-304-7404

MANAGERS: George Mairs, Bill Frels
This homebody fund specializes in companies with headquarters literally within an hour's drive of its base in St. Paul. Deep into healthcare and financial firms like Medtronic and U.S. Bancorp, Mairs & Power owns only 30 stocks and keeps them for eons. It's held 3M since 1958 and has bought only one new stock within the past year: Minneapolis-based chemicals company Valspar. To discourage short-termers (and keep its expense ratio a low 0.79%), Mairs & Power does not allow shareholders to redeem their shares by telephone. And it's sold in just 20 states (including New York and California). A website? You've got to be kidding. **Three-year return: 15%**

Marsico Focus

888-860-8686	www.marsicofunds.com

MANAGER: Tom Marsico

 Marsico runs a tight portfolio (between 20 and 30 stocks) that holds rockets like EMC and Qualcomm and tugboats

like Sony and Wal-Mart. He was up 51% in 1998 and 55% in 1999. **Three-year return: N.A.**

MAS Mid Cap Growth

800-354-8185	www.msdw.com

MANAGERS: Arden Armstrong, Steve Chulik, David Chu

  Lead manager Armstrong has turned in one of the best 10-year performances among midcap growth funds. She balances what she calls stable growth stocks (such as medical equipment firm Lincare Holdings) with aggressive growth plays (such as chipmaker Maxim), all the while limiting her bets on any one stock. **Three-year return: 56.6%**

MAS Small Cap Growth

800-354-8185	www.msdw.com

MANAGERS: Arden Armstrong, Steve Chulik, David Chu

 Armstrong and company's two-year-old small-cap vehicle roared out of the gate with a 300% gain in 1999. They're unlikely to repeat that IPO-charged performance, but their history at MAS Mid Cap suggests this one will grow into a consistent winner. **Three-year return: N.A.**

Masters' Select Equity

800-960-0188	www.mastersselect.com

MANAGERS: Shelby and Christopher Davis, Sig Segalas, Foster Friess, Mason Hawkins, Bill Miller, Richard Weiss

Miller had better watch out for the jinx: He's just replaced ex-Oakmarker Robert Sanborn (who last year replaced the underperforming Jean-Marie Eveillard) in the value slot of this multimanager fund. The idea here is to put the best picks of the best managers (all of whom happen to be in the MONEY 100, by the way) into one fund. So far, so good: Not only did this fund beat the market in '99, it beat these managers' combined returns at their own portfolios. **Three-year return: 26.8%**

MFS Capital Opportunities

800-637-2929	www.mfs.com

MANAGER: Maura Shaughnessy

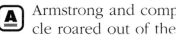 Shaughnessy overcame plenty of skepticism when she took over in early 1999 by driving the fund to a 58% one-year return. She quickly tossed out a huge bet on troubled conglomerate Tyco International and pumped up tech from a smidgen of

assets to a full third. No newbie, Shaughnessy has managed money at MFS for eight years, notably at top-performing Utilities (which she continues to run). **Three-year return: 40.6%**

MFS Massachusetts Investors Trust

800-637-2929	www.mfs.com

MANAGERS: John Laupheimer, Mitch Dynan
The oldest mutual fund couldn't keep up with the New Economy last year. Late to the tech game, the managers were punished for favoring the likes of Pfizer and Hartford Financial Services. While they've upped tech, they stick to the big name brands (like GE and Bell Atlantic) that have produced rock-solid returns and held this fund steady over many, many years. **Three-year return: 20.3%**

Neuberger Berman Partners

800-877-9700	www.nbfunds.com

MANAGERS: Robert Gendelman, Basu Mullick
After this midcap fund surpassed $3 billion in assets in 1998, Gendelman and Mullick began buying bigger stakes in larger companies like Merck, Cigna and GTE. Yes, we suppose that makes them guilty of style drift, but their shift in stock size has proved to be a sound move. The fund performed in the top half of its value category last year after wallowing in the bottom quarter in 1998. **Three-year return: 13.5%**

New Perspective

800-421-0180	www.americanfunds.com

MANAGERS: Team
  The seven managers are generalists, but their analysts, who cover specific sectors like domestic telecoms or international pharmaceuticals, also have responsibility for investing portions of the fund's assets. As the numbers show, it works. **Three-year return: 29%**

Nicholas

800-227-5987	www.nicholasfunds.com

MANAGERS: Albert Nicholas, David Nicholas
A piddling 1.7% gain was all this fund could muster in 1999, but the longer record shows that father and son do well by such market share leaders as General Motors, Motorola and American Home Products. They hold a 23% health-care stake and 18% in financial stocks, so when pharmaceuticals and banks bounce back, so will Nicholas. **Three-year return: 17.3%**

Nicholas-Applegate Growth Equity

800-551-8643	www.prudential.com

MANAGER: William Chenoweth

  When Chenoweth took over in 1998, he brought the same methods he had successfully deployed at now closed Turner Small Cap Growth. Looking for earnings surprises and price momentum, he has accumulated a 55% tech stake, with midcap companies like Veritas Software and e-commerce security outfit VeriSign. **Three-year return: 51.8%**

Oakmark

800-625-6275	www.oakmark.com

MANAGER: Bill Nygren

Value legend Robert Sanborn, who launched this fund, could not convince enough investors to stick with him—and picks like Mattel and Philip Morris—during this long growth-market rout. If there's a silver lining behind his recent departure, however, it's that new manager Nygren's bargain-hunting instincts at sister fund Oakmark Select have been so keen he's found undervalued stocks even in the tech sector. Nygren plans to broaden the flagship portfolio back to 40 or 50 stocks from a low of 20. (Sanborn had been selling off many of his stocks to meet heavy redemptions that helped slash the fund's assets from $8 billion at the end of 1998 to about $2 billion this spring.) And for those considering Nygren for a taxable account, accumulated losses at Oakmark should forestall capital-gains distributions for a while. **Three-year return: 2.5%**

Oakmark Select

800-625-6275	www.oakmark.com

MANAGER: Bill Nygren

Nygren's value strategy actually beat the S&P 500 during the past three years, thanks to savvy choices like newspaper chain Times Mirror and software company Sterling Commerce, both recently bought out at fat premiums. If Nygren gets one wrong, however, the consequences can be dire: Oakmark Select won't hold more than 20 names. **Three-year return: 28.3%**

Oak Value

800-622-2474	www.oakvaluefund.com

MANAGERS: David R. Carr Jr., George W. Brumley III

Along with an 11% stake in Warren Buffett's Berkshire Hathaway,

Carr and Brumley have grabbed cheap cash-generating small-caps (such as insurer RLI) and have tiptoed into tech, recently buying Compaq. **Three-year return: 15.2%**

Oppenheimer Main Street Growth & Income

800-525-7048	www.oppenheimerfunds.com

MANAGERS: Charles Albers, Nikolaos Monoyios

Albers and Monoyios use computer models, but it's not strictly numbers. They avoided JDS Uniphase and Qualcomm because they felt the stocks were speculatively priced. Albers concedes that this led to "mediocre" performance between October and March, but with recent market volatility, their decision looks pretty smart. **Three-year return: 23.9%**

Putnam International Growth

800-225-1581	www.putnaminv.com

MANAGERS: Team

[M] With 20% of assets in Japan, another 17% in the U.K., and technology, energy and consumer staples dominating a smartly diversified portfolio of 120 large-caps, this is one of the best international plays out there. It has passed its benchmark (Morgan Stanley's Europe, Australasia and Far East index) in seven of the past nine years. **Three-year return: 32.1%**

Rainier Core Equity

800-248-6314	www.rainierfunds.com

MANAGERS: Team

Alcoa, Baxter and Citigroup are major holdings in this large-cap vehicle, which has 20% of its assets in mid-size stocks. Returns have barely beaten (and have even trailed) the S&P 500 during the past few years, but the 100-stock fund is still firmly in the top quarter of its category. **Three-year return: 29%**

Royce Premier

800-221-4268	www.roycefunds.com

MANAGER: Charles Royce

Royce's commitment to low-priced small-fry is paying off again. Over the 12 months ended March 31, he beat the S&P by more than 12 percentage points. These days, he hunts for bargains among insurers like Aon and downmarket retailers like Ross Stores. **Three-year return: 12.9%**

RS MidCap Opportunities

800-766-3863	www.rsim.com

MANAGER: John Wallace

N A With nearly half its assets in tech, RS MidCap can be volatile, but it's steadier and cheaper than Wallace's other charge, RS Diversified Growth (up 129% last year). At RS and former employer Oppenheimer (where he ran Main Street Growth & Income during much of the 1990s), Wallace racked up one of the best management records of the entire decade. He sets high standards, buying only stocks he thinks can double in 18 months. And if one drops 15%, it's outta there. Says Wallace: "We cut our losses quickly." **Three-year return: 37.5%**

Safeco Equity

800-624-5711	www.safecofunds.com

MANAGER: Richard Meagley

N This 68-year-old fund survived the Great Depression, so we think it can handle a few bumpy months in the Nasdaq. Richard Meagley, who's been running things since 1995, oversees the $1.9 billion mix of blue-chip growth and value stocks. Washington Mutual is No. 1 in a portfolio that should be subtitled, "Slow and steady wins the race." **Three-year return: 18.1%**

Schwab 1000

800-435-4000	www.schwab.com

MANAGER: Geri Hom

Veteran indexer Hom may well deserve a lifetime achievement award in tax-efficiency: The $5.3 billion asset fund, which owns the thousand largest U.S. companies, has not paid a capital-gains distribution since its inception in 1991. **Three-year return: 27.5%**

Scudder International

800-225-2470	www.scudder.com

MANAGERS: Irene Cheng, team

N Cheng seeks good buys in thriving industries and emphasizes specific countries when trends look good. (Her Japan stake, for instance, zoomed from 10% to 30% this past year—a bold move that paid off big-time.) Also helping matters is Scudder's notably deep international research department.
Three-year return: 25.5%

Selected American Shares

800-243-1575	www.selectedfunds.com

MANAGERS: Christopher Davis, Ken Feinberg

Davis and Feinberg prefer their value stocks with a growth twist, scooping up blackened blue chips and hanging on for the inevitable rebound. About 41% of Selected American Shares recently was in financial stocks, including American Express and Citigroup, and 31% was in tech stocks such as Hewlett-Packard, Oracle and Texas Instruments. Davis fans take note: Legendary manager Shelby Davis (Chris' 63-year-old dad) still guides the fund as its senior research adviser. **Three-year return: 27.2%**

Sound Shore

800-551-1980	www.soundshorefund.com

MANAGERS: Harry Burn III, T. Gibbs Kane Jr.

Sound Shore trailed the average midcap fund last year thanks to sour picks like Bank One (since sold). But in their 15-year run, Burn and Kane have forged one of the best records in their class, with a streamlined collection of 40 pure value picks. They picked up Safeway when it hit bottom late last year, figuring that the grocery chain's new Web strategy should keep earnings strong. **Three-year return: 13.5%**

SSGA Emerging Markets

800-647-7327	www.ssgafunds.com

MANAGER: Brad Aham

Aham, an analyst at the fund before taking the reins in September, is keen on financial and service companies in this 405-stock portfolio. Diversification muffles his gains but also limits risk: Investors get truly global exposure while avoiding the blowups that have bedeviled other emerging markets funds. Samsung is the top holding in a portfolio that ranges from Korea Telecom to DeBeers. **Three-year return: 5.1%**

SSGA Growth & Income

800-647-7327	www.ssgafunds.com

MANAGER: L. Emerson Tuttle

When Tuttle is high on an industry, he'll load up heavily, as he's done in communications and energy with stocks like Lucent, WorldCom, Duke Energy and Arco. Still, since most of his assets come from employee savings plans, he's designed the fund as a core holding that owns a reasonable 60 or so stocks. "Our first job," he explains, "is to beat the S&P consistently, not to hit a home run and then strike out three times." **Three-year return: 31.7%**

Stein Roe Young Investor

800-338-2550	www.steinroe.com

MANAGERS: David Brady, Erik Gustafson

It's a fund designed for kids (with a $100 minimum investment under a $50-a-month savings plan), but its returns would impress any grown-up. The savvy Brady and Gustafson invest in the products and services that teens live by, like McDonald's and AOL. **Three-year return: 31.2%**

Strong Opportunity

800-368-1030	www.estrong.com

MANAGER: Dick Weiss

Weiss looks for companies selling for less than what he figures a takeover price would be. This year, he's buying cheap Old Economy stocks that'll benefit from New Economy technologies, such as W.W. Grainger. He's also waiting to pounce as dotcoms get even cheaper. But he won't name which ones just yet.
Three-year return: 27.9%

Strong Schafer Value

800-368-1030	www.estrong.com

MANAGER: David Schafer

This one has been a disappointment, losing 16.4% last year. But Schafer, who survived the 1973-74 bear market as a pension manager, is confident that his value style will return. "My stocks keep delivering earnings," he notes. "And sooner or later Wall Street will catch on." Signs are, it'll be sooner. As the market broadened this spring, the fund suddenly soared into the top 25% of its value category, thanks to names like distributor Arrow Electronics and pharmaceuticals company Alza. **Three-year return: 0.3%**

TCW Galileo Select Equities

800-386-3829	www.tcwgroup.com

MANAGER: Glen Bickerstaff

This is a year-old retail version of an institutional fund that has outshone the S&P 500 six years straight.

Bickerstaff moved to TCW in 1998 after shining at Transamerica. He hunts for companies that will dominate their field, such as Intel, Home Depot and Kansas City Southern (the railroad that owns Janus Funds). Bickerstaff holds fewer than 40 stocks in just six sectors, so he's not for the timid. His largest stake these days? Dell Computer. **Three-year return: N.A.**

Templeton Developing Markets

800-342-5236   www.franklintempleton.com

MANAGERS: J. Mark Mobius, Tom Wu, H. Allan Lam
Patience helps when riding the swings of emerging markets. And patience really pays when your money manager is Mobius. This fund was pummeled in 1997 and '98 after investing aggressively in the ruins of Asia. But in '99, as Asia started to recover, so did the fund, which posted a sweet 51.6% gain. **Three-year return: -1.5%**

Third Avenue Value

800-443-1021   www.mjwhitman.com

MANAGER: Martin Whitman
 A timely 40% stake in semiconductor companies, scooped up during 1998's tech meltdown, led Third Avenue to a category-stomping 12.8% gain last year. "I was lucky," says Whitman, "since the other 60% of my portfolio had terrible underperformance." Not to worry. Over the past five years, Whitman's policy of buying safe and cheap has kept the fund in the top 10% of its small-value peers. **Three-year return: 18.6%**

TIAA-CREF Growth Equity

800-223-1200   www.tiaa-cref.org

MANAGERS: Nancy Wadelton, Ted Wolff
 This youngster is a clone of excellent TIAA-CREF institutional accounts. The managers want high growth, but "don't go for broke," says Wolff. Translation: They won't buy Pets.com, but will play the Internet with companies that can fill the cybermaw, such as Liberty Media. And if they can't find the right stock, they won't sit on cash. A chunk of the fund's assets always tracks the Russell 3000 growth index, which makes this growth portfolio more consistent than most. **Three-year return: N.A.**

TIAA-CREF Social Choice Equity

800-223-1200	www.tiaa-cref.org

MANAGERS: Joan Deneher, Russell Gregory-Allen

  Barely a month old, this instantly became one of the best choices around for investors who want to track the S&P 500 while avoiding companies in the index that, among other things, sell weapons (GE) or fail environmental screens (Exxon Mobil). A skimpy 0.27% expense ratio is an enormous edge in the pricey social-funds market. **Three-year return: N.A.**

Torray

800-443-3036	www.torray.com

MANAGERS: Robert Torray, Douglas Eby

Torray and Eby look for what they call "superior" businesses that can grow 15% a year but may have been tossed aside by Wall Street because of earnings disappointments or other kinds of performance blips. With stalwarts like Kimberly-Clark and Illinois Tool Works—as well as newer holdings like Disney and Abbott Laboratories—the value fund returned 24% last year. **Three-year return: 22.7%**

T. Rowe Price Emerging Markets Stock

800-638-5660	www.troweprice.com

MANAGERS: Team

N You won't find these managers plopping 20% of their assets in Korea or any other single hot market. They pick stocks, not countries, targeting growing companies that are selling at respectable prices. Tech and telecom were the winning plays last year, of course, but management trimmed companies like China Telecom and Egyptian Mobile Phone Network as prices got heady, and added to steadier stocks like Teléfonos de México and Teva Pharmaceutical Industries. **Three-year return: 11.1%**

T. Rowe Price Equity Income

800-638-5660	www.troweprice.com

MANAGER: Brian Rogers

A dividend-income approach was not the path to success in 1999. But Rogers has a solid 15-year record, and the portfolio is full of dependable names backed by steady dividends. March and April's nasty markets really could make an investor appreciate this fund's conservative charms. Equity Income held up much better than the market during the roughest days—and has a history as a strong performer in bearish times. **Three-year return: 11.3%**

T. Rowe Price International Stock

800-638-5660	www.troweprice.com

MANAGERS: Team

The strategy: Buy blue chips and hold them as long as earnings grow steadily. Also: Avoid dramatic country or sector bets. Management moved slowly into hot areas like Japan and tech, so this fund lagged in 1999. But modest risks and moderate expenses have made it a long-term leader. **Three-year return: 17.3%**

T. Rowe Price Mid-Cap Growth

800-638-5600	www.troweprice.com

MANAGER: Brian Berghuis

Berghuis holds a diverse group of companies expanding at least 12% a year. It's moderate stuff for a growth fund, but Berghuis has kept pace with his peers during his eight-year tenure while keeping risk below average. His low-turnover style also leads to above-average after-tax returns. **Three-year return: 28.1%**

T. Rowe Price Science & Technology

800-638-5660	www.troweprice.com

MANAGER: Chip Morris

This diversified techie returned "only" 101% in 1999, lagging those with more dotcoms. Yet it wasn't hit as hard as other tech funds were when the Nasdaq nosedived in April. Morris is taking advantage of the confusion to bulk up on cheap Internet infrastructure, while trimming PC-related positions to less than 5%. **Three-year return: 55.7%**

T. Rowe Price Small Cap Stock

800-638-5660	www.troweprice.com

MANAGER: Gregory McCrickard

Technology is only a quarter of this 230-plus stock portfolio, which offsets growth bets with classic value plays. Disciplined diversification has led to top-half performance year in, year out—translating to top third overall returns in the long run. You'd be hard-pressed to find a more reliable and less expensive performer. **Three-year return: 17.4%**

T. Rowe Price Value

800-638-5660	www.troweprice.com

MANAGER: Brian Rogers

Rogers is more aggressive here than he is at T. Rowe's Equity Income (see page 93). This is a midcap portfolio of stocks that were found, as he puts it, "on the trash heap"—such as medical-equipment maker Hillenbrand Industries, bought as it bottomed in 1999. **Three-year return: 13.7%**

Tweedy Browne American Value

800-432-4789	www.tweedy.com

MANAGERS: Chris Browne, Will Browne, John Spears

This 80-year-old value shop has seen its share of market cycles. The managers feel comfortable avoiding high-flying tech stocks in favor of names like American Express and municipal bond insurer MBIA. Longtime investors are certainly comfortable with a sterling record that outpaces 80% of midcap-value peers over the past five years. **Three-year return: 13.5%**

Tweedy Browne Global Value

800-432-4789	www.tweedy.com

MANAGERS: Chris Browne, Will Browne, John Spears

This fund keeps just 10% or so of its assets in U.S. stocks vs. the typical 30% held by most global funds. But the value mavens at Tweedy Browne minimize risk—and deliver solid returns—with their skinflint style. In late 1998, for example, they placed an 18% stake on beaten-down Japanese stocks and reaped outsize gains when the market took off. The bulk of the portfolio, however, is in Europe. Recent purchases include Diageo, the conglomerate that owns Pillsbury, Burger King and (to wash it down) Guinness. They slurped it up for 10 times earnings. **Three-year return: 18.6%**

Vanguard 500 Index

800-851-4999	www.vanguard.com

MANAGER: George "Gus" Sauter

Worried that S&P 500 indexing leaves you overexposed to overinflated tech stocks? Don't be, counsels Sauter. "The 500," he notes, "is a little light on tech relative to large-cap active managers." Fun fact: Vanguard 500, with about $107 billion in assets as of March 31, is neck and neck with Fidelity's Magellan ($109 billion) in claiming the largest-fund spot. **Three-year return: 27.4%**

Vanguard Global Asset Allocation

800-851-4999	www.vanguard.com

MANAGERS: Eric Bendickson, Michael A. Duffy

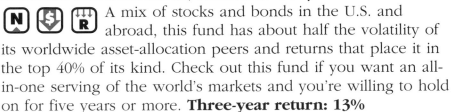 A mix of stocks and bonds in the U.S. and abroad, this fund has about half the volatility of its worldwide asset-allocation peers and returns that place it in the top 40% of its kind. Check out this fund if you want an all-in-one serving of the world's markets and you're willing to hold on for five years or more. **Three-year return: 13%**

Vanguard Health Care

800-851-4999	www.vanguard.com

MANAGER: Edward P. Owens

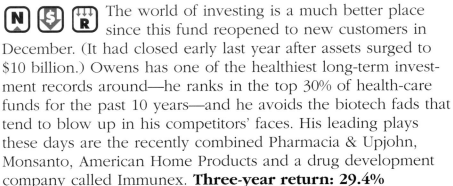 The world of investing is a much better place since this fund reopened to new customers in December. (It had closed early last year after assets surged to $10 billion.) Owens has one of the healthiest long-term investment records around—he ranks in the top 30% of health-care funds for the past 10 years—and he avoids the biotech fads that tend to blow up in his competitors' faces. His leading plays these days are the recently combined Pharmacia & Upjohn, Monsanto, American Home Products and a drug development company called Immunex. **Three-year return: 29.4%**

Vanguard International Growth

800-851-4999	www.vanguard.com

MANAGER: Richard Foulkes

Foulkes lagged the EAFE foreign benchmark recently, largely because he didn't jump into Japanese tech stocks. He says he prefers "well-managed companies," like Samsung and Vodafone AirTouch and takes comfort in being "a steadier performer" whose fund has easily outpaced most of its peers during the past 10 years. This is a worthy choice for folks who feel uncertain in overseas markets. **Three-year return: 16.8%**

Vanguard Small-Cap Index

800-851-4999	www.vanguard.com

MANAGER: George "Gus" Sauter

Sauter not only strives to mimic the performance of the Russell 2000 index, he has actually beaten that benchmark in four out of the past five years by as much as 2.2 percentage points. (That kind of performance can quickly add up to sizable amounts of money, considering the fund's low 0.3% expense ratio.) The fund's three-year gains here rank it in the top 20% of its peer group. **Three-year return: 18.9%**

Vanguard Total Stock Market Index

800-851-4999	www.vanguard.com

MANAGER: George "Gus" Sauter

You could consider this a tasting menu of the whole market—in this case, the stocks in the Wilshire 5,000 index. And you get them all at rock-bottom Vanguard costs. **Three-year return: 27.3%**

Vanguard U.S. Growth

800-851-4999	www.vanguard.com

MANAGERS: John Cole, David Fowler, J. Parker Hall III

  Although this portfolio of steady growers represents the old reliable approach to large-cap growth investing, last year the managers moved beyond Microsoft to spunkier plays like JDS Uniphase. **Three-year return: 31.1%**

Vanguard Windsor II

800-851-4999	www.vanguard.com

MANAGERS: James Barrow, team

Barrow's deep-value picks (Philip Morris, Imperial Tobacco, Waste Management) dragged him 6% into the red in 1999. But over 15 years, he has proved to be a master of the style. Value believers have reason to keep the faith. **Three-year return: 12.6%**

Wasatch Core Growth

800-551-1700	www.wasatchfunds.com

MANAGER: Samuel Stewart

Stewart has consistently beaten the Russell 2000 the past seven years by holding small companies that promise 15% to 20% earnings growth. Making a comeback, he says, are lower-quality credit companies. (AmeriCredit is the No. 1 holding in his portfolio.) He's also betting on health care, which gets a weighty 31% stake. One small-cap favorite: Orthodontic Centers of America. **Three-year return: 15.6%**

Washington Mutual Investors

800-421-0180	www.americanfunds.com

MANAGERS: Team

 Last year stank: a 1.2% return. But Wash-Mu isn't looking to chase fads. "In runaway markets, we will not keep up," says James Dunton, one of eight "portfolio counselors." The team sticks to NYSE issues that have paid a dividend in nine of the past 10 years. That's the reason the fund has a 16% annualized return—since 1985. **Three-year return: 15.7%**

Weitz Value

800-232-4161	www.weitzfunds.com

MANAGER: Wally Weitz

In the early 1990s, Weitz scooped telecom and cable stocks out of the bargain bin, and he let these winners ride: At year-end, Liberty Media, Telephone & Data Systems and Adelphia Communications totaled more than 18% of assets. But Weitz has also bought cheap names in banking, financial services and real estate. (Risk alert: The fund has more than 40% in financials and could be singed as interest-rate fears are fanned.) **Three-year return: 27.2%**

Westport Small Cap

888-593-7878	www.westportfunds.com

MANAGERS: Andrew Knuth, Ed Nicklin

This young small-cap blend fund grew 15.4% in 1998 and 42.7% in '99. Turnover last year was shockingly low for a small-capper—all of 10%—and holdings include lesser-known service and tech stocks like Conexant Systems and Emmis Communications. **Three-year return: N.A.**

White Oak Growth Stock

888-462-5386	www.oakassociates.com

MANAGERS: James Oelschlager, Donna Barton, Douglas MacKay

These two dozen big-name, big-return stocks tend to deliver on their big growth estimates. A teeny turnover rate means just one thing: These folks buy with conviction. When Eli Lilly, a top holding, took a plunge, the team added to its position. **Three-year return: 47.7%**

Life-Cycle Funds

Does investing ever seem like too much of a hassle for you? Would you rather visit the dentist than comb through thousands of mutual funds—or even 100 specially selected mutual funds—in search of winners? Would you rather *become* a dentist than fret about asset allocation? Then you, or a loved one who feels this way, should consider a life-cycle mutual fund.

"They're designed for reluctant investors who say, 'Take care of my money for me, and leave me alone,'" explains Patrick Reinkemeyer, investment consulting director at Morningstar.

Many investors have said just that. Assets in all life-cycle funds tracked by Morningstar hit $25.0 billion in May 2000, up about twelvefold since 1995. That makes this one of the fastest-growing mutual fund categories in the country.

Life-cycle funds hold stocks, bonds and cash in proportions that are considered appropriate for investors at specific ages, somewhat like those dog food brands that offer one nutritional mix for puppies and other blends for older pooches. So is it just a marketing gimmick? Yes and no. The funds do offer some value for a particular kind of investor. One definite advantage: Even the most conservative life-cycle funds tend to outperform CDs or money-market funds, those refuges of the risk averse. Adds Sheldon Jacobs, editor of the *No-Load Fund Investor* newsletter: "Funds that allocate your money among both stocks and bonds can be ideal for investors in the 15% tax bracket"—people who often can't afford big risks and want a balanced portfolio for a minimum investment.

How they work. About 70 such funds have allocations pegged to investors' ages. The typical mix: an aggressive version with more stocks than bonds (for those up to age 55 or so); a moderate combo that's evenly balanced (age 55 to retirement); and a conservative portfolio with more bonds than stocks (for retirees). Your sole burden is to switch funds as you age. Otherwise, you don't have to do a thing. For example, Dreyfus LifeTime Portfolios (800-645-6561) are available in growth, growth and income, and income versions. The growth portfolio returned an average of 14.8% annually over the past three years, fourteenth highest among life-cycle funds, according to Morningstar.

Some life-cycle offerings are funds of funds. The growth version of Vanguard LifeStrategy Funds (800-662-7447), for instance, buys only shares of four other Vanguard portfolios, three of them low-cost index funds. (The funds are Vanguard Total Stock Market Index, Vanguard Total Bond Market Index, Vanguard Total International Stock Index and Vanguard Asset Allocation.) Vanguard LifeStrategy Growth returned 15.6% annually during the past three years, ninth highest among its peers. But, given that about 20% of the portfolio is in high-quality bonds, Morningstar says the fund is "not designed for aggressive investors."

Some life-cycle funds try to make investing easier still. So-called targeted life-cycle funds ask you merely to select a fund named for the year when you expect to retire. As you approach that target date, the portfolio is weighted more heavily toward bonds. The third-ranked three-year performer among all life-cycle funds was Barclays Global Investors LifePath 2040 (available through Charles Schwab's OneSource, 800-435-4000), which yielded 18.0% annually for investors who are roughly 40 years from retirement. Of course, its return should decline, and you can guess why: LifePath 2040 is 90.2% in stocks. LifePath 2010, a companion fund with a more imminent retirement target, keeps only 45.0% in stocks, and it delivered 11.2% annually over the same three years.

Oddly enough, the cookie-cutter approach taken by these funds can be an advantage for some people. A 25 year old who plans to retire in 2040 might be investing too conservatively for his own good. He would never put 90.2% of his retirement money in equities—unless the Barclays Global Investors LifePath 2040 did it for him. Similarly, life-cycle funds could help an investor who would otherwise neglect to make prudent asset allocation adjustments as he aged.

But life-cycle funds do have drawbacks. For starters, they are meant to be all-in-one investments. If you have other money in taxable accounts or in sheltered portfolios such as IRAs or 401(k)s, those funds will throw your allocation off balance.

Moreover, age is hardly the only investment consideration. "I think appetite for risk is more important than age," Jacobs says. Also worth taking into account: how wealthy you are and how much risk you can afford.

For us, though, the chief drawback is this: You buy both stocks and bonds so that when you need to raise cash, you can choose which to sell, depending on market conditions, but a life-cycle fund never lets you make that choice. When you cash in each share, you unload stocks and bonds at the same time.

When It's Time to Sell a Fund

You just met the funds we like the most. But, if you are like most investors, there are probably some funds in your portfolio that *you* don't like anymore. Should you sell them? The answer might be yes—but not so fast.

If stock investors tend to hold losers too long, as we suggested in Chapter 2, mutual fund investors are often too quick to sell their underperformers. A study by the Boston market research firm Dalbar found that between 1984 and 1995 the average stock fund posted a yearly return of 12.3%, while the average investor in those funds earned just 6.3%. The problem, says San Diego money manager Michael Stolper, is that many investors bail out of funds in the hope of catching the next hot manager. That's a foolish game of follow the leader. But there are sound performance reasons to consider dumping a fund:

The fund is a consistent laggard. One quarter of poor performance does not a bad fund make. In fact, even one year's may not, either. "You should examine a fund's relative record over several different periods before selling," says Roy Weitz, whose website offers advice about mutual-fund-selling decisions (www.fundalarm.com). If your fund has underperformed its peer group average by one percentage point or more in the past year, he says, go back further. If it's lagged by two points in three years, or three points in five years, it may be time to sell.

The fund's style changes. If your fund portfolio is meant to spread your bets among several asset classes, that strategy can be thwarted if your large-cap fund's manager invests in, say, small technology companies to add sizzle to his or her record. Another problem: Top-performing funds sometimes get flooded with assets and begin to increase the size of the typical companies in which they invest. "It's not good for shareholders because you're not getting what you bargained for," says San Francisco money manager Kurt Brouwer, who oversees $500 million in fund portfolios for wealthy clients. Check with rating services such as Morningstar to determine if a fund is sticking to its knitting. Examine your fund's holdings for out-of-place stocks. Compare the median market cap of your fund's holdings today to that of a year ago.

A new manager fails to make the grade. Brouwer

thinks it's usually time to abandon ship when a new boss assumes the helm of an actively managed fund. A less severe response is to scrutinize performance more closely. "Large fund companies often have plenty of talent on the bench who can carry on the previous manager's philosophy," says Susan Belden, editor of the *No-Load Fund Analyst*. "So you don't have to assume the new guy will fall on his face." Her advice: Consider dumping the fund if it lags its peers by at least three percentage points over 18 months.

CHAPTER 4

The Case for Bonds

*S*tocks, stocks, stocks, stocks, stocks. Over the last decade, the equities market has captured the hearts and imaginations of the American investor. The mere suggestion that you should put even a cent of your money in bonds is often met with incredulous stares. After all, almost everyone knows that over the past seven decades, stocks have returned an annualized 11.4%, which is more than twice bonds' 5.3% gains. So who needs bonds? Smart investors, that's who. True, bonds don't regularly deliver gangbuster gains or offer stocks' long-term inflation protection or make for scintillating cocktail-party chat. But they do have their virtues. Here are some of the benefits bonds can provide:

■ **Diversification:** Although stocks historically return more than bonds, equities are also more volatile. That's why combining stocks with bonds will net you a more stable portfolio. In fact, portfolios that include stocks and bonds can give you much of the upside of equities while limiting risk— a definite plus in today's volatile market. During the past decade, a blend of 25% intermediate-term U.S. Treasuries and 75% large-company stocks would have provided almost 90% of stocks' return while reducing the jumpiness of your portfolio by nearly 20%.

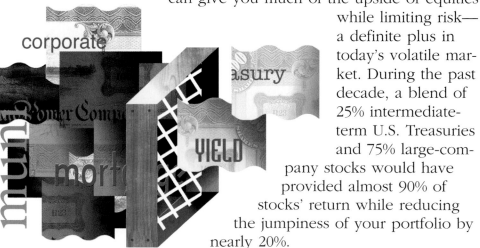

Bonds are also capable of beating stocks' performance when interest rates drop or when the stock market enters the doldrums. For instance, from 1969 to 1982, the 7.8% annual average return of medium-term U.S. bonds surpassed the 6.7% average gain of U.S. stocks. No surprise, then, that back in 1982 many investors were selling stocks to buy bonds. And guess what: 1982 also began the biggest bull market stocks have known. Just as you would have been wrong to put all your money in bonds in 1982, when stocks were stone cold, you might be wrong to put all your money in stocks today. As an investor, you should always consider buying what most people shun. Could anything be more ignored than bonds are at this stage of the bull market?

Still not convinced? Well, consider these two examples: In 1973 and 1974, when stocks fell 37.2%, bonds went up 10.6%. And in the murderous month of October 1987, stocks lost 21.5% of their value, but medium-term bonds rose 3%. As you can see, when stocks zigged, bonds zagged—providing a cushion when investors needed it.

Aggressive investors may balk at committing a full 25% of their portfolio to bonds—however, 20% is probably the lowest you should go to get the full benefit of bonds.

■ **Income.** Because bonds pay interest regularly, they are a good choice for investors—such as retirees—who desire a steady stream of income.

■ **Security.** Next to cash, U.S. Treasuries are the safest, most liquid investments on the planet. Short-term bonds are a good place to park an emergency fund or money you'll need relatively soon—say, to buy a house or pay college tuition in a few years.

Bonds provide a more subtle form of protection, as well. "Many investors," says Harvard economist John Campbell, "are unaware that their financial portfolio is dwarfed by the value of their human capital," by which he means their current and future job income. Most people's labor earnings are dependent on the health of the U.S. economy, since even a mild recession retards salary growth and a bad recession puts people out of work. Unless you're a minister, a mortician or a prison guard, your job income is probably tied to the stock market more closely than you think. Therefore, says Campbell, "if your labor earnings move with the aggregate stock market, you should take less risk in your financial portfolio."

U.S. Treasuries are the safest bonds of all because the interest and principal payments are guaranteed by the "full faith and credit"—that is, the taxing power—of the U.S. government. Interest is exempt from state and local taxes, but not from federal tax. Because of their almost total lack of default risk, Treasuries carry some of the lowest yields around.

Treasuries come in several flavors:

- **Treasury bills**, or T-bills, have the shortest maturities—13 weeks, 26 weeks and one year. You buy them at a discount to their $10,000 face value and receive the full $10,000 at maturity. The difference reflects the interest you earn.
- **Treasury notes** mature in two to 10 years. Interest is paid semiannually at a fixed rate. Minimum investment: $1,000.
- **Treasury bonds** have the longest maturities—10 to 30 years. They pay interest semiannually, and are sold in denominations of $1,000.
- **Zero-coupon bonds**, also known as "strips" or "zeros," are Treasury-based securities that are sold by brokers at a deep discount and redeemed at full face value when they mature in six months to 30 years. Although you don't actually receive your interest until the bond matures, you must pay taxes each year on the "phantom interest" that you earn. For that reason, they are best held in tax-deferred accounts. Because they pay no coupon, zeros can be highly volatile in price.
- **Inflation-indexed Treasuries (TIPs).** Issued in 10- and 30-year maturities (plus some five-year bonds issued earlier that are still trading on the secondary market), these pay a real rate of interest on a principal amount that rises or falls with the CPI. You don't collect the inflation adjustment to your principal

- **Tax savings.** Certain bonds, such as municipal bonds, provide tax-free income. Although these bonds usually pay lower yields than comparable taxable bonds, investors in high brackets (generally, 28% and above) can often earn higher after-tax returns from tax-free bonds. For instance, according to the fund firm T. Rowe Price, an investor in the 31% tax bracket would have earned returns equivalent to an annualized 10.3% in munis for the 10 years ended Sept. 30, 1999 vs. 8.5% in corporates and 7.9% in Treasuries. To figure out whether you should be in munis or taxables, calculate the muni's **taxable equivalent yield** using the worksheet on page 129.

until the bond matures or you sell it, but you owe federal income tax on that phantom amount each year—in addition to tax on the interest you receive currently. Inflation bonds are best held in tax-deferred accounts.

Mortgage-backed bonds represent an ownership stake in a package of mortgage loans issued or guaranteed by government agencies such as the Government National Mortgage Association (Ginnie Mae), Federal Home Loan Mortgage Corp. (Freddie Mac) and Federal National Mortgage Association (Fannie Mae). Interest is taxable and is paid monthly, along with a partial repayment of principal. Except for Ginnie Maes, these bonds are not backed by the full faith and credit of the U.S. government. They generally yield up to 1% more than Treasuries of comparable maturities. Minimum investment: typically $25,000.

Corporate bonds pay taxable interest. Most are issued in denominations of $1,000 and have maturities ranging from a few weeks to 100 years. Because their value depends on the creditworthiness of the company offering them, corporates carry higher risks and, therefore, higher yields than super-safe Treasuries. Top-quality corporates are known as **investment-grade bonds**. Corporates with lower credit quality are called **high-yield**, or **junk**, **bonds**. Junk bonds typically have higher yields than other corporates.

Municipal bonds, or munis, are America's favorite tax shelter. They are issued by state and local governments and agencies, usually in denominations of $5,000 and up, and mature in one to 30 or 40 years. Interest is exempt from federal taxes and, if you live in the state issuing the bond, state and possibly local taxes as well. Note, though, that Illinois, Kansas, Iowa, Oklahoma and Wisconsin tax interest on their own municipal bonds. No matter where you live, any capital gain you realize when you sell a municipal bond is fully taxable.

The Way Bonds Work

Back to Basics. Understanding the virtues of bond investing is only part of what you need to learn about fixed-income investing. To get the full benefit, you must understand how bonds work. Otherwise, you can get burned in ways you never imagined.

When you buy a bond, you're essentially lending money to a bond issuer, such as a corporation, municipality or the federal government, in return for the issuer's promise to pay a fixed rate of interest (the **coupon rate**) and to repay the principal or face

Bonding with Munis

You probably think municipal bonds are like an Oldsmobile—a conservative investment vehicle that only your father could love. Think again. Tax-exempt issues can be very attractive.

Even investors in the 28% federal tax bracket come out ahead with muni bonds. Here are some specifics. At first glance, a 6.44% yield on a 10-year Treasury, for instance, looks a lot better than the 5.50% yield on a 10-year insured muni. But you know what they say about looks. In reality, that 5.50% is equivalent to a taxable yield of 7.64% for investors in the 28% bracket, and 7.97% for those in the 31% bracket.

The muni payoff becomes even juicier if you live in a high-tax state, since residents usually don't pay state income tax on muni income, and in many large cities your yield will also be free from local levies. (The muni bond calculator at www.money.com can help you figure out taxable-equivalent yields.)

For most investors, mutual funds are the best way to buy munis. For an initial ante of $3,000 or less, you can find a solid bond fund that provides instant diversification, low fees and professional management.

YIELD OF DREAMS

Factor in the tax savings on munis, and their yields become alluring.

What a muni is really worth for an investor in the . . .

- 10-year Treasury note yield: **5.5%**
- High-grade muni yield: **4.7%**
- **6.5%** — 28% tax bracket
- **6.8%** — 31% tax bracket
- **7.3%** — 36% tax bracket

amount of the bond (typically $1,000) at the end of the bond's term (usually one to 30 years). While the coupon rate remains fixed after the bond is issued, the bond itself almost always sells for more or less than its face amount. As a result, a bond's **current yield**—the annual coupon payment divided by the current price—fluctuates daily. To evaluate whether a bond is paying a competitive return, ask your bond dealer or broker for its **yield to maturity**. This is the return you will earn based on the bond's coupon rate and current price if you hold the bond to maturity.

When shopping for a bond fund, focus on three questions: How long? How good? How much?

"How long?" refers to the average maturity of the bonds that a fund owns. The longer the maturity, the more the fund will suffer when rates rise. Intermediate-term issues with maturities of 10 years are your best bet. "You get 95% of the yield of longer maturities but with just 65% of the market risk," says Chris Ryon, who runs three Vanguard muni funds.

"How good?" is a matter of ratings. Stick with funds that own investment-grade issues, that is, those rated at least BBB by Standard & Poor's.

The answer to the question *"How much?"* should be zero—that is, you should not pay a sales load for a bond fund. If you live in a state with high income taxes, you can duck local levies by going with a fund that buys only munis issued in your own state.

Although it's theoretically more cost-effective to buy individual muni bonds, it can get tricky. Complicating the issue is the fact that investors have more muni bond choices than ever before. Of course, many of the 1.5 million outstanding issues are of topnotch quality—about half the new issues are insured, for example, and therefore rated triple A. But there is also a plethora of new, unrated health-care, hospital and industrial-development bonds. Their yields are attractive, but historically these bonds default at quadruple the rate of the overall muni market. "These days, issuers are using muni bonds for aquariums, racetracks, housing in the middle of the desert, anything to gin up economic development," says bond expert Joe Mysak.

The result: Lacking reliable price information, too many investors have simply chased the highest available yields and wound up holding dubious bonds. "You get these little old ladies canvassed by telephone in California, offered 8% bonds that are too good to be true," says bond pro Zane Mann.

How can you avoid getting snared? Buy a fund or buy highly-rated individual bonds at reasonable prices (check www.investinginbonds.com for comparable price quotes).

Generally, long-term bonds (those with 10- to 30-year maturities) have higher yields than intermediate-term (four to 10 years) issues, which, in turn, carry higher yields than short-term (one to four years) bonds. Under certain economic conditions, the Treasury curve can "invert," in which case this relationship would be temporarily reversed.

Similarly, because of the risk involved, the weaker the financial health of the issuer, the higher the rate investors demand. Junk bonds—or to use the euphemism preferred by junk issuers, "high-yield" bonds—typically pay two to $2^1/_2$ percentage points more than Treasury bonds, while high-quality corporate bonds usually yield one-half a percentage point or so more than Treasuries. Those margins change with market conditions.

Municipal bonds work pretty much the same way. But since the income they pay is free of federal (and sometimes state and local) tax, their yields are lower than taxable bonds'. (For a listing of types of bonds, see box on page 106.)

Risky business. Despite their wimpish image, it's not hard to lose money in bonds. Although the interest payments you'll get from owning a bond are "fixed," your return is anything but. One pitfall you've got to be on guard against is **credit risk**, also known as default risk—that is, the chance that the issuer won't pay interest when it's due or won't repay the principal when the bond matures. This isn't a concern if you invest in Treasury securities; Uncle Sam makes sure that we taxpayers pay his debts.

The danger of defaults is also relatively low for investment-grade corporates. A recent Standard & Poor's study of more than 7,300 bonds it has rated since 1981 found that just 2.1% of investment-grade corporates defaulted within 15 years of being issued.

Default rates are generally far lower than 2.1% for high-quality muni bonds. By contrast, 23% of junk bonds had defaulted within 15 years. To gauge credit risk, check out the ratings assigned by firms such as Standard & Poor's (see box on page 113).

But another type of risk is more likely to wreak havoc with your bond holdings—**interest-rate risk**. To get a handle on this hazard, think of a seesaw. When interest rates go up, bond prices go down, and vice versa. As the chart on the opposite page shows, the longer the bond's maturity, the more its price rises or falls in response to a change in interest rates.

But maturity gives you only a general idea of how a bond reacts to fluctuating rates. **Duration**, a technical measure that's too complicated and boring to go into here, provides a more accurate gauge. The higher a bond's duration (a figure that you can get from your broker), the more sensitive it is to interest rates. The price of a bond with a duration of seven years, for example, will decline a bit less than 7% if interest rates rise by

The Interest-Rate/Bond-Price Seesaw

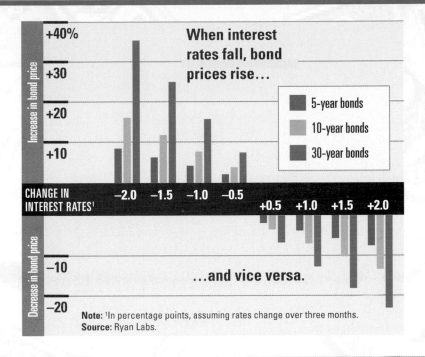

When interest rates fall, bond prices rise...

Increase in bond price

+40%
+30
+20
+10

- ■ 5-year bonds
- ■ 10-year bonds
- ■ 30-year bonds

CHANGE IN INTEREST RATES[1]   −2.0   −1.5   −1.0   −0.5   +0.5   +1.0   +1.5   +2.0

Decrease in bond price

−10
−20

...and vice versa.

Note: [1]In percentage points, assuming rates change over three months.
Source: Ryan Labs.

one percentage point and rise a bit more than 7% if rates drop by the same amount.

You should also be aware that some bonds have a **call provision** that allows the issuer to repay the principal on specified dates before maturity. If you own a callable bond with a coupon rate of 8% when new bonds are paying 6%, you can pretty much bet that the issuer will redeem it, leaving you to reinvest your money at lower rates. Before you buy a callable bond, ask the broker for its **yield to call** for each call date. This will tell you the return you'll earn if the issuer repays the bond early.

Bond strategies. If you're looking to bonds for income or to dampen the jumpiness of a stock portfolio, you're probably better off in short- to intermediate-term issues. Over the past 20 years, intermediate-term Treasuries provided almost 90% of long-term Treasuries' return with only half as much volatility.

You may also want to spread your money around by investing in a variety of bonds with different maturities. You could do

Top Bond Funds

Picking among more than 3,700 bond funds is a chore. Most just aren't worth bothering with, and many are carbon copies, especially those in the same sector. Therefore, look for funds that keep costs low. Here are some of our favorites:

FUND	1-YR	5 YEARS	10 YEARS	800 #
American Century Inflation-Adjusted Treasury	5.59	4.12[1]	—	345-2021
Fremont Bond	6.25	6.34	—	548-4539
Heartland Short-Duration High-Yield Muni	-1.39	3.44[2]	—	432-7856
Loomis Sayles Bond Retail	-0.33	10.97[2]	—	633-3330
Vanguard Total Bond Market Index	1.91	5.88	7.63	851-4999
Vanguard Tax-Exempt Intermediate-Term	0.16	4.52	6.56	851-4999

Notes: [1]Since inception, June 1998   [2]Since inception, January 1997.
All returns through May 31, 2000.

this by buying several bond funds (see below for more on bond funds) or by buying a half-dozen or more individual bonds to build a laddered bond portfolio, where each rung consists of a different maturity bond, from one year right on up to 10 years. When the one-year matures, you reinvest the money in a new 10-year issue. In this way, you always have more money to reinvest every year, and you are somewhat protected from interest rate shifts because you have locked in a range of yields.

If you want to go big-gain hunting, long-term issues are the place to be. Here you're betting that interest rates will fall. Remember, though, you can lose big if rates seesaw against you.

Bonds vs. bond funds. Next, consider whether bonds or bond funds are best for you. Conventional wisdom says bond funds are bad because, in almost every case, you have no assurance of getting your money back. If you buy a bond fund and interest rates rise, your net asset value will crash. But if you buy an actual bond, you can simply hold it to maturity and get your money back (barring the unlikely event of a default), no matter how much rates skyrocket.

As it so often is, the conventional wisdom is wrong. Individual bonds are better than bond funds only if you have a sizable sum to invest—say, a minimum of $75,000—to get the diversification you need. For the rest of us, bond funds with low expenses beat individual bonds hands down.

Here's why: the power of compounding. True enough, any rise in interest rates will temporarily depress the fund's value, as investors learned to their shock in 1994, when a jump in rates knocked the average bond fund for a 4% loss. But in the long run, higher rates mean a fund's income can be reinvested at greater yields.

Let's say you invest $1,000 in a 30-year Treasury bond at 6%. Between now and 2030, you'll get $30 in interest every six months. Now let's say interest rates rise one percentage point. If you put each of your bond's interest payments into an investment yielding the new rate of 7%, you'd actually earn 6.54% annually over the life of your 6% bond.

Here's where being a small investor is a big problem: The interest payments on your bond are only $30 apiece, and no one will sell you a bond for a lousy 30 bucks. Instead, you'll have to put your little nubbins of interest into the bank or a money fund, where they're likely to earn far less than the rate on new bonds. And thus you fail to harness the full power of compounding.

But a good fund manager will sweep together all the interest payments and reinvest them in bulk purchases of new, higher-yielding bonds. For this management service, funds charge annual expenses that average 1% or so of your account value.

Buy bonds on your own, and you sidestep the management fee. With the exception of Treasuries, however, most bonds don't trade every day, so it's hard to gauge their value. And although access to bond prices has improved a bit, bonds are still in the dark ages compared with stocks. Bond dealers are more than happy to exploit this situation. Treasuries aside, when you buy bonds in small amounts—and less than $1 million is small in the bond world—price variations of 2% to 6% among dealers for the same bond are all too common.

Buying Treasuries shouldn't be a problem, especially if you buy directly from the federal government through its Treasury Direct program. With corporates, the difficulty of getting a decent price, plus the need to diversify because of credit and call risk, argues in favor of a bond fund. As for munis, if you shop carefully—get price quotes from three brokers and check out recent prices (see the box listing bond websites on page 113)—you should get your bonds at a good price. And if you stay with the highest-rated issues and buy the bonds of four or five states, your risk of being decimated by a default is relatively low.

CHAPTER 5

Winning the Battle of Risk vs. Return

*T*he market turmoil in the first half of 2000 reminded us that stocks can go down—way down. There's not a whole lot you can do about that, except for two things: You can run your portfolio by a variety of risk indicators to see how it might behave when the days of reckoning come—and perhaps you can fine-tune your holdings ahead of time.

There are three risk indicators that all investors should be on a first-name basis with. All three are based on past performance, and they can tell us something—but by no means everything—about the future. "If an investment has been volatile in the past, it will likely be volatile in the future," says New York University finance professor Martin J. Gruber. Of course, we're talking probabilities here, not certainties.

With that warning in mind, here's a rundown of the three risk measures.

■ **Beta.** Originated in the early 1960s by Nobel laureate economist William Sharpe, beta tells you how much an investment's returns go up and down in relation to a specific benchmark. Beta is typically used to monitor the volatility of stocks and stock funds, and the benchmark of choice is the Standard & Poor's 500 index. The benchmark you use is assigned a beta of 1; investments with betas higher than 1 fluctuate more than the benchmark, while those with lower betas fluctuate less. If the S&P 500 gained 10%, you'd expect a stock fund with a beta of 1.2 to rise 12%. If the S&P 500 lost 10%, the stock fund should fall 12%.

Before you get too thrilled about beta, though, you should know about one of its shortcomings: It works better for portfolios of stocks than it does for individual issues. "While beta explains about 90% to 95% of the volatility of a diversified portfolio of stocks, it explains only 30% to 35% of the volatility of an individual stock," says Gruber. That's because beta captures only movements triggered by underlying market forces, not those caused by other factors, such as inept management, industry-wide slumps and the like. These nonmarket factors tend to cancel each other out in a diversified group of stocks.

■ **Standard deviation.** This seemingly oxymoronic concept (Can something be standard and a deviation?) measures volatility regardless of what drives it—the market, interest rates, sinister outside forces, whatever. Conceived in the early 1700s by Abraham de Moivre, a probability pioneer, standard deviation tells you how much the short-term returns of a security or portfolio of investments have jumped up and down around its long-term average—and are therefore likely to do so in the future. It can be calculated in a variety of ways, but the most common method today is to figure the deviation from an average monthly return over a three-, five- or 10-year period and then annualize that number. Mathematical gobbledygook aside, the bigger an investment's standard deviation, the more volatile that investment has been and will probably be in the future.

The real beauty of this measure is its flexibility. Using standard deviation, you can compare the volatility of two different types of securities—stocks vs. bonds, for example—or you can apply this yardstick to similar investments. Take the Oberweis Emerging Growth and Fasciano small-growth funds. Both posted comparable annualized gains for the 10 years through July 31, 1999—13.7% and 13.3% respectively. But Oberweis had a standard deviation of 32.1% vs. 14.6% for Fasciano. So while both funds took their shareholders to similar places, Fasciano offered a much smoother ride.

■ **Downside risk.** Standard deviation treats upward and downward variations equally. But have you ever heard anyone complain, "This fund's returns are too high. The volatility is killing me!" No. Most of us worry about losing money. That's why Morningstar created a gauge for mutual funds called Morningstar risk, or downside risk. To come up with this stat, Morningstar analysts first measure the extent to which a fund has earned less than risk-free Treasury bills on a monthly basis over the past three, five and 10 years. They then calculate a risk score for each fund based on how its record vs. T-bills compares with the average for its peers. A score of 1.2 means the fund has 20% more downside risk than its peers—that is, the average amount by which it underperformed T-bills was 20% higher than for similar funds—while a score of 0.9 shows a fund has 10% less downside risk.

Though helpful, this measure can be used only to compare similar funds. For example, a bond fund with a score of 1.1 is 10% riskier than the average bond fund. But since bonds aren't nearly as volatile as stocks, a bond fund with a score of 1.1 will be much less risky than a stock fund with a 1.0 score.

Consider two caveats when assessing the risk in your portfolio. First, while it makes sense to check out the risk of individual securities, it's more important to monitor the volatility of your portfolio overall. Standard deviation is the best way to do that. But calculating standard deviation for a portfolio of investments is tricky. Many financial planners have software for this sort of heavy-duty number crunching, and Morningstar's Principia software will calculate the standard deviation of portfolios of funds.

Another alternative: Go to the Financial Engines calculator (developed by beta man Nobel laureate William Sharpe) at www.financialengines.com. You won't get a standard deviation. But if you plug in your holdings, plus how much you'd like your nest egg to be worth when you retire, the calculator will tell you how risky your portfolio is compared with the holdings of investors overall and estimate the odds of your portfolio hitting the target you've set.

Finally, while these risk measures are useful gauges for building a portfolio, don't fall into the trap of sacrificing long-term gains to avoid short-term risks. Sticking all your retirement savings in T-bills, for example, may guarantee you a low standard deviation. But this move virtually guarantees puny returns and increases the risk that you may have to shelve your dreams of a lavish retirement with no money worries. In other words, sometimes the biggest risk of all is trying to play it too safe.

Dealing with Uncertainty

Because you just don't know. In investing, the rational choice is to avoid extreme positions and to diversify among several asset classes, including bonds. If it turns out the next 30 years are like the past 30, adding bonds to your portfolio would mean building less wealth than you would get by going 100% into stocks. If it turns out, however, that the future isn't as kind to stocks, then you could come out way behind by making an all-or-nothing bet.

Why diversification pays. Of course, it's impossible to know in advance what mix will give you the best trade-off of risk and return. So the best you can do is limit risk by diversifying the assets in your portfolio.

The idea of diversification—which goes by the equally euphonious name asset allocation—has been around for centuries. Check out Act 1 of *The Merchant of Venice*, and you'll find Antonio, the 16th-century version of a global trader, explaining that his "ventures are not in one bottom trusted, nor to one place." Our Elizabethan English is a bit rusty, but we think that translates into "I don't put all my eggs in one boat."

But, these days, many investors have come to believe that diversification is as outdated as Shakespeare's dialogue. And, forsooth, anyone who threw all his money into a Standard & Poor's 500 index fund 10 years ago did better than the prudent soul who spread his dough among large- and small-caps, foreign shares and bonds.

On the other hand, buying only Japanese stocks seemed foolproof back when the seemingly invincible Nikkei index peaked at 38,957 in 1989. By mid-2000, the Nikkei was 56% below that lofty level. As the Bard might say, the fault is not in our markets, dear investors, but in ourselves—that is, in our inability to pour all our money into winning investments while avoiding the losers.

How, then, are we to cope in a world where hot sectors turn frigid overnight? Where emerging market funds lure billions of investor dollars with a 73% return in 1993 and then lose roughly 7% annually for the next five years? A world where the only certainty is uncertainty?

Well, you can turn to a Ouija board. Or you can try something a bit more practical—diversifying your portfolio among a variety of asset classes. "A diversified portfolio will not give you a grand slam in any given year," says Roger Gibson, a Pittsburgh investment adviser and author of *Asset Allocation: Balancing Financial Risk*. But, he explains, it should help you avoid a shutout.

Now, diversification seems intuitively obvious to some—and a colossal waste of opportunity to others. Rather than rely on intuition, though, here's a more detailed explanation of how diversification works in investing—and the academic theories behind it:

Benefiting from the zigzag effect. As we discussed earlier in Chapter 4 on bonds, the key premise underlying diversification is that all assets don't move in lockstep with one another, or to put it another way, some zig as others zag. To quantify this zigzag effect, market pros use a statistic called the coefficient of correlation.

We'll spare you the formula, but the basic idea is this: If two investments move precisely in tandem, they have a correlation of 1; if they move precisely in opposite directions, their correlation is -1. A correlation of zero means their movements are unrelated.

Most, but not all, of the assets individual investors own are positively correlated, although the extent to which they move together varies substantially. Over the past 10 years, for example, Standard & Poor's 500 index had a correlation of 0.79 with domestic small-caps. The returns don't move in lockstep, but they do follow each other somewhat—not surprising since both track the fortunes of the U.S. economy. The less that two investments react in the same way to the same forces, the lower their correlations. The S&P 500's correlation with foreign stocks is only 0.53 and even lower with real estate investment trusts (0.44) and intermediate-term government bonds (0.36).

When volatility can help. As scintillating as math freaks might find such statistics, correlation lay dormant on the investing front until the early Fifties, when Harry Markowitz came to a remarkable counterintuitive insight: Adding volatile assets with low correlations to your portfolio could actually lower the volatility of your holdings overall. The riskiness of a portfolio is less than the sum of the riskiness of its parts because of that zigzag effect. Markowitz then went on to prove that you could get the biggest gain with the least pain by blending assets that have low correlations to one another so that some parts of your portfolio chug along while other parts stagnate or get clobbered. Markowitz's work eventually won him a share of the Nobel Prize in 1990.

You can use science or seat-of-the-pants. As a practical matter, then, how should you create a diversified portfolio? We see two approaches: the quantitative method and the seat-of-the-pants strategy. To go the quant route, you'll have to consult with an adviser with optimization software, who will create a portfolio

Asset Allocation Resources on the Web

- **Fidelity's Asset Allocation Planner (www.fidelity.com)**
  Diversification advice, a risk questionnaire and five model portfolios

- **The Intelligent Asset Allocator (www.efficientfrontier.com)**
  Comprehensive information on how to build a diversified portfolio

- **Schwab Investor Profile (www.schwab.com)**
  Investor profile questionnaire that matches you to one of six model portfolios

based on such factors as your time horizon (the number of years before you expect to dip into your investments and the length of time you'll be drawing on them), the level of volatility you're comfortable with and the size of the returns you would like to earn.

If you're already in or near retirement, you can try T. Rowe Price's Retirement Income Manager Program (www.troweprice.com). T. Rowe Price generates 500 simulations, or patterns of returns, based solely on historical performance. These simulations are then used to come up with combinations of assets with a high "success rate"—that is, portfolios that will provide a target level of income without running out of money during the investor's lifetime. (You can also check out the asset allocation advice on the websites listed above.)

For the seat-of-the-pants approach, begin by setting a stocks/bonds mix appropriate for your time horizon. If you're investing for a goal that's less than three years away, you can pretty much forget stocks (and stock funds). Why? Because you might not have enough time to bounce back from short-term losses in the stock market. If you're looking at a three-to-five-year horizon, you might go 20% or so in stocks; 50% or so is reasonable for five to 10 years; and 70% or more makes sense for longer-term investing. You can vary these percentages depending on how much volatility you can stand. Even if you do nothing beyond a simple stocks/bonds combo, you can get some of the risk-reducing benefits of diversification. For the 20 years through Sept. 30, 1999, for example, a mix of 60% large-cap stocks and 40% intermediate-term bonds would have earned a 14% annual return, giving you 85% of an all-stock portfolio's gains while reducing volatility by 35%.

Divide and Conquer

Diversifying gives you a better trade-off between risk and return. For example, going from an all-Standard & Poor's 500 portfolio to the 75% stocks/25% bonds mix below yielded a slightly lower return but reduced volatility even more. Diversifying beyond large stocks and bonds into small-cap and foreign shares, on the other hand, generated virtually the same returns as the S&P 500 but with lower risk.

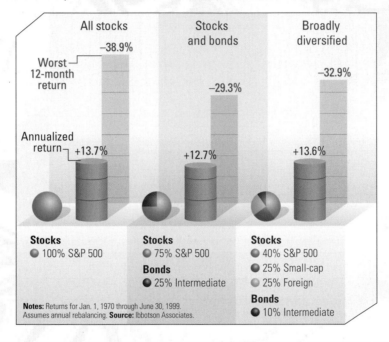

All stocks

Worst 12-month return −38.9%

Annualized return +13.7%

Stocks
- 100% S&P 500

Stocks and bonds

−29.3%

+12.7%

Stocks
- 75% S&P 500

Bonds
- 25% Intermediate

Broadly diversified

−32.9%

+13.6%

Stocks
- 40% S&P 500
- 25% Small-cap
- 25% Foreign

Bonds
- 10% Intermediate

Notes: Returns for Jan. 1, 1970 through June 30, 1999. Assumes annual rebalancing. **Source:** Ibbotson Associates.

Feel free to branch out into other asset classes, but don't act as if you're at an all-you-can-eat buffet and load up on everything from Finnish bonds to platinum futures. Simpler is better. A portfolio that includes both large- and small-cap stocks, as well as bonds and foreign shares, should do just fine. As a guide to creating your own mix, check the performance of the model portfolios on the Charles Schwab and Fidelity sites listed in the box on page 121.

Rebalance your portfolio. Inevitably, your portfolio will get out of whack. If you had started with an 80/20 blend of S&P 500 stocks and bonds four years ago and let your money ride, stocks' gargantuan gains would have brought your mix to nearly 90/10 today. To keep your proportions on track, rebalance your portfolio annually, either by selling some winners and plowing the profits into laggards or, ideally, by adding new money to the asset classes that are trailing. Rebalancing also forces you to buy investments when they're out of favor and more likely selling at bargain prices.

Whichever approach you choose, make sure that the blend you end up with passes the smell test. Are the investments themselves sensible? Are the proportions reasonable? Given their relatively low correlations, a combination of tech stocks and emerging markets funds might seem like a low-risk route to high returns—in theory. But do you really want your future riding on such a wacko combo? We wouldn't. After all, the reason for diversifying in the first place is to lower risk, not to create a new set of uncertainties that could turn your portfolio into a comedy of errors.

Avoid Diversification Pitfalls

Even the best make mistakes. Harold Evensky may be the best financial planner in the country. He is almost certainly the best known—a ubiquitous guy with a bow tie and a big brain who can effortlessly explain the mathematical complexities of investment theory. He's also living proof that it's a lot easier to talk about a diversified portfolio of mutual funds than it is to build one. Every three months, the *New York Times* periodically asks Evensky and four other experts to pick a basket of mutual funds, then compares their results to the return of Standard & Poor's 500-stock index. At one point, Evensky's *Times* portfolio included Schwab 1000, an index fund of the 1,000 largest U.S. stocks; Vanguard Index Value, an index fund that owns the cheapest stocks in the S&P 500; and Wilshire Target Large Company Growth, a third index fund that holds the fastest-growing members of the S&P 500.

These three funds are all stalwarts, but owning them together makes no sense—as Evensky now readily concedes. That's because at the time, 324 of the 364 stocks in the Vanguard fund and 214 of the 227 in the Wilshire fund were included in Schwab 1000. In other words, 89% of the stocks in the Vanguard fund and 94% of Wilshire's were already in Schwab's. "There's a huge overlap," Evensky recalls sheepishly. "I sort of backed into it over time. It's not a perfectly intelligent and straightforward portfolio."

He hastens to add that he does not use this combination of funds for his real clients. But if a renowned expert like Evensky can make a mistake like this, you know the rest of us can too.

It's a good reminder that we all need new and better ways to think about diversifying our portfolios. That's especially urgent because diversification is just about the only tenet of modern finance that has proved to be unassailably true.

But fund investors tend to make two serious errors when they try to diversify. First, they forget that their funds need to complement all their investments. Second, they fail to check, when buying a new fund, how much it overlaps with those funds they already own.

Remember, you are an egg. For diversification to work its magic, you need to consider all the sources of risk and return in your total portfolio. And your portfolio does not consist only of investments in funds, stocks, bonds and cash. If you're like most people, the single biggest investment in your portfolio is you. That's because your career is an asset—and your total labor income constitutes the return on that asset.

Economists call this your "human capital," and you need to make certain that it harmonizes with your investment capital. Mike Henkel, president of Chicago's Ibbotson Associates, the leading investment consulting firm, explains it this way: "If you're 30, you have probably got 35 years of labor income ahead of you. You've got a big chunk of your total portfolio tied up in your own human capital. So it's important for you to have a very well diversified investment portfolio."

If, for instance, you work as a software engineer in Silicon Valley, your human capital is dependent on the health of the technology industry: A recession in the computer business (like the one that hit in 1983-84) would not only cripple your salary growth, it might also throw you out of work entirely. The recession could last months or years. Even the value of your home might drop. That's just when you'd want your investments to be there for you—but if you were paid partly with options on your company's stock, and you allocated much of your 401(k) into company stock, and you even bought a technology mutual fund to boot, then your investments will be down at the same time you are.

In short, when you're making sure not to put all your eggs in the same basket, remember to count yourself among the eggs. Timothy Kochis, a financial planner at Kochis Fitz Wealth Management in San Francisco, says, "If you work for a very large company like GM or IBM, we may recommend that you begin investing more heavily in small stocks. If your company does

Which Industries Move in Lockstep?

Here's how to find industry sectors that can balance your portfolio:
This table shows the similarity of stock returns for 10 industries for the decade ended Dec. 31, 1997. The lower the number, the less similar the returns and the better the diversification. To find a good diversifier for each industry, look across to the cell highlighted in white. If you work for, say, an electric utility, computer stocks may cut your risk and lift your return. If you work for a health-care company, automobile stocks would provide needed diversification.

	Automobiles	Banks	Computers[1]	Distribution[2]	Electric Utilities	Entertainment	Health Care[3]	Home Building	Household Prods.	Insurance[4]	Oil[5]	Telephone
Automobiles	1.00	0.47	0.29	0.29	0.14	0.41	0.21	0.35	0.25	0.31	0.26	0.16
Banks	0.47	1.00	0.58	0.38	0.33	0.55	0.36	0.58	0.42	0.73	0.36	0.41
Computers[1]	0.29	0.58	1.00	0.35	0.08	0.54	0.28	0.52	0.53	0.52	0.16	0.26
Distribution[2]	0.29	0.38	0.35	1.00	0.37	0.46	0.39	0.37	0.44	0.40	0.28	0.35
Electric Utilities	0.14	0.33	0.08	0.37	1.00	0.22	0.22	0.38	0.50	0.45	0.41	0.69
Entertainment	0.41	0.55	0.54	0.46	0.22	1.00	0.32	0.49	0.47	0.53	0.18	0.30
Health Care[3]	0.21	0.36	0.28	0.39	0.22	0.32	1.00	0.29	0.39	0.31	0.22	0.36
Home Building	0.35	0.58	0.52	0.37	0.38	0.49	0.29	1.00	0.46	0.54	0.13	0.29
Household Prods.	0.25	0.42	0.53	0.44	0.50	0.47	0.39	0.46	1.00	0.50	0.39	0.53
Insurance[4]	0.31	0.73	0.52	0.40	0.45	0.53	0.31	0.54	0.50	1.00	0.39	0.50
Oil[5]	0.26	0.36	0.16	0.28	0.41	0.18	0.22	0.13	0.39	0.39	1.00	0.45
Telephone	0.16	0.41	0.26	0.35	0.69	0.30	0.36	0.29	0.53	0.50	0.45	1.00

Notes: [1]Software and services [2]Food and health-care products [3]Hospital management [4]Diversified [5]Composite
Source: Schwab Center for Investment Research.

most of its business in the U.S., we'll suggest you add some international stocks to your portfolio."

By the same token, says Kochis, you should think twice about buying a real estate fund if you already own a home. After all, he points out, that means your home is already a large part of your net worth. Do you really need to own even more real estate?

The table on this page, which shows the correlation between stock returns in 10 industries over a decade, will help you mix and match investments. Let's say you work in home-building. By running your eye across the row labeled "Home building," you can see that banking stocks have had a fairly high correlation with yours (0.58), while oil-industry stocks have had a very low correlation (0.13). (The lower the number, the less similar the returns and the more effective the diversification.)

If you think about it, this makes sense: Since new homes are financed with the mortgages that banks provide, those two industries should prosper when inflation is low and borrowing is cheap. But when inflation is high, both industries will suffer. On the other hand, oil companies tend to prosper when inflation is high, and that should make oil stocks a pretty good diversification tool for you. (An interactive version of this table, featuring more than 60 industries, is available at www.money.com.)

Two funds can be worse than one. Now let's tackle the second big problem in diversifying a fund portfolio: overlapping holdings. What's wrong with owning funds that overlap? Not too long ago, one of MONEY magazine's rival publications recommended that you pair Vanguard Specialized Health Care with T. Rowe Price Blue Chip Growth. Not only did both of these funds count Pfizer, Warner-Lambert and Bristol-Myers Squibb among their top 10 holdings, but Blue Chip Growth had 20% more of its assets in health-care stocks than does the market as a whole.

Thus, instead of complementing the Vanguard fund, Blue Chip Growth threw it out of kilter. Remember, the whole point of diversification is to produce the highest possible return at the lowest possible risk. By making a double bet on health care, you would have certainly increased your potential return if those stocks did well—but you would have done nothing to reduce your risk if they fared poorly.

When buying a new fund, don't make the classic mistake of looking only at its performance. Instead, check to see what it owns and whether those holdings duplicate what you already have. You can get a rough idea of how much your funds overlap by eyeballing their annual and semiannual reports. Look at the tables of their 10 largest holdings, then note how much they have in each industry sector (see the "schedule of portfolio investments"). If they share three or more top holdings or their biggest industry weightings are within a couple percentage points of each other, you've got an overlap problem. For an instant analysis of the overlap among funds, use Morningstar's Portfolio X-Ray feature at www.morningstar.com.

CHAPTER 6

The Secrets of Tax-Smart Investing

*T*axes can take a toll on your investment returns in many different ways. Take mutual funds. "The return you get after taxes is often nowhere near the return you see reported," says Vanguard fund taxation specialist Joel Dickson. He estimates that over the past decade, domestic stock funds have lost 2.5 percentage points of return a year on average to taxes—effectively reducing annual returns by more than 15%. How? Much of the problem comes from managers' frenetic trading, which generates taxable capital gains. This must be what T.S. Eliot had in mind when he called April the cruelest month.

Although radical moves to avoid taxes often lead to lousy investment decisions—witness investors who got burned in fee-heavy limited partnerships in the 1980s—there are many tax-wise strategies that can help you keep the Internal Revenue Service's hands off your investment gains.

Put munis in your mix. If you own bonds in your portfolio, tax-free municipals are probably a better choice than taxable alternatives like Treasuries and corporates. The reason: Munis give you a shot at higher returns once you factor in their tax savings. The higher your tax bracket, the more munis can help. To find out whether you should be in munis or taxable bonds, review the section on municipal bonds in Chapter 4, and then calculate the muni's taxable equivalent yield using the worksheet on the opposite page.

Play the indexes. You've no doubt heard index funds extolled for their superior long-term performance. But you should also consider them for their high "tax efficiency." That's a fancy way of saying that index fund shareholders keep a higher

Taxable or Tax-Exempt?

To find out whether you're better off in munis or in taxable bonds or bond funds, fill out the worksheet below.

		EXAMPLE	YOUR FIGURES
1	Enter yield on muni bond or fund	**5.1%**	
2	Enter your marginal federal tax rate[1]	**31%**	
3	Subtract line 2 from 100% (100%-31%=69%)	**69%**	
4	Divide line 1 by line 3 (5.1%÷69%=7.4%)	**7.4%**	
5	Enter yield on taxable bond or fund.	**6.5%**	
6	If line 5 is larger than line 4, you're better off in taxables. Otherwise, munis are the better bet.	**Munis!**	

Note: [1]If the bond or fund is also exempt from state and local taxes, multiply your combined state and local tax rate by 1 minus your marginal federal tax rate (example: 6% x 69%) and then add the result (4.1%) to your federal rate (31% + 4.1%). Enter this figure (35.1%) on line 2 and continue with steps 3, 4 and 5.

percentage of their gains after paying taxes than shareholders in regular stock funds do.

What makes index funds efficient is their low portfolio turnover. Most stock fund managers are constantly trading securities, typically replacing 80% or more of their holdings each year. When these trades are profitable, they create realized (read: taxable) short- and long-term capital gains.

By law, funds must distribute these gains to shareholders, who in turn pay taxes at a rate of up to 39.6% for short-term gains and as much as 20% for long-term gains. But since index funds engage in the "passive" strategy of simply buying and holding the stocks of whichever index they follow, they have much lower turnover than actively managed funds—often 5% or lower annually. This translates to fewer realized capital gains and smaller taxable distributions to shareholders. (Of course, index funds must also pass along dividend payments, if any, but there's not much they can do about that.)

In fact, there are only two reasons an index fund might create capital gains: The manager has to sell stock to raise cash for investors redeeming their shares, or the fund's portfolio requires rebalancing to reflect a change in the underlying index. But even in the case of departing shareholders, funds can employ techniques to keep taxable distributions down.

Vanguard 500 Index fund manager Gus Sauter, for example, uses "hifo" or high-in-first-out accounting, which essentially means selling shares with the highest cost to minimize realized gains and distributions. So far, taxable distributions from the fund, which tracks the S&P 500, have been minimal.

You can also get the tax efficiency of index funds via ETFs, or exchange-traded funds. (See page 61 for more details.) You should have no trouble finding one to match your investing style.

Capitalize on losses. While index funds' tax efficiency stems naturally from their low turnover, another breed of funds—tax-managed funds—purposely try to minimize, if not eliminate, taxable distributions. To accomplish this, managers rely on a few specific strategies. First, they tend to emphasize stocks with no or low yields, which reduces dividend income. Second, they buy and hold. This way, the fund has fewer realized gains, and those it has tend to be long term, which qualifies them for the lowest tax rates. Finally, managers will occasionally sell some stocks for losses, which they can later offset against gains in other stocks. "Those losses provide a tax shield that can be used to shelter future gains," says Donald Peters, who manages T. Rowe Price Tax-Efficient Growth and co-manages Tax-Efficient Balanced, a fund that invests in a roughly 50-50 mix of stocks and muni bonds (T. Rowe Price: 800-638-5660).

If you like the idea of indexing but also want the benefits of a tax-managed fund, you can find both those qualities rolled into one in what we suppose you could call tax-managed index funds, although, thankfully, nobody does. The Schwab 1000 fund (800-435-4000), for example, tracks a Schwab index of the 1,000 largest U.S. companies. But in an effort to avoid taxable distributions, manager Geri Hom also employs proprietary software to harvest losses in certain stocks that can cancel realized gains in others.

Gus Sauter employs similar strategies at Vanguard's stable of tax-managed funds. Vanguard's Tax-Managed Growth & Income, for example, follows the S&P 500 index, much as the Vanguard 500 Index fund does, although the tax-managed version occasionally deviates from the index to take losses in some stocks (Vanguard: 800-851-4999). So far, tax-managed funds have pretty much lived up to their promise of limiting taxable distributions.

Look for funds with hidden tax breaks. Under IRS rules, mutual funds must distribute capital gains to shareholders each year. Unless those funds are in an IRA, 401(k) or other tax-sheltered account, shareholders may then owe taxes on the distributed gains. On the other hand, funds that incur capital losses do not distribute them. Instead, the funds can use them to offset future gains for up to eight years. So a fund that recently realized $50 million in losses will not have to distribute its next $50 million in capital gains, giving shareholders a free ride.

In looking for these built-in tax breaks, it's important to understand that only funds that booked their losses by selling stock are entitled to the benefit; funds that held on to losing stocks will get no relief.

How can you tell if a fund you're interested in has large tax losses? You'll have to do some digging. If you become interested in a fund that had a negative return, check its annual report. You can get one from the fund company, or at websites such as www.freeedgar.com, where SEC filings are available. In the footnotes to the fund's financial statement, you will usually find an item describing the fund's tax loss carry-forwards (also called "capital loss" carry-forwards), if it has any.

Of course, you don't want to latch on to a fund simply because it has a potential tax break; tax strategy should never drive investment decisions. "But if you're buying funds in a taxable account," says Russ Kinnel, an analyst at Morningstar, "a large carry-forward is a good thing to look for."

Build your own tax shelter. This strategy is simple yet effective—and it goes against the prevailing putative wisdom that frequent trading is the route to success. All you do is buy stocks that have superior long-term prospects and pay little or no dividends—then hang on to them unless their prospects sour or you need the money. As a practical matter, this strategy involves buying companies with fast-growing earnings, since they're least likely to burden you with taxable dividends.

Following this strategy accomplishes two things. First, you get tax-deferred compounding of gains. "You're earning a rate of return on money you otherwise would have sent to Uncle Sam," says Neil Wolfson, national partner in charge of investment consulting at KPMG LLP. Second, by holding a stock longer than a year before selling, any gain is taxed at the maximum long-term capital-gains rate of 20% rather than at ordinary income rates of up to 39.6% (not including state taxes). This combination of deferral and lower rates does not eliminate taxes, but as the chart on page 133 shows, it dramatically reduces the IRS' take.

One more thing: Bequeath a stock or fund to an heir, and appreciation in the share price during your lifetime escapes income taxes (although confiscatory estate taxes could still apply).

Five Year-End Tax-Cutting Strategies

At one time or another, even the most tax-conscious investor has worried about buy-and-sell decisions that could force you to write a big check to the IRS on April 15th. In fact, if you're not careful, Uncle Sam could abscond with up to 40% of your annual gains—unless you intervene before year-end. Luckily, it's not all that hard to shield your profits from tax. But there's no one-size-fits-all tax-avoidance strategy. What you need to do at year-end depends on what you've done with your investments throughout the year—or plan to do before Dec. 31.

Did you sell appreciated stock or mutual funds shares this year? Did you sell stocks or funds at a loss? Are you holding onto bonds that have dropped in price? Below are five typical investing scenarios, followed by the appropriate tax-saving strategy. Take our advice before the New Year and the only grinch in your holidays will be the one starring in the television special.

■ **SCENARIO NO. 1:** *You recently sold stock, and your gains exceed your losses.* Say, for example, that you sold shares earlier this year for a $5,000 capital gain, but that you haven't sold any investments at a loss. Before year-end, you should identify securities in your portfolio on which you're $5,000 in the hole—and sell them. By pairing a $5,000 gain with a $5,000 loss, you shield the gain from tax, for a savings on your return of $500 to $1,980, depending on your top income tax rate and how long you owned the profitable stock before you sold it.

The problem with this strategy is that you may not want to sell your loser(s). If so, here's your out: Sell the loser stock and use the proceeds to buy new shares of the same stock after 31 days, counting the date of sale—but no sooner. Under the tax law's so-called wash-sale rule, you can't write off the loss if you purchase substantially identical securities within 30 days before or after the sale. There's a risk, of course, that the stock will go up during the time you don't own it. If you're uncomfortable

Taxes Are a Drag

The bars below show the growth of $10,000 earning 10% annually under three different scenarios: no taxes on gains (green); taxes paid on the entire gain each year at ordinary-income rates of 31% (gold); and taxes deferred until the end of the period and then paid at the 20% capital-gains rate (brown). You can't eliminate taxes, but buying and holding as long as you can is the next best thing.

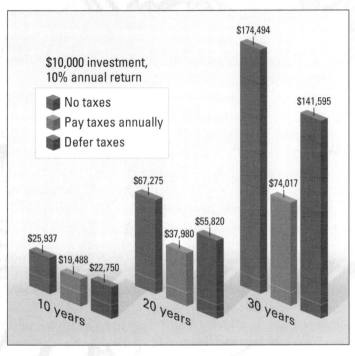

$10,000 investment, 10% annual return

- No taxes
- Pay taxes annually
- Defer taxes

$174,494

$141,595

$67,275

$74,017

$55,820

$37,980

$25,937

$19,488

$22,750

10 years

20 years

30 years

Source: Money estimates.

with that prospect, you can reinvest as soon as you wish in a security that would not be considered substantially identical to the one you sold. For example, if you sold shares from a stock mutual fund, you can choose a fund from a different company but with a similar investment objective.

■ **SCENARIO NO. 2:** *You sold stock this year, and your losses exceed your gains.* The tax law lets you deduct your capital losses dollar for dollar against your capital gains; if your losses exceed your gains, you can deduct up to $3,000 of the excess against your other income, such as salary and interest. Say, for example, that you haven't realized any capital gains this year and your losses come to $3,000 or less. You don't need to monkey with your investment portfolio at all. Simply write off the loss against your ordinary income when you file your 2000 return. The savings on a $3,000 write-off: $450 to $1,188, depending on your top tax rate.

If your capital losses total more than your capital gains plus $3,000, you have two choices. One option is to sell stock on which you have enough of a gain to absorb the excess loss. If you don't want to part with your appreciated stock permanently, sell it and then buy new shares of the same stock. Doing this works to your advantage in two ways: You'll generate a capital gain to absorb your loss, and you'll have a higher cost basis on the new shares than you had on the ones you sold. Assuming the stock continues to appreciate, you'll have a lower gain—and hence lower taxes—the next time you sell. What makes this strategy even more attractive is that you don't have to wait any length of time to buy those new shares, since the wash sale's wait period applies only to stock that you've sold at a loss.

Your second option for dealing with excess losses is to do nothing—for now. The tax law lets you carry forward unused losses to later years. Just be sure to keep track of your carry-forwards so that you remember to use them in the future.

■ **SCENARIO NO. 3: *You're holding on to appreciated stock—and you have some big cash outlays coming up.*** If you intend to give to charity this holiday season, your best tax move may be to give the stock instead of cash. Or, if you were planning to sell stock soon to pay a big expense for a child, such as college tuition, you may be better off taxwise giving the stock to the child. Consider:

If you've owned the stock for more than a year and you give it to charity by year-end, you can claim its full fair market value as an itemized deduction and you avoid tax on the gain. Say you paid $1,000 years ago for stock now worth $5,000. If you sell the stock and give the proceeds to charity, you could deduct the $5,000 donation. But you would also owe $800 in tax on the long-term gain ($400 if you're in the 15% income tax bracket). If, instead, you donate the stock, you get the $5,000 deduction and pay no tax.

Alternatively, you could give the stock to a child who is age 14 or older. Your child can then sell it and pay tax at his or her

A Little Forethought Can Save Money

Before selling shares in a mutual fund, think about the tax implications. The tax law contains four different accounting methods for computing your capital gain (or capital loss) when you sell mutual fund shares. Surprisingly, these methods—known as **specific identification**, **single-category averaging**, **double-category averaging** and **first-in, first-out (FIFO)**—can yield vastly different results. So before you redeem shares in a fund, you (or your tax pro) should project your tax using each of the methods, and then structure the sale to use the one that is best for your taxes.

In many cases, specific identification gives you the best tax result. With specific ID, you specify in writing the particular shares you want to redeem—at the time you sell. By selling your costliest shares, for example, you generate the smallest possible taxable gain, or the largest possible tax-deductible loss. To identify the shares you're selling, note their purchase date and the price you paid. Also ask the fund for a confirmation that you traded shares bought on those dates and keep a copy of your letter and the confirmation.

If you don't use specific ID, you can wait until the time you file your return to choose one of the other three methods to calculate your tax. It's possible that one of those methods will yield a better tax result than specific ID. But you can't know that unless you examine the tax consequences of the sale before you sell.

Note: Specific ID and FIFO are off limits if you sold shares from your fund in the past and used averaging back then to figure the tax. In that case, you must continue to use averaging for every subsequent sale from that fund.

rate, generally 10% on a long-term gain vs. a 20% hit for you. A few caveats: The tax savings don't add up as nicely if the child is 13 or younger, because his or her unearned income above $1,400 will be taxed at your rate. Moreover, think twice before you give stock to a college student who qualifies for financial aid, since your gift could reduce the amount of aid.

That said, be aware that giving stock to family members is also a simple way to lighten the potential tax on your estate, since you can give away assets worth up to $10,000 per person per year free of gift tax, $20,000 per person each year if you and your spouse make the gift together. (When the recipient sells the stock, he or she will owe tax based on the price of the stock when you bought it.) Note: To ensure that such a gift is "made" this year, you must complete all of the paperwork transferring your securities and the recipient must assume full ownership of the assets before year-end.

■ **SCENARIO NO. 4:** *Your bonds have slumped.* Now could be a good time to sell them and reinvest in a different bond. Done right, such a swap can save taxes and preserve your investment position, says Hugh R. Lamle, president of Chase & M.D. Sass Partners, an investment management firm in New York City, who prepared the following example:

Assume you paid $106,500 in January 1999 for Treasury notes with a par value of $100,000, a coupon rate of 5.5% and a maturity date of Feb. 15, 2008. As interest rates rose during the year, those Treasuries would have declined in value to $96,125. If you sold at the end of 1999, you would have a short-term capital loss of $10,375. If you used that loss to offset gains on your 1999 return, you would have saved from $1,038 to $4,109, depending on your top income tax rate and whether the gains you're offsetting are long term or short term.

Now assume that you turned around and paid $96,687 for Treasury notes with $100,000 face value, a coupon of 5.625% and a maturity date of May 15, 2008. True, the new notes cost $563 more than the price you got for the old ones, but your tax savings from claiming the $10,375 loss outweigh that extra cost. More important, your income over the life of the notes increases by $1,077. Indeed, when you factor in both your net tax savings and your extra income, the swap leaves you ahead by $1,552 to $4,623.

A warning: You can't claim the tax loss if you buy a new bond that is substantially the same as the old one during a 30-day period before or after the sale. If you don't want to wait, you can buy a new bond that differs from the old one in at least one—and preferably two—of the following ways: the issuer, credit rating, maturity and yield.

■ **SCENARIO NO. 5:** *You have fresh money to invest in a mutual fund.* Be careful. Near the end of the year, funds pay their shareholders a pro rata share of the taxable income and capital gains realized by the fund during the year. If you invest shortly before the annual payout, you'll owe tax on a year's worth of earnings—even though you just bought the fund and your investment isn't likely to have increased much in value. So, before you invest, be sure to call the fund and ask for the "ex-dividend date," and then hold off on investing until that date has passed.

CHAPTER 7

Your Online Toolkit

*T*he Web has forever changed the world of investing. Thanks to the Internet, it is now a snap to buy and sell stocks and mutual funds, to find and read breaking news and insightful commentary and to access company documents as soon as they are filed with government regulators.

Although such changes are undeniably beneficial, the Web can also create problems for investors. Online brokers are not always reliable, and the quality of their service varies widely. But the biggest problem for online investors may be the sheer quantity of financial stuff that is now available online. Talk about information overload!

To help you get your bearings in the cyberworld of personal finance, the editors surfed their way through more than 1,000 websites and 20 online brokers. Our first-hand findings will help you evaluate the quality of information you'll find on the Web. We've also assembled a list of the best financial sites and provided guidance on finding the best online broker for your needs.

The Perils of Analyst Research on the Web

There may be no better symbol of the mixed blessings of the too-much-information age than the sudden ubiquity of stock analysts' ratings and reports on the Web. Once the exclusive province of institutional investors and favored individuals, stock analysis and news about ratings changes from firms like Goldman Sachs and Merrill Lynch are now all but unavoidable online. Every major financial site carries listings of analysts' buy-sell-hold ratings on virtually every stock traded. And those unsatisfied with mere ratings can buy complete research reports online from clearinghouses like Multex Investor (www.multexinvestor.com) and Zacks Investment Research (www.zacks.com) for between $5 and $300. In other venues there's no cost at all: Several online brokerages, including Schwab, DLJdirect, Merrill Lynch and MSDW.com now offer their own or other brokers' research to clients.

These reports, despite their dry tone and their often arcane subject matter, have proved surprisingly popular with online investors. Granted, some reports can yield data or insights you may not find elsewhere, and access to such research is a nice account perk when provided for free. However, the truth is that there's generally far less to analysts' research than meets the eye, especially as it's currently presented on the Web. Below we've highlighted the major drawbacks of the analyst info that you'll encounter online and how, if possible, to overcome them.

The news is always good. Tap in the ticker symbol of any major company at your favorite financial site and you'll most likely find, mixed in with your price quote and P/E ratios, a little box devoted to the company's "consensus rating." Given the certainty that such specific numbers imply, you'd be forgiven for thinking that the rating represents something meaningful about the company compared with others. Unfortunately, most analysts seem to take their inspiration from the Dodo's call of the caucus-race in *Alice's Adventures in Wonderland*: "Everybody has won, and all must have prizes." Roughly two-thirds of all analyst recommendations are "buys" or "strong buys" and less than 1% are "sells," according to Boston research firm First Call, the leading collector of such data. That's because sell-side analysts, as they're tellingly called, labor under a considerable conflict of interest. They have a financial incentive to help their brokers sell more stock by writing favorable reviews about the companies they cover. Positive coverage helps stocks go up, and a company is more likely to take its banking business to a firm already saying nice things about it.

Frequent rating changes can cause portfolio fatigue. In an attempt to appeal to would-be day-traders—and to fill up all those empty Web pages demanding an endless supply of content—financial websites have begun reporting analyst upgrades and downgrades as breaking news. But using ratings changes to inform your investment decisions is a dubious strategy at best.

Researchers at four San Francisco area universities examined what sort of results investors would have gotten had they adopted a strategy of buying the most heavily recommended stocks and selling the dogs. The results? Highly rated stocks do perform slightly better, but to keep up with every change in analyst opinion you might have to turn over your portfolio four times or more in a year, generating enormous trading costs that would cancel out your profits and guarantee you a tax return more complicated than Bill Gates'.

Stock reports are rarely worth the money. The one good thing you can say about the ubiquitous upgrade and downgrade lists and consensus rankings is that you can get them for free. That's not always the case with analyst reports themselves—and if you're not careful they can cost you plenty. If your broker doesn't provide research gratis, or if you want to supplement what's available through your broker with a wider array of material from other sources, the best place to go is Multex Investor. It offers more than half a million reports from 400 sources, including big names like Merrill Lynch and Prudential Securities.

About a third of the site's material is free, though much of that is available to users only on a limited trial basis. The catch? You have to provide detailed personal information to each brokerage house whose research you want access to—and you must be willing to take a call from their brokers, who are eager to sign you up as a client. How long the free ride lasts varies from broker to broker and most are over in a month or so.

But the quality of institutional research varies widely, and it's virtually impossible to tell which reports are valuable and which are worthless until after you've laid down your money.

Anything you find online is old news. No matter whether you get your research free from your online broker, or pay-per-view with Multex or Zacks, these reports are neither as complete nor as timely as you might think. Much of the most important information that the analysts uncover may never find its way into their reports in the first place, notes Lehman Brothers analyst Daniel Niles, and may really come out only in the detailed conversations analysts have with portfolio managers and others. Moreover, the reports you see generally arrive in your hands days or even weeks after a broker's big clients have seen them. As much as they like to pay homage to the investor revolution, full-service brokerage houses don't want to upset their favorite clients.

In all, you'd do well to treat analyst reports the way you might treat real estate listings—or personal ads. They can be useful documents, but only if you assume from the start that what rough truths they contain may well be hidden underneath layers of embellishment.

The Top Financial Websites

In our view, there are far more useful Web features than access to analyst research, and many financial websites are so good that we're eager to share them with you. After visiting nearly 1,000 different sites, we emerged with the best websites that no person who cares about money can afford to ignore. They are a diverse collection. Some, like Microsoft's MSN MoneyCentral, are backed by the richest corporations in the world. Others are the passion of one person, like the Superstar Investor directory that Terry Silver runs from his home in San Ramon, Calif. But they all have this in common: They are the very best financial sites the Internet has to offer.

We placed only one limit on our search: To earn a spot on the list, a site's best features had to be free of monthly or annual subscription fees.

The Supersites

There are more than a dozen megasites vying to be your one-stop financial portal, but Yahoo! Finance, Microsoft's MSN MoneyCentral and Intuit's Quicken.com run circles around the rest. All three deliver quotes, research, news and other investing essentials and can help you with additional personal-finance tasks like shopping for a mortgage or estimating taxes.

Of course, no single site can do it all, and each of the supersites has features that will appeal to some users more than others. We recommend you give all three a test drive; you'll likely find that one becomes your first stop whenever you hit the Web.

■ Yahoo! Finance (finance.yahoo.com)

With its no-frills design and nonstop data, Yahoo! Finance is the pinnacle of utility and the best place to go when you need factual financial information fast. Want to check out a stock? Punch

Okay, so we can't be objective about our own website. But we couldn't put together a guide to the best of the Internet without telling you about the many features available at our award-winning website www.money.com.

One of money.com's top goals is to harness the interactive potential of the Web by creating tools that let you get more personalized advice than you can in a paper magazine. One of our many stock and fund screeners, for example, helps you hunt for stocks using principles developed by value-investing legend John Neff. We have calculators that can help you assess your retirement portfolio and buy a car, insurance or a home. You'll also find updated news feed from CNNfn, website reviews, online investing how-tos and stories on Internet culture.

---

in its ticker at the top of the home page (or look it up by name). Volumes of additional info are just another link away. From the first screen you can also see how the Dow and other indexes are doing or head for breaking stories from Reuters and the Associated Press.

The site is organized into broad categories such as research and world markets. And while Yahoo! hosts its own information centers and marketplaces for products like loans, insurance and real estate, it's also one of the best directories on the Net. If it can't give you what you need, it will point you to the sites that can.

■ **MSN MoneyCentral (www.moneycentral.com)**
MoneyCentral places a greater emphasis on editorial content and step-by-step guides than Yahoo! does. MoneyCentral's real strength, however, lies in its wide range of interactive tools and research. You have to download a small program to your hard drive on your first visit to take full advantage of the tools, but they are well worth this inconvenience. The Research Wizard (which walks you through the basics of fundamental analysis) makes the site accessible to newcomers, while its stock screener, charting capabilities and other free onscreen gadgets are among the most sophisticated available anywhere, at any price.

■ **Quicken.com (www.quicken.com)**
While Yahoo! focuses on data and MoneyCentral is big on tools, Quicken.com excels at broad coverage and consistency. Here, you can get the scoop on all personal-finance topics without

having to dig far. The site is logically laid out, with major categories tabbed at the top of every page, allowing easy access from virtually any other part of the site. And each area, be it retirement, banking or taxes, is complete in itself, with bulletin boards, reference materials, solid (if generic) advice and, in many cases, a marketplace where you can shop for items like insurance and mortgages.

Investing Sites

Directories: If there's an investing destination worth your time, you'll probably find it at **Superstar Investor** (www.superstarinvestor.com), which contains 7,500 links organized by topics ranging from annual reports to technical analysis, and provides thumbnail reviews of leading sites in key categories. Other directories may rival Superstar in size, but many are cluttered with paid links and none are so smartly organized.

If you prefer to spend less time vetting sites on your own, the critics at the **Dow Jones Business Directory** (www.businessdirectory.dowjones.com) offer up only those they consider best of breed, and they add new reviews every week. Although the directory is designed primarily as a business resource, it has sections spanning most personal-finance topics.

Financial News: **CBS MarketWatch** (www.marketwatch.com) and **CNNfn** (www.cnnfn.com) both offer timely, accurate, well-written updates on the day's top news and make it easy to find in-depth articles on specific industries or trends. CNNfn (which, like MONEY, is owned by Time Warner) is particularly diligent about supplementing stories with links to company profiles or previous articles. MarketWatch isn't as well organized, making it harder to navigate than CNNfn, but it does offer a broader collection of stock market and financial data, and it features lively commentary written by a stable of regular columnists.

Stock Quotes and Research: The hands-down favorite quote site of the MONEY staff, **Yahoo! Finance** (finance.yahoo.com) is the best place for quick access to stock price, P/E, volume and other fundamental information. Company profiles, news, charts, insider trades, analyst ratings and SEC filings are then just one more click away.

MSN MoneyCentral (www.moneycentral.com) serves up much of the same data in a format that's slightly harder to use. It does, however, offer a few notable research extras, such as its "advisor FYI alerts," which supplement your quote with significant developments, such as analyst recommendation changes, quarterly earnings filings dates and unusual trading volumes.

Some of **Thomson Investors Network** (www.thomsoninvest.net) is fee-based, but much of the best info is free, including commentary from insider-trading expert Bob Gabele; a weekly earnings newsletter from First Call; and I-Watch, which tracks institutional trading activity. The site's TipSheets give quotes a new dimension: Enter a ticker and get a handy one-page overview of the company that includes charts, earnings estimates and tables comparing its key ratios to its competitors'.

Quarterly and annual earnings reports filed with the SEC often disclose crucial corporate info not available anywhere else. **10K Wizard** (www.10kwizard.com) is the best place to get them. Search here for filings by company name, ticker or any other keyword.

Portfolio Tracking and Analysis: Virtually all financial sites feature portfolio trackers that let you follow a group of stocks. The best ones are easy to set up, include cost-basis comparisons (so you can see how much money you've made or lost), offer tools to help identify asset-allocation weaknesses and alert you to news that affects your holdings.

CNBC.com (www.cnbc.com) has an outstanding tracker for active investors, with real-time quotes, alerts that notify you when a stock hits a price you specify and a customizable ticker tape that, like the cable network's, scrolls across the bottom of the screen. The site also has a bunch of flashy, graphical valuation tools that can help you decide whether to adjust any of your holdings.

The tracker at **Quicken.com** (www.quicken.com) alerts you whenever an analyst upgrades or downgrades one of your stocks. More useful for mainstream investors is its portfolio analyzer, which can pinpoint diversification shortfalls, using easy-to-read pie charts.

Stock Screeners: Screeners, which allow you to search a database of stocks by price, growth rates, key financial ratios and other customizable criteria, are widely available on the Net.

Despite the proliferation, two screeners stand out from the pack—and one of those is overwhelmingly superior.

MSN MoneyCentral's Investment Finder (www.investor.msn.com) has long been one of the most powerful stock-screening tools available in any venue and the closest Web-based rival yet to the kinds of tools for which professionals pay hundreds of dollars to use every month. The Investment Finder is worth a bookmark for just about any stock investor.

Although it offers users a set of 17 pre-defined screens, the Investment Finder's true power lies in its Custom Search section, where you can build complex searches relatively simply. You can choose from an impressive assortment of criteria, ranging from basics like P/E ratios and earnings-per-share data to such arcana as short-interest ratios. MoneyCentral's software stores old screens so that you can tinker with them later.

While not as versatile or powerful as MoneyCentral's, Quicken.com's (www.quicken.com) stock screener is still an easier-to-use alternative, appealing especially to beginners and anyone wanting to perform quick, uncomplicated searches. Quicken presents a page of 33 criteria with blank fields into which you enter the maximum and minimum acceptable number of factors you wish to screen for. While Quicken.com may not let you find a company with decreasing inventory turnover and a low price-to-cash-flow ratio the way MoneyCentral will, it can do an admirable job finding, for example, all S&P stocks with earnings growth rates greater than 25% and P/Es lower than 25.

Mutual Funds: Many destinations offer mutual fund advice, and most fund families have competent, informative sites, but **Morningstar.com** (www.morningstar.com) is the must-have bookmark for every fund investor. Access Morningstar's massive database to compare funds' performances, holdings and returns. Cool extras include Portfolio X-Ray, which lets you see the extent to which your funds hold the same stocks, and Q&As with fund managers and analysts.

FundAlarm (www.fundalarm.com) is not just the place to go for a gossipy inside look at the fund industry, it's a great source of info on foundering funds. The site maintains a list of "3-Alarm" funds that have underperformed their benchmarks for the past 12 months, three years and five years.

Charts: The best online chart programs let you draw good-looking, easy-to-read charts easily and compare many stocks on one page over multiple time periods. **MSN MoneyCentral** (www.moneycentral.com) serves up rich, informative charts that download in a jiffy and update on the fly. You can choose from 10 time periods or pick your own dates, and get high, low, close and volume stats for any date with a point of your cursor.

BigCharts (www.bigcharts.com) is a close contender to MSN—and a top choice for Mac users. You can choose among several styles (such as bar, candlestick or fever line) and plenty of backgrounds. One minor drawback: You must hit a button to reload the page every time you make a change in your chart.

Bonds: If you're not as familiar with bonds as you are with stocks, **Investing in Bonds** (www.investinginbonds.com), brought to you by the Bond Market Association, is a great starting place. The site not only explains how bonds work, it gives advice on identifying investing objectives and finding the right mix of stocks, bonds and cash.

Our top destination for buying and selling bonds: the **Bond Center at E*Trade** (www.etrade.com). Offerings include munis, corporates, zero coupons and Treasuries, among others. (There's a $40 fee for trades of fewer than 20 Treasuries or 10 munis or corporates; as with all bonds, the commission is embedded in the selling price.) E*Trade's searchable database organizes bonds according to price, yield, credit rating and maturity. Bonds are not as liquid as stocks, but E*Trade's quick-pick feature calls up lists of all bonds that are available for immediate purchase.

IPOs: **IPO Central** (www.ipocentral.com) is a one-stop information clearinghouse on IPOs, with comprehensive data and hype-free news. Get the scoop here on postponed offerings, recent pricings and the first-day trading details of new issues.

Missed out on a hot IPO and want to pick up shares after the trading begins? Check out **IPO Edge** (www.quote.com/ipo), part of the Quote.com supersite, which tracks aftermarket performance for every company that's gone public over the past 18 months. It rates each new issue on 36 criteria, including the quality of a firm's underwriter and buying habits of executives.

International: Keep up with global investing trends by visiting **Worldlyinvestor.com** (www.worldlyinvestor.com). The site's best feature is its ranking of ADRs (American Depositary Receipts, shares of foreign firms traded in the U.S.), which is searchable by industry or country.

If you're looking for the latest developments on the Nairobi Stock Market or other exotica, the **Emerging Markets Companion** (www.emgmkts.com) is the place to go. The site covers global investing instruments like Brady Bonds and euros, along with news, research and a hodgepodge of links you probably couldn't find elsewhere.

Miscellaneous: With data on more than 1,000 dividend-reinvestment plans, **Netstock Direct** (www.netstockdirect.com) is the ultimate guide to buying stock directly from companies.

Investing newsletters are rarely worth the cost, but **Investools** (www.investools.com) lets you sample many of the most popular ones. The site's goal is to sell subscriptions, but you can browse for free.

Stock Detective (www.stockdetective.com) scours the Web for info on stocks that investors would do well to avoid. Visit the site for an education on how not to get burned, or just for the spectacle of how shameless stock promoters can become.

The monthlong stock market simulation games at **MarketPlayer.com** (www.marketplayer.com) are a great way to test your most daring strategies without risking real money.

ClearStation (www.clearstation.com) is the place for learning the specifics of technical analysis.

Taxes: **MSN MoneyCentral** (www.moneycentral.com) has sections devoted to topics like audits and property tax, with up-to-date information and tips, plus links to relevant publications and forms from the Internal Revenue Service. Use the tools to estimate next year's taxes or to find out what deductions you might be missing.

To make sure the IRS doesn't eat up all of your market gains, go to **Fairmark Press Tax Guide** (www.fairmark.com). The site focuses specifically on investing taxes, offering advice to begin-

Visit any financial message board on the Net, and you may feel as if you've stepped out of the bus terminal and into the streets of some teeming, unfamiliar city. Where do you go first? How do you get acquainted with the locals? And who's the freak named Food Stamps in a Bodybag screaming "Awesome earnings run!!!"?

Most boards are filled with irrelevant chatter, but there are some pockets of community and civilized discussion if you know where to look. To help you find them, follow us on a guided tour of the Web's four dominant investment chat sites, then head to money.com/contents for a more detailed interactive guide with additional help and links to where the action is.

■ Silicon Investor (www.techstocks.com)

Best discussion topics: Most large-cap Nasdaq stocks.

Lay of the land: Nicknamed SI by its users, Silicon Investor is the upscale neighborhood in town, attracting a high percentage of advanced investors and active traders. Anyone can read the messages for free, but to post your own thoughts you have to pay ($200 lifetime, $60 half-year). The fee may give SI an elitist air, but it's just steep enough to deter the less serious from joining, and many discussion threads are earnest indeed.

Highlights: Not surprisingly, considering the site's address, tech discussions are by far the most popular forums. Some, like Dell, Intel and Compaq, have attained near legendary status, thanks to the variety and intelligence of their posts. But there are also good forums that are not focused on individual stocks, such as Market Gems, with its bent toward short-term trading, or Ask Michael Burke, where a guy named, yep, Michael Burke, opines on subjects ranging from economics to John Travolta.

Fitting in: Like a gated community, SI quickly escorts rule breakers out of town. Those who violate the site's hallowed Terms of Use by posting advertisements or abusive or obscene comments get booted without a refund. It's probably no accident, then, that unlike at most message sites, many participants here feel comfortable enough to post under their real names rather than kooky handles.

Warning: Even the best neighborhoods have back alleys. You should avoid the $5-and-under forums not only here but wherever you travel, since those areas tend to attract users more interested in pumping stocks than analyzing them.

■ Motley Fool (www.boards.fool.com)

Best discussion topics: America Online, Amazon.com, CMGI.

Lay of the land: If The Fool were a neighborhood, Old Glory would grace the Victorian homes and lemonade stands would dot the sidewalks. Its mainstream denizens are generally true believers in the religion of buy and hold. More than half a million users have registered at The Fool, but the regular participants are a much smaller, tight-knit bunch.

Highlights: Although posters usually make polite and intelligent comments, there are far fewer hot spots here than you might expect. The Fool has fallen out of fashion among board aficionados, garnering only a fraction of its competitors' daily traffic, and the bulletin boards of stocks as widely held as Sunoco and Gillette often remain cavernously empty for days. Start at the section that lists the 25 most active threads over the past seven days to zero in on the action.

Fitting in: Five full-time constables—The Fool calls them strollers—patrol the streets, stirring conversations, reprimanding troublemakers and welcoming newcomers.

■ Raging Bull (www.ragingbull.com)

Best discussion topics: IPO General Discussion, CMGI Traders Talk, Dr. Bob's Stock Timers.

Lay of the land: Raging Bull is like that hot city neighborhood where all the new restaurants are opening up. Think New York City's East Village or Chicago's Wicker Park. It has attracted members who seem looser and less formal than those at SI or The Fool while being no less informed. And as at SI, discussions about tech companies and megacap stocks reign supreme.

Highlights: Though its focus and membership aren't all that different from SI's, Raging Bull has distinguished itself with some unique amenities. Its best innovation is the ignore button, which lets you filter out that guy who keeps haranguing you for being long Compaq. Likewise, a search bot digs through the day's posts, deleting spam, ads and profane posts.

Fitting in: So-called community developers surf the site, scolding riffraff, moderating threads and listing the day's top five posts at the Herd on the Board area. Looking for a trustworthy insider to show you the way? The weekly Behind the Boards column highlights those deemed to be valuable contributors.

■ Yahoo! (messages.yahoo.com/yahoo/business_and_finance)

Best discussion topics: The ones you create and monitor yourself.

Lay of the land: Watch your wallet here, because you're hanging out on the wrong side of the tracks, and there's not a cop in sight. This is where an engineer posted a link to a phony Bloomberg story in 1999 announcing a buyout of PairGain Technologies, sending its stock soaring before the fraud was unveiled.

Yahoo! is easily the most popular site (Yahoo!'s Amazon board, for example, attracted 1,176 messages on one randomly selected day, compared with 220 at SI's Amazon board). More is not more. Unless you're 11 years old, you will quickly tire of the you-suck-no-you-suck banter that most often passes for investment conversation.

Highlights: There aren't any. What with thousands of threads on penny stocks and spurious trading systems, the only reason to stick around is to start your own discussion through the Yahoo! clubs feature and rigorously limit access.

Fitting in: Are you sure you want to? People do get booted for foul or threatening language, but troublemakers can simply create new aliases and log right back on. Save yourself some grief and hail a cab back to the nicer parts of town.

ners struggling with their IRAs, active traders looking to minimize capital-gains taxes and anyone in between.

Calculators: The most complete collection of calculators on the Web resides at **FinanCenter** (www.financenter.com)—more than 100 in all. Use them to answer questions on everything from bonds (which are better for me: taxable or tax-exempt?) to cars (should I lease or buy?). It uses text and graphics to help you make sense of the results.

Retirement Planning: The Retirement and Workplace Services area at **American Express** (www.americanexpress.com) offers a good general overview of various retirement planning issues along with clever interactive features. You can, for example, calculate the impact that any habit (be it smoking or eating out) will have on your retirement savings.

If you're only a few years away from retirement, head to the money section of **ThirdAge** (www.thirdage.com), a community site that's designed for "active older adults." Everything here is tailored for the over-50 set, from chats to news articles to links to other resources.

The Best Online Brokers

Today 3 million households invest online, up from 2.2 million a year ago. To fuel that growth, brokerages are luring customers with a wider array of products and perks than ever. Yet many are ignoring the basics that customers want most: reliability and attentive customer service. "A lot of people have two or three accounts because they've been trained that they can't rely on an online broker," says Datek Online CEO Ed Nicoll.

For our online-brokerage survey, we decided that the only way to evaluate which brokers are keeping pace was to become their customers. So our reporters opened real accounts at 20 leading Web-based brokerages, made trades and grilled customer service departments with questions via e-mail and over the phone, rating response time, accuracy and manners.

Once our testing was complete, we sorted more than 150 subjective and concrete variables into five categories: ease of use, customer service, system responsiveness, products and tools, and costs. Then we reweighted the categories to determine the best broker for each of our four investor types—mainstream investors, frequent traders, wealthy investors and beginners.

For Mainstream Investors

First Place: Fidelity   Second Place: Ameritrade   Third Place: Merrill Lynch

For mainstream investors—whom we define as those with $25,000 to $75,000 in investable assets and making between two and 20 trades a year—we emphasized ease of use, customer service and system responsiveness while underweighting product offerings. That's because mainstream clients are most interested in common stocks and a solid assortment of funds and banking services, all of which are offered by virtually every e-broker. We also under-weighted costs. Despite the industry's (and some traders') obsession with $8 vs. $14.95 trades, such differences are, in fact, almost negligible to people who make only a few trades a year.

Service has slipped at most online brokers, which may be victims of their own success. One of our reporters heard Mozart's Symphony No. 40 in G minor for 65 minutes as he dangled on hold at DLJdirect. The rep who finally answered advised, "Never call after 3 p.m. We're understaffed during those hours." Fortunately, our moments of frustration were eclipsed by our winners' superlative performance.

Despite a wide array of offerings (stocks, funds, options, bonds, credit cards, banking services and on and on), Fidelity's Powerstreet site is extremely easy to navigate. We were especially impressed by the real-time quote feature on the same page as the trading screen. Other sites do offer this all-in-one layout, but the trading data is often difficult to read. Fidelity also makes it easy to keep track of a portfolio by posting holdings like cash management accounts and IRAs on a single page. Best of all, Fidelity never kept us waiting long when we wanted to talk to a live person, and its reps answered our queries quickly and accurately.

For all its attractions, though, Powerstreet still has room to improve. We did not find the site particularly responsive, and its commission schedule, frankly, penalizes buy-and-hold investors. Limit orders cost $30, but Fidelity cuts that rate to $19.95 for folks who trade 36 or more times a year. And customers who trade less than that can't get intraday account balance updates.

At Ameritrade, pages loaded quickly, and helpful customer service reps picked up calls in about a minute. Ameritrade's commissions are low, just $13 for a limit order, and its site is a snap too. We also liked that stock price alerts can be sent via e-mail or text pager. With so many other offerings at the site itself, however, it's surprising that Ameritrade still lacks portfolio trackers and watch lists.

Hitting the ground running, Merrill Lynch Direct, Merrill's new online offering, grabbed third place. Many initially doubted that the full-service firm could compete online, but Merrill is pulling it off with flying colors. Commissions start at $29.95 for up to 1,000 shares, and the firm gives ML Direct clients free access to its coveted buy-sell-hold stock reports. Moreover, reps picked up the phone in seconds and answered e-mail queries within three hours. Merrill doesn't offer wireless or after-hours trading, but we applaud its precise order confirmations, intraday account balances and excellent cash management accounts.

For Frequent Traders

First Place: **Datek Online**   Second Place: **Ameritrade**   Third Place: **A.B. Watley**

Fast and cheap. When it comes to e-brokers, those are the two crucial characteristics for active investors. We also looked for easy navigation, real-time quotes, low margin rates, after-hours trading, immediate balance updates, options, precise time stamps on orders and fast trade confirmations.

Datek was the winner, thanks to free streaming real-time quotes, accelerated trading systems and a 12-hour trading day via Island, its affiliated electronic communication network (ECN). And we love the firm's to-the-second trade confirmations listing when orders are entered, processed and executed. Limit and market orders are just $9.99 (and your market order is free if it isn't filled in less than a minute). Datek is one of the few brokerages that don't accept what's called payment for order flow, the practice by which brokers are paid by large trading firms known as marketmakers for directing market orders to them. This practice can widen the spreads on market orders, a hidden cost of trading that's passed on to investors. One drawback: Datek still doesn't offer options.

With some of the lowest commissions around, easy navigation, after-hours trading, good site performance and (unlike Datek) access to options, Ameritrade has many of the elements active traders prefer (except real-time balance updates).

A.B. Watley came in third, thanks to its $9.95 limit orders, pre- and after-market trading, unlimited free real-time quotes and fast trade confirmations. Like Ameritrade, Watley offers options and lacks real-time balance updates. But its customer service desks aren't open on weekends.

Online Brokers Scorecard

The table details how 20 online brokers rate in five crucial categories. The overall rankings reflect category weightings geared toward mainstream investors—with ease of use, customer service and system responsiveness counting for more than the other two categories.

Company website (www.) telephone (800)	Ease of use	Customer service	System responsiveness	Products and tools	Cost	Overall ranking
Fidelity fidelity.com 544-7272	●●●●●	●●●●●	●●	●●●●◗	●●	●●●●●
Ameritrade ameritrade.com 454-9272	●●●●	●●●●●	●●●●	●●●◗	●●●●◗	●●●●●
Merrill Lynch mldirect.com 653-4732[1]	●●●	●●●●◗	●●●●●	●●●●●	●●	●●●●◗
Datek Online datek.com 823-2835	●●●	●●●●◗	●●●●	●●	●●●●●	●●●●◗
Charles Schwab schwab.com 225-8570	●●●●	●●●●	●●●●	●●●●◗	●●	●●●●
JB Oxford & Co. jboxford.com 782-1876	●●●●	●●●●	●●●	●●●	●●●	●●●●
Quick & Reilly quickandreilly.com 831-7220	●●	●●●●◗	●●●◗	●●●◗	●●●	●●●●
DLJdirect dljdirect.com 825-5723	●●●◗	●●	●●●●◗	●●●●◗	●●●	●●●◗
Morgan Stanley Dean Witter msdwonline.com 680-6896	●●●	●●	●●●●●	●●●●●	●●	●●●
Web Street Securities webstreet.com 932-8723	●◗	●●●●●	●◗	●●●●	●●●●◗	●●●
E*Trade etrade.com 387-2331	●●●	●●◗	●●◗	●●●●●	●●●	●●◗
TD Waterhouse waterhouse.com 934-4448	●●●◗	●●	●●◗	●●●●●	●●●●◗	●●◗
Suretrade suretrade.com 909-6827	●●	●●●	●●●	●●●●	●●●●●	●●●
A.B. Watley abwatley.com 229-2853[2]	●●●	●●	●●●◗	●●●	●●●●◗	●●
National Discount Brokers ndb.com 888-3999	●●●◗	●	●●●	●●●●◗	●●●	●●
American Express americanexpress.com/trade 297-7378	●	●●●●	●●	●●●●	●●●●●	●●
Muriel Siebert & Co. siebertnet.com 872-0711	●●	●	●●●	●●●●	●●●●	●
Mydiscountbroker.com mydiscountbroker.com 882-5600[2]	●	●●●	●●	●●●◗	●●●●	●
Dreyfus edreyfus.com 421-8395	●◗	●	●●●●◗	●●	●●●●	◗
Scottrade scottrade.com 619-7283	●●◗	●	●◗	●●●	●●●●◗	◗

Notes: [1]Area code 877. [2]Area code 888.

For Wealthy Investors

First Place: **Merrill Lynch**   Second Place: **Morgan Stanley Dean Witter**   Third Place: **Fidelity**

To find the best brokers for people with at least six figures to invest, we looked for firms with a wide array of products, personalized service and perks like better access to IPOs, free proprietary research and reduced margin rates. Merrill Lynch Direct finished first for many of the reasons we named it a top mainstream site, including good customer service and incisive free research. But what cemented the decision in Merrill Lynch's favor is actually a related offering called the Unlimited Advantage account, which blends the best of online investing with the hands-on attention wealthy investors sometimes demand. For a fixed annual fee, you get virtually unlimited trading plus personal attention and planning from Merrill Lynch financial consultants. Anyone can sign up, but its pricing structure ($1,500 a year for accounts less than $150,000; 1% for accounts between $150,000 and $1 million; between 0.75% and 0.5% thereafter) really only makes sense for investors with more than a couple hundred thousand dollars.

Morgan Stanley Dean Witter came in second. Clients with $100,000 receive access to IPOs, enhanced tax statements and e-mail alerts about analyst reports or ratings changes. Those with $500,000 get a dedicated customer service team, a priority 800 number and a Palm V organizer (the Palm is for existing customers only). Like Merrill, MSDW also has a fixed-fee option, called MSDW Choice. The plan, which charges 2.25% down to 0.3% of assets annually depending on your balance, offers nearly unlimited trading and your own financial adviser. (Although anyone with $50,000 can qualify, note that MSDW Choice is much more expensive than Merrill's Unlimited Advantage for clients with less than seven figures to invest.)

Fidelity, our top pick for mainstream investors, also offers attractive perks to customers with high balances. Preferred Services clients with $100,000 get $19.95 trades (normally, they're $30), and their calls are routed to the top of the line. Customers with $500,000 or more have access to financial representatives who answer questions over the phone and in person.

For Beginners

First Place: **Ameritrade**   Second Place: **Datek Online**   Third Place: **DLJdirect**

The best online brokers for newcomers have low minimum balances and fees, copious online help, primers, easy site navigation and attentive customer service. Ameritrade impressed us as

So You Want To Try After-Hours Trading

Carl Quick of Orlando likes the idea of trading after the stock market closes at 4 p.m. ET. The 52-year-old software engineer for Lockheed Martin wants to control his investments, but he's too busy to deal with them during the day. So he put a small slice of his funds, about $6,000, with Datek Online and recently signed up for after-hours access. "I can come home, at my leisure, and play around with it," he says. "I am interested in that kind of freedom."

While institutional investors have long had access to trading after the closing bell, online brokerages are increasingly offering after-hours access to clients like Quick. And though a fair and stable after-hours stock market is a virtual certainty in the long run, this brave new world is currently rife with risks; small shareholders wanting to join in need to take extra precautions to protect themselves.

If you decide to give after-hours trading a try, keep these guidelines in mind.

- **Know what your marketplace offers.** Some systems admit only individuals, while others are open to institutions too. Likewise, not all stocks trade on all systems.
- **Watch the order book.** Your system's order book shows each stock's current pricing info. Both Island ECN (www.isld.com) and MarketXT (www.marketxt.com) post their books online—free for all, regardless of whether you trade there. Keep an eye on them.
- **Name a price you're comfortable with.** All after-hours orders are limit orders. That means you must specify a price at which you will buy or sell. If there are no takers at your price in your marketplace, the order will expire unexecuted.
- **Beware of market manipulation.** A market with few participants is easier to manipulate. Be wary of stocks that are moving fast for no apparent reason.
- **Remember your goals.** Forget the hype. Ultimately, your reasons for buying or selling a stock should be no different after hours than during the day.

the best place for newbies. Its $18 fee for broker-assisted trades is not a lot of money for some extra hand-holding, and its low minimum deposit encourages beginners to trade online without ponying up most of their assets.

Datek came in second, thanks to its customer service, low fees and uncluttered site. Some may criticize Datek for not offering options, IPOs or bonds, but we think this simplicity encourages novices to focus on the basics. Datek's cheap commissions and no-minimum balance are big pluses, and the firm doesn't slam small or inactive accounts with penalties.

Our 65-minute Mozart concert aside, DLJdirect is a good place for neophytes, largely because of its no-minimum-balance require-

Online Cons: A Field Guide

A glossary of popular Internet securities scams

■ **Illegal touting.** When a promoter praises a stock without disclosing that he is being paid to do so.

■ **Pump-and-dump.** Touts drive up demand in a stock by lauding it on bulletin boards or using e-mail. When the price soars, the touts dump their shares at the inflated price. Newer investors take the hit when the stock inevitably collapses.

■ **Pyramid schemes.** A marketing ploy in which promoters claim you can profit by sending in small sums of money for signing up, and then get paid to recruit new participants. Later investors eventually get stuck with losses.

■ **Exotic frauds.** Solicitations that offer an "opportunity of a lifetime" to invest in obscure vehicles like ostrich farms or so-called prime bank securities thrive online. Sometimes, the investments don't exist. Other times, they wind up being worth almost nothing.

ments, low incidental fees, simple site and flat $20 commission for any trade up to 1,000 shares. Just remember: If you want to talk to a customer service representative, call before 3 p.m.

The Darkest Side of the Internet

The Internet can do many wonderful things for investors, but if you're not careful you can get scammed. Consider the case of John Famularo.

Famularo was playing around on his home computer one day when he came across some message-board threads discussing a company called Uniprime Capital. The firm had recently made the astounding announcement that it was successfully developing a cure for AIDS. True believers were posting glowing comments about it on message-board sites like Raging Bull at a furious pace. Within two days, Uniprime's over-the-counter shares had spiked from around $1.50 to a midday high of just under $8. More than 5.2 million shares changed hands on the stock's busiest day, vs. a typical daily volume of well under 100,000 shares. It was into that buying frenzy that Famularo, a 37-year-old air-traffic controller at the Dallas/Fort Worth airport, called in his market order for 1,000 shares. It was filled at $5 apiece. An active trader, Famularo says he didn't bother to research Uniprime. He

10 Questions to Ask Before You Invest

Found a hot investment tip online? Consult this checklist before buying.

1. Is the investment registered with the Securities and Exchange Commission and your state's securities agency?
2. Have you read audited financial statements about the investment? (Find public company filings at the SEC's website, www.sec.gov, or at FreeEDGAR, www.freeedgar.com.)
3. Is the person recommending this investment a registered broker? If so, have you seen his or her Central Registration Depository (or CRD) regulatory record? CRD records are available from the National Association of Securities Dealers (www.nasdr.com) or your state securities regulator. (Find yours at www.nasaa.org, the North American Securities Administrators Association website.)
4. What does the person promoting the investment have to gain? It is not illegal for a promoter to receive cash or securities if the payment is disclosed, but consider it a big red flag. The Stock Detective (www.stockdetective.com) keeps tabs on many paid Web promoters.
5. If the tip came from an online bulletin board or e-mail, is the author identifiable or using an alias? Is there any reason to trust that person?
6. Are you being pressured to act before you can check an investment out?
7. Does the investment promise you'll get rich quick, using words like "guaranteed," "high return" or "risk free"?
8. Does the investment match your objectives? Could you afford to lose all the money you invest?
9. How easy would it be to sell the investment later? Stocks with few shares are easy for promoters to manipulate and hard for investors to sell if the price starts falling.
10. Does the investment originate overseas? If yes, beware: It is tougher to track money sent abroad and harder for burned investors to have recourse to justice.

---

just believed no company could be allowed to lie about having a cure for AIDS if it didn't. "I got suckered," he says today. "I got into that mental state that it had to be real, and I couldn't get out, so I just watched it." Uniprime shares eventually traded at just 3¢ each, making Famularo's $5,000 investment worth $30.

Uniprime, it turns out, was no health-care company but a Las Vegas car dealership—a fact that went unnoticed by many investors. According to fraud charges filed in related civil and criminal cases, Uniprime and a major shareholder allegedly lied about the company in a series of press releases. Not only was the major shareholder not the medical researcher he claimed to be, according to court papers, but he had actually been convicted of conspiracy to commit murder and was in prison in Colorado when the research was supposedly done. Both Uniprime and the major shareholder are contesting the charges.

The case would be funny if it weren't so serious—and so common. Age-old money frauds of all types are flourishing on the Internet. No longer do con men need rooms full of cold-calling brokers. Now, with just an e-mail address list and a chat-board alias or two, penny-stock promoters can spam tens of thousands (if not millions) of investors, run up a stock's price and sell their shares to unwitting buyers—only to disappear into cyberspace. The cost to pull off such a fraud: less than one-tenth of a cent per name for the e-mail addresses; most everything else is free. "You just need one person, and they just need to have access to a computer somewhere," says John Stark, head of the Securities and Exchange Commission's office of Internet enforcement.

Online and off, investors get ripped off to the tune of an estimated $10 billion a year—that's more than $1 million an hour—according to the North American Securities Administrators Association (NASAA). In spite of the cops' best efforts, however, the complaints just keep pouring in. The SEC's Internet complaint hotline (e-mail address: enforcement@sec.gov) gets up to 300 messages a day, a thirtyfold increase since its June 1996 founding.

Who falls victim to these promotions? The money losers represent the broad range of American investors of all ages, locales, occupations and net worths. "It is anybody who has got Internet access and is following these message boards or is capable of receiving e-mail," explains Cameron Funkhouser, vice president of market regulation at the National Association of Securities Dealers. "With all this information on the Internet, people are doing their own research and getting sucked into these schemes."

The best way to avoid getting taken in a cyberscam is to protect yourself before you plunk down your hard-earned cash. Get hold of financial documents, read them, find out about the people behind the investments, and learn more about what you're planning to get than you would to, say, buy a car. If, despite your best efforts you do get burned, don't be embarrassed. You're surely not alone. Save all your documents and alert the securities cops at the SEC (www.sec.gov), the NASD (www.nasdr.com) or the North American Securities Administrators Association (www.nasaa.org). You may not get your money back, but at least you'll clue others in to the problem.

CHAPTER 8

Avoiding the Biggest Investment Mistakes

*C*hantakarn Barsch thought her boyfriend seemed like a smart enough guy. He was a doctor who exuded confidence. So when he sang the praises of one stock to Barsch, an inexperienced investor, she figured he knew what he was talking about. Besides, she knew she needed to diversify. At the time, Barsch, a 36-year-old systems analyst, had about $50,000 in savings, but it was all in two mutual funds. So she took her boyfriend's advice and pulled $20,000 out of one fund, added $5,000 in cash and bought shares in the recommended company: Atari Corp.

A year later, she watched the stock (then merged with JTS Corp.) slowly tank, figuring all the while it couldn't fall any lower. The following year, the company that had birthed such video-game classics as Asteroids, Battlezone and Centipede had taken a direct laser shot to its bottom line, transforming Barsch's investment into little more than fiscal space debris. By the time she sold the shares, her $25,000 investment, minus Charles Schwab's $29.95 commission, was worth $9.47.

Game over.

To make matters worse, the fund Barsch had pulled the money out of, Safeco Growth, had risen nicely. Had she left all her money in the fund instead of buying Atari, it would now be worth well over $30,000. "I'd heard about people losing money all the time," says a humbled Barsch. "I just never thought it would happen to me."

The fact is, every investor makes some mistakes. And with more and more people taking charge of their own finances, more mistakes than ever are being made. Perhaps our newfound financial empowerment has emboldened us too much. Maybe the long-running bull market has created a strain of optimism so potent that care and caution are increasingly ignored.

company nest egg than Schafbuch did. The reason? His colleague had invested his retirement money in equities, whereas Schafbuch had mostly steered clear, preferring to stick to fixed-income investments. He suddenly realized he'd been far too worried about risk.

Kay Shirley, a financial planner in Atlanta, sees one client after another who errs on the side of caution when it comes to retirement planning. "My typical clients are too conservative with their 401(k)s," she says. "They think of it as safe money, as sacred money. They forget that it's long-term money. Most 401(k) options are not wildly aggressive. It's a good place to take a little risk."

Schafbuch took a much larger risk than he realized in another area, however: company stock. By the time he retired at age 53, 25% of his total portfolio was in Monsanto. Soon after he left the company he hired a financial planner, who immediately flagged the trouble spot. It was true that Monsanto stock had done well, but Schafbuch's planner convinced him to reduce his stake to 5%, simply for the sake of diversification. (And it's a good thing: The stock subsequently declined.) Schafbuch acquiesced, though not without some reluctance. "You have a sense of loyalty and attachment to the company," he explains. And he's not alone in feeling that way.

Larry Carroll, a financial adviser in North Carolina, sees it all too often among his retired clients. "They're psychologically married to the stock," he explains. "But when you're retired, you can't have that many eggs in one basket." He says he's seen clients with 75% to 100% of their portfolio in one company's stock. Most planners advise clients not to have more than 10% of their portfolio in company stock.

Mistake No. 3: Taking a Flier on a Start-Up

Recently, Don Chambers, a certified financial planner in Salt Lake City, got a tip from a client about a start-up venture in Utah that a friend was orchestrating. The details were a little fuzzy. In what would prove to be an ironic twist, it had something to do with a game that taught biblical principles of creating wealth. Chambers had previously invested in two start-ups that had proved profitable for him, and he was open to new opportunities.

His client was investing about $20,000 and, based on little more than his client's opinion, Chambers put $10,000 of his IRA money into the new venture, as well as $1,000 for each of his three kids. "I had spoken with the owner once for about two minutes," Chambers recalls. "The company wasn't established. It had no revenues. I really didn't investigate the company." Even his 19-year-old daughter Julie said don't do it.

Within months, the Securities and Exchange Commission was investigating, the CEO was in jail and Chambers was out $13,000. It was his pride that was damaged the most. His daughter's response: "I told you so, Dad." He may be a little chagrined, but he also believes his kids learned an important lesson early on about risky investments. For himself, he feels that he has a solid enough portfolio to allow him to take on a high-risk investment every once in a while. But he's quick to note, "I think these deals are inappropriate for most investors."

Mistake No. 4: Ignoring the Fine Print

Sometimes you hear about a deal that seems perfect: high potential, low risk, perhaps even a tax break. What could possibly go wrong? Plenty—especially if it's complicated and you're locked in for a set amount of time.

Dee Fornaro, a sixtysomething retired secretary living in Littleton, Colo., has learned this the hard way through several investments she's made over the years in limited partnerships. Although she has made some money in them, twice she's invested $10,000, only to get nothing in return.

Her most recent unfortunate experience occurred when she bought into a limited partnership that was investing in distressed rental properties. The investment was supposed to return 13% a year. But when she wanted to divest in order to put a down payment on a townhouse, she found that she couldn't. "If you buy a stock at $20, and it goes down to $18, you can sell it," she says. "With these partnerships, there's no control."

5 Questions to Ask Before You Take Advice

1. Who is giving the advice?
Some advisers are more reliable than others. If the person is merely a name—or a pseudonym—on a message board, be wary.

2. Is the person qualified?
Find out if the person is a registered broker (and, if so, what his or her disciplinary history is) or a financial planner (and, if so, whether he or she is certified). Request and check references.

3. Does the person have something to gain?
There's nothing inherently wrong with this, but you should know what's at stake. If the adviser is a broker, ask about commissions and other incentives for advising you to buy or sell a particular security.

4. Does the adviser know the company and the stock?
Request research reports and financial documents to back up any claim.

5. Does the person understand my goals and risk tolerance?
If the person can't explain why the investment is suitable for you, it may not be. Professional brokers are required to ask what your goals are.

In the end, she lost her entire investment, and now feels these partnerships are too risky for the average person. "You need to know everything about them," she says, "and no one can. It's too complicated. There's just not enough time to learn about everything that's involved."

Mistake No. 5: Trading Too Often

It seems that as investors are becoming more empowered through the Internet, they're also more prone to mess up. After all, with commissions as low as $8 a trade, you can afford to take chances, right? But more chances means the potential for more mistakes. In some cases, a lot more.

Darrell Mak, a 34-year-old computer programmer in Annapolis, Md., sometimes wishes he could stop trading—or at least slow down. "I start getting mesmerized," he says of the ability to track stocks in real time on the Web. "It feeds your emotions and is bad for your financial health."

5 Questions to Ask Before You Give Advice

1. **Do I know what I am talking about?**
   The person who's listening to your off-the-cuff advice may really take it to heart. Be sure you know what you are saying—and why—before putting someone else's finances at risk.

2. **Do I understand this person's financial goals?**
   A stock that's good for you may not be right for everyone. Before you start blabbing about a volatile Internet stock, consider that you may be speaking with a divorced mother trying to safeguard her kids' future. Brokers must determine suitability; a friend should too.

3. **What do I know about this person's investing aptitude?**
   Some investors know how to evaluate a tip, others don't. Make sure your advice is right for your friend's level of sophistication.

4. **Do I have an ulterior motive?**
   If you're talking about a stock that you own or are short, tell the person seeking your advice.

5. **Am I prepared to back up my advice?**
   The person listening to you can—and should—get more information. Be prepared to respond to such requests.

With the constant access to the market that online trading affords, Mak finds it hard to watch his stocks topple, if only for a day, without doing something about it. "When something goes down, I keep telling myself over and over to ignore it," he says. "But I get so hooked on looking at it that I make a bad move." One such bad move was selling 400 shares of Dell when it was still a high-flier. On a day after the market had plunged several hundred points, Darrell got an itchy trading finger when Dell dropped $5 by 10:30 a.m. Was he questioning the company's fundamentals? No. But the falling stock price scared him, and with a few keystrokes on his Suretrade account, Mak immediately sold half his holdings, which he'd had for over a year. It finished up $8 for the day and subsequently moved much higher.

Since that day, Mak fights the urge to sell right away when one of his holdings starts falling. In fact, he'll actually turn the computer off and go for a walk or to the gym to get his mind off trading. He'll also think back to the day he sold his Dell stock and use that experience to strengthen his willpower. "I try not to get suckered into what the crowd's doing," he says. "I tell myself to do the opposite, but it's easier said than done."

And though he's devoted to online trading, Mak says he can appreciate the benefits of having a broker at times. "Ideally, you'd be talked out of making a bad move," he says. "Online, there's no one to stop you."

Mistake No. 6: Relying on Message Boards

The classic hot-tip mistake has evolved into a high-tech nightmare for some investors who rely on advice from the ubiquitous financial message boards found on the Internet today. With some participants trying to influence a stock's price on these boards, it's easy for unsuspecting visitors to buy into tall tales. Even responsible investors looking for an edge can get taken in by the plethora of bad advice. Kent Newsome knows this all too well.

A 38-year-old lawyer (and part-time country music songwriter) in Houston, Newsome is relatively new to the stock-picking world, having started around two years ago. But he considers himself a serious buy-and-hold investor, having sold only three stocks out of the 32 he's invested in. Doing good research has helped him achieve sizable returns. But like many investors today, a part of him was itching to score big on the next high flier.

That's when Newsome noticed that a group of investors on the Yahoo! message boards were talking up a microcap company called Saratoga Brands, which is best known for its cheese. "My wife loves cheese," he laughs, applying Peter Lynch's logic that if you're going to buy stock, do it in a field you understand. And vicariously, Newsome knew his cheese. So after listening to this particular group of "investors" talking up the company, Newsome did a little research. But not enough. "Part of me knew it sounded a little fishy," he says, mainly because of the stock's low volume mixed with the high level of interest in it on the boards. Still, eager to score, he bought 200 shares at just over $2.

Within weeks, the cheerleaders on the board disappeared. And soon the stock, which had been inching upward, started dropping precipitously. About a year later, it hit 59¢ per share and Newsome bailed out, now convinced that the anonymous message posters had been trying to run up the stock price. "I don't know for a fact that they were pumpin' and dumpin'," he says in his marked Texas drawl, "but they talked a lot of people into buying that stock. And I bought into it hook, line and sinker. There were so many reasons I shouldn't have invested." Today he won't even look at message boards and suspects that most are tainted in some way by manipulative opportunists.

Mistake No. 7: Paralyzed by Indecision

For some investors, the pain and loss associated with negative stock market experiences drive them away from investing altogether. For Kerry Kuehner, a 49-year-old graphic designer in Chesterfield, Mo., it was a missed opportunity that sent her over the edge. For her, the consequences went way beyond losing a few thousand dollars.

Three years ago, Kuehner got a tip from a friend in the real estate business that Brooks Fiber was expanding and might be a takeover candidate. He encouraged her to take a look at the stock. Kuehner was hesitant. Having lost nearly $30,000 in tech stocks in the early '90s, she'd become increasingly gun-shy about stocks, especially tech stocks. But feeling she had a great tip, she called her broker and asked her to look into it. When a few weeks passed and her broker hadn't called her back, Kuehner assumed it probably didn't check out. Just as well, she figured. The last thing she needed was another tech stock loser. The company, however, was soon bought out by WorldCom. The stock soared.

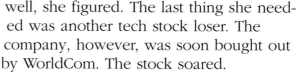

Kuehner confronted her broker about it and discovered that she had purchased the stock for another client (who had inquired about the stock independently, the broker says). In fact, Kuehner's broker had received a favorable report on the company just days before the takeover was announced but says she didn't have enough time to research it thoroughly before the buyout.

The episode shattered Kuehner's confidence. She hasn't invested another dime since, missing out on some huge potential gains, and she hasn't reallocated the investments she already had. And because she's been paralyzed by indecision, her money is still with the same broker. "I feel stupid to have my money with someone I feel bad about," she says now. "I'm just frozen by not having a darn idea of what to do next."

Last but not least. The final mistake in this series may be the most common of all. It is investors' predilection for thinking that their results are very good even when they are not. The obvious danger of such misguided perception: An investor will fail to change a plan that really isn't working.

Mistake No. 8: Overrating Yourself

If you listen to CNBC, market websites or your lunch pals, you might think the whole point of investing is to beat the market. Many people who think they are outperforming the averages really aren't. And, no offense, you might be one of them.

To succeed as an investor you've got to understand yourself at least as well as you understand the financial markets—and most of us don't. In fact, one of the most powerful steps you can take to improve your investing results is to stare long and honestly into a mirror to see whether you really are the investor you think you are.

Two groups of investors have been caught looking into a mirror recently, and the findings are fascinating. A team of professors at the Northwestern, Duke and Harvard business schools asked investors how their mutual funds had performed, then compared those answers with the funds' actual returns. MONEY also asked investors whether they had beaten the market and by how much. In both cases, like fishermen recounting the great catches of years gone by, investors wildly overstated how well they had done.

The academic study gave 80 investors continuous feedback on how their mutual funds were faring compared with the market (as measured by Standard & Poor's 500-stock index). Then, at the end of the experiment, the investors estimated how their portfolios had performed relative to the S&P 500 over the whole period.

Nearly a third claimed that their funds had beaten the market by at least 5%, and one of every six said they had outperformed by more than 10%. But when the researchers checked the portfolios of the people who claimed to have beaten the market, it turned out that 88% of them had exaggerated their returns. More

Ambushed by Margin Debt

The Internet makes trading on margin easier than ever. You've probably heard or read stories about people who have used margin debt to turbo-charge their stock returns. There is an important flip side to these stories, however. Margin debt can be harmful if you use it recklessly or without knowing all the rules, and even a small amount of margin can greatly increase your stress level if the market turns against you.

All it takes to open a margin account is a $2,000 balance and a click of the mouse. There's usually a questionnaire in place of a credit check. And there's no human broker to raise a judgmental eyebrow. No wonder margin debt has soared in recent years.

And it seems there's no bottom to the well of available cash. Despite the alarming rise in borrowing, the Fed has been unwilling to alter the margin requirements set in 1974, which allow investors to borrow up to 50% of the purchase price of a stock. Though brokerages are free to raise their own requirements, many of them are reluctant to cut into the easy profits they make from the 7% to 10% lending rates.

The attraction of margin trading is devilishly simple. Say you've got $10,000 to invest in XYZ.com. Borrowing an equal amount from your broker, you buy $20,000 of the stock. Now say XYZ.com shoots up 50%. Suddenly, you have $30,000 in shares. When you pay back the $10,000 you borrowed, plus the loan rate, you wind up with nearly $10,000 in gains. Had you traded on your savings alone, your gains would amount to only $5,000.

But say XYZ.com tanks by 50%. The $20,000 investment drops to $10,000. After paying back your $10,000 loan, your initial investment is decimated. Had you declined to borrow money in the first place, you would have salvaged $5,000.

Trading on margin is risky not just for you but for the brokerages too. If your bet goes sour, so too might their loan. When a sinking stock approaches the level where selling it wouldn't raise enough money to repay your loan, brokers can issue what's known as a margin call. Here's how it works: In an investment made on margin, a drop in the stock's value eats into your contribution first. When the stock price falls so far that the amount you had put up is less than 25% to 35% of the current value of the investment, the broker can order you to sell the stock at a loss to repay the loan (even if you still think the stock will go up) or to deposit more cash into your account immediately. If you don't, the broker can liquidate your other stocks to cover the loan without your assent, without your input and, in fact, without even bothering to tell you.

That's what happened to investor Lael Desmond. He had about $50,000 and an equal amount on margin in his nine-month-old Ameritrade account, all riding on Internet stocks like Yahoo!, Excite and AOL. Then 27, Desmond had recently quit a $40,000-a-year job in chemical sales, hoping his investments would yield enough money for his medical school tuition. Desmond's thin grasp on how margin loans worked didn't stop him from using them. "My understanding at the time was that it was like a loan at a bank," he says. "You pay interest on the amount you borrow."

He got a brutally swift education two years ago. After a drop in the market, Desmond received a letter demanding a prompt infusion of about $9,000. When he called the brokerage, the demand had risen to $13,000. He scrambled to collect cash advances from five credit cards to make the payment. A swoon in the market soon upped the amount he owed to $21,000. He rushed to the bank and wired the money, just making Ameritrade's three-day deadline. When he called later that day to check up, he learned that his entire portfolio had been liquidated at nine that morning.

Desmond took his dispute to arbitration and won, but the victory is bittersweet. After lawyer's fees, he will wind up with $25,000, about half his original investment. Had his stocks been left untouched, he figures his portfolio could be worth about $300,000.

Desmond's experience scared him off margin trading—forever.

BEFORE YOU BORROW

It has to be said: Trading stocks with money that isn't yours is not investing—it's speculating. But if you're thinking of giving it a try anyway, keep these essentials in mind.

- **Learn all your broker's rules before you take a loan.** Even if you've traded on margin before, each firm has its own maintenance requirements, restricted-margin stocks and margin call rules.

- **Be prepared for the consequences of a margin call.** Your broker has the right to sell your stocks to cover its loan if you can't come up with extra cash fast enough.

- **Only borrow amounts you can afford to lose**—or are able to cover easily with cash from other accounts.

- **Keep your holdings diversified.** If you concentrate all your margined stocks in one sector—especially a volatile one—then the stocks are likely to rise or fall in tandem. If they all fall at once, there's an increased chance you'll get hit with a margin call.

- **Never buy an IPO (or newly issued stock) on margin.** In today's seesaw IPO environment, it's too risky to even contemplate. Fortunately, many brokerages won't even let you.

than a third of the investors who thought they had beaten the market actually lagged it by at least 5%—and a fourth of all the self-described market beaters finished at least 15% behind the S&P 500!

"This shows a shocking lack of learning," says Max Bazerman, a Northwestern and Harvard professor who was one of the leaders of the study. "It's easy to have illusions about the future if you don't even have a grip on your own recent past."

MONEY's survey found strikingly similar results. Approximately eight out of 10 investors who thought they had outperformed the Dow during a specified period actually had not.

Separately and decisively, these studies show that the overwhelming majority of investors are kidding themselves when they claim to beat the market. "Everybody wants to believe they're better than average and they can beat the market with their own special something," says Don Moore of Northwestern, co-leader of the study. "It's remarkable how this illusion persists, even in the face of evidence to the contrary."

Welcome to Lake Wobegon. Part of being human is to think we're better than we really are—at just about everything. In general, if you ask a group of people "who's above average here?" roughly three-quarters will stick up their hands—even though, by definition, half of the group has to be below average (or the median). This view of life is like Garrison Keillor's Lake Wobegon, where "all the children are above average." For decades, psychologists have been amassing mountains of evidence for what they call overconfidence or "the optimistic bias":

A 1965 study asked drivers who'd had severe car crashes how skillful they were behind the wheel. These drivers—including those the police had found responsible for the car wrecks and even those who'd been so severely injured that they had to answer the survey from their hospital beds—insisted they were more skillful than average.

In late 1997, the Montgomery mutual funds surveyed 750 investors nationwide and found that 74% of them expected their own funds to beat the S&P 500 every year—even though most funds fail to beat it any year.

Who Cares? I'm in Boca

Add it all up and it's clear: We think we're better than we really are because it's good for our self-esteem. While positive thinking can be useful, unrealistic optimism is not. The reality is that your odds of beating the market over time are no better than one in four, and they're probably worse. And chasing hot funds, or hot stocks, in a frenzied attempt to beat the market is the best way to get burned—or turned off investing entirely.

The attempt to beat the market often leads investors to miscalculate their performance. You're so eager to tell yourself or your friends that you've beaten the market that you forget to look at how your entire portfolio has done. The craving to beat the market can lead you to count your winners and ignore your losers: Sure, your three tech stocks are up 171% in the past year—but how are your AT&T shares doing? Ignoring your losers ("That one doesn't count; I won't make that mistake again") may be common, but it isn't financially healthy. You can't learn from your mistakes if you refuse to admit you've made any.

If you really think you've been beating the market, then it's time you looked hard into the mirror by measuring the actual return of your whole portfolio: Don't forget to subtract all your commissions, fees and taxes, and make sure you include any money you added in over the period. Chances are, you'll find that you too—like 80% of the investors who've recently been studied—have been exaggerating.

Finally, ask yourself why you want to beat the market anyway. Consider the words of a man who lived in Boca Raton, one of Florida's richest retirement communities. Amid the elegant stucco homes, the manicured lawns, the swaying palm trees, the sun and the sea breezes, he was asked if he had beaten the market over the course of his investing lifetime. His response: "Who cares? All I know is, my investments earned enough for me to end up in Boca."

Can you imagine a better answer? After all, the whole point of investing is not to earn more money than average, but to earn enough money to reach your own goals. The best way to measure your investing success is not by whether you're beating the market but by whether your investments are growing steadily and rapidly enough to get you where you want to go. That means that staying put, in an index fund or even in a fund that is underperforming the S&P by a point or two, is better than climbing onto the whizzing treadmill of trying to beat the market. In the end, what matters isn't crossing the finish line before anybody else but just making sure that you do cross it.

CHAPTER 9

Navigating the Maze of Employee Stock Options

*E*mployee stock options (ESOs) used to be reserved for the executive suite. No longer. From cash-poor Silicon Valley start-ups to old-line manufacturing and service firms, more and more companies are offering stock options to the rank and file as well.

The National Center for Employee Ownership (NCEO) estimates that employees control at least 10% of total U.S. corporate equity, up from about 8% just a decade ago, and that employee stock ownership plans account for at least $500 billion. Ten years ago there were only about 1 million workers covered by a few hundred stock option plans. Today there are probably seven times that many employees participating in some 3,000 plans.

What Are Your Options, Anyway?

Learn the ABCs of ESOs. An employee stock option is the right given to you by your employer to buy ("**exercise**") a certain number of shares of company stock at a pre-set price (the "**grant**," "**strike**," or "**exercise price**") over a certain period of time (the "**exercise period**").

Most options are granted on publicly-traded stock, but it is possible for privately-held companies to design similar plans using their own pricing methods. Usually the strike price is equal to the stock's market value at the time the option is granted, but not always. It can be lower or higher than that, depending on the type of option.

Employees profit if they can sell their stock for more than they paid at exercise. NCEO estimates that employees covered by broad-based stock-option plans receive an amount equal to

How to Exercise Your Options

Options can be exercised in three different ways.

■ **Cash.** This is the most straightforward route. You give your employer the necessary money and get stock certificates in return. But what if, when it comes time to exercise, you don't have enough cash on hand to buy the option shares and pay any resulting tax?

■ **Stock swaps.** Some employers let you trade company stock you already own to acquire option stock. Say your company stock sells for $50 a share and you have an incentive stock option to buy 5,000 additional shares for $25 each. Instead of paying $125,000 in cash to exercise the option, you could exchange 2,500 shares (with a total market value of $125,000) you already own for the 5,000 new shares. This strategy has the additional benefit of limiting your concentration in company stock. Note: You must have held the swapped incentive stock option shares for the required one- and two-year holding periods to avoid having the exchange treated as a sale and, thus, incurring tax.

■ **Cashless exercises.** This is the most common method. A broker helps the optionholder to buy the stock at the exercise price and simultaneously sell it at the market price without putting up any money. The optionholder pockets the difference between the market price and the exercise price less taxes and brokerage fees.

between 12% and 20% of their salaries from the "spread" between what they pay for their option stock and what they sell it for.

Most stock options have an exercise period of 10 years. This is the maximum amount of time during which the shares may be purchased, or the option exercised. Restrictions inside this period are prescribed by a "vesting" schedule, which sets the minimum amount of time that must be met before exercise. With some option grants, all shares vest after just one year. With others, 20% of the total shares are exercisable after one year, another 20% after two years, and so on. This is known as "staggered" or "phased" vesting. Most options are fully vested after the third or fourth year, according to a recent survey by consultants Watson Wyatt Worldwide.

Whenever the stock's market value is greater than the option price, the option is said to be "in the money." Conversely, if the market value is less than the option price, the option is said to be "underwater."

During times of stock market volatility, a company may "reprice" its options, allowing employees to trade in underwater options for in-the-money options. For example, if options were originally exercisable at $50 and the stock's market price dropped to $30, the company could cancel the first option grant and issue new options, possibly fewer than originally granted, exercisable at the new $30 share price. Investors generally frown upon this practice, although, of course, employees welcome it.

Options must be handled with care. Most managers below the executive ranks receive *nonqualified options*, which have immediate tax consequences when they are exercised (see box on opposite page). You can exercise these at any time over a defined period, but income taxes are due when the option is cashed in, whether you hang on to the stock or sell it.

Although lower-level employees get a fraction of the options that the boss in the corner office does, the money provided by stock options can be extremely important. By carefully exercising annual stock options for a growing company, you may accumulate enough funds to foot the bill for your child's college education. But here's the problem: "Managing stock options is the most complex financial task employees face," says financial planner Michael Beriss at American Express Financial Advisors in Bethesda, Md. "And middle managers are largely on their own to figure out how to benefit from them." Unlike top executives, most employees seldom qualify for company-paid financial planning advice.

As a result, too many employees cash in their options way too soon and spend the money. "Their distaste for risk outweighs any desire to hold on to the options for long-term profit," says Mark Lang, an associate professor of accounting at the University of North Carolina at Chapel Hill. Lang is the co-author of a 1996 study of 60,000 employees who received options at eight companies. The study found that many workers cashed in their options within six months of becoming eligible to do so. By cashing in early, the typical employee in the study sacrificed an estimated $1 in future value for every $2 he realized.

Types of Options

Not all ESO plans are alike. The way a plan is set up can make a big difference to the value of the options, and the way you'll be taxed on them.

■ **Nonqualified stock options:** These are the stock options of choice for broad-based plans. Generally, you owe no tax when these options are granted. Rather, you are required to pay ordinary income tax on the difference, or "spread," between the grant price and the stock's market value when you purchase ("exercise") the shares. Companies get to deduct this spread as a compensation expense.

After that, any subsequent appreciation in the stock is taxed at capital gains rates when you sell. Keep the stock for more than a year and you'll have a long-term capital gain, taxed at a top rate of 20%; hold for one year or less and your gain is short-term, taxed at higher, ordinary income tax rates. Nonqualified options can be granted at a discount to the stock's then market value. They also are "transferable" to children and charity, provided your company permits it.

■ **Incentive stock options (ISOs):** These are also known as "qualified" stock options because they qualify to receive special tax treatment. No income tax is due at grant or exercise. Rather, the tax is deferred until you sell the stock. At that point, the entire option gain (the initial spread at exercise plus any subsequent appreciation) is taxed at long-term capital gains rates, provided you sell at least two years after the option is granted and at least one year after you exercise.

ISOs give employers no tax advantages and, so, generally are reserved as perks for the top brass, who tend to benefit more from ISO's capital gains tax treatment than workers in lower income tax brackets. High-paid workers also are more likely than low-paid workers to have cash to buy the shares at exercise and ride out the lengthy holding period between exercise and sale.

If you don't meet the holding period requirements, the sale is a "disqualifying disposition" and you are taxed as if you had held nonqualified options. The spread at exercise is taxed as ordinary income, and only the subsequent appreciation is taxed as capital gain.

Unlike nonqualified options, ISOs may not be granted at a discount to the stock's then market value, and they are not transferable, other than by will.

Two warnings apply here: 1. No more than $100,000 in ISOs can become exercisable in any year. 2. The spread at exercise is considered a preference item for purposes of calculating the dreaded Alternative Minimum Tax (AMT), increasing taxable income for AMT purposes. A disqualifying disposition can help you avoid this tax.

Options are so complex that it's easy to make mistakes when cashing them in. Here are three questions to ask yourself before exercising your options:

■ **Do I need the money now, or can I wait to maximize my return?** Typically, you become eligible to cash in 20% of your options a year after you receive them, another 20% the following year and so on. Conventional wisdom holds that you should sit on your stock options as long as possible, assuming you expect the stock to climb. Odds are you'll snare bigger profits this way than if you cash in and invest after-tax proceeds elsewhere.

However, there are reasons to cash in options before they expire. For instance, if the options (based on today's stock price) make up more than 25% of your investments, consider cashing in some of them to diversify your portfolio and reduce risk. One smart way to do this is to exercise about 20% annually over a four-year period and reinvest the money. The remaining unexercised options will allow you to participate in any future stock appreciation.

Financial planner Beriss points out that the discipline of cashing in systematically prevents people from becoming emotionally attached to company shares. "Sometimes employees whose stock has enjoyed a big run-up are reluctant to diversify," he says. "They don't think they can do as well in other investments."

There are two other reasons to sell early. The first is if you become less positive about your employer's prospects. Says Beriss: "Once you think your company shares have peaked, liquidate all your options right away to lock in your gains." Second, if you leave the company, you'll have to cash in your vested options within 60 days of departure or lose them, a standard practice.

■ **Will cashing in my options bump up my tax bracket?**
Most employees outside of the executive suite receive nonqualified stock options that are taxed as ordinary income. Your tax bill will depend on where you live and your federal income tax bracket, but, generally, you should expect to turn over about 40% of your options' profits to the government. The key is to plan ahead so you don't give Uncle Sam a penny more than necessary.

■ **What do I want to do with this money?** Don't cash in your options until you have specific plans for the money, such as paying for college. Otherwise, you'll be more likely to exercise your options in a knee-jerk response to gyrations in the share price. For instance, many workers cash in their options as soon as company shares notch a new 52-week high in the mistaken belief that the stock won't run up any further. Setting goals will also help you avoid viewing options' profits as found money to fritter away.

CHAPTER 10

Five Steps to the Retirement of Your Dreams

When it comes to planning for your future, it's easy to feel overwhelmed. Is it too late to capitalize on the bull market? Should you take a flier on Net stocks, or retreat into cash? Are you on track to retire well—or are you well behind?

Take a deep breath. Retirement is not a race. And there are many ways of getting there. Here's your five-step approach to a great retirement:

Step One: See Where You Stand

To figure out where you're going, you need to know where you are. We're not suggesting that you spend every Sunday night poring over the stock tables with a calculator. It makes sense to add up your retirement assets once a year—no more, no less. Yes, the markets are volatile and your totals can jump around from week to week. But obsessing over every blip in the market could drive you nuts; all you need to do is make sure you're on course.

There's nothing wrong with taking the low-tech route and simply tallying your holdings on paper. But if you fire up financial planning software like Quicken or Microsoft Money or online programs like DirectAdvice.com and the portfolio tracker on MONEY's website (www.money.com), the computer will do much of the work for you in future checkups.

First, round up the accounts clearly labeled for use in retirement. (This is also a good time to make sure you're taking advantage of every tax-sheltered account you are eligible for; see the box on page 184 for a rundown.) Add the stocks, bonds and mutual funds in accounts that aren't tax protected but that you've earmarked for retirement.

More than 7 million employees now include stock options among their perks. If you're one of them, count these assets only if you intend to use the gains toward your retirement (you'll probably have to exercise the options long before then). Financial planner Dee Law of Harvard, Mass. says hundreds of pre-retirees she sees assume their homes will help fund that golf-club membership. It's not a bad plan: You can now shelter as much as $500,000 in capital gains from the sale of your primary residence from Uncle Sam. But when it comes time, "very few actually want to abandon their home sweet home," says Law. "Don't count on the cash until you've got a for sale sign out front."

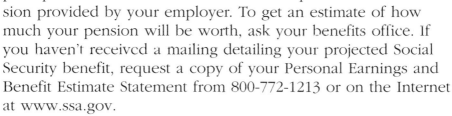

On the other hand, despite all the scary talk about the system going bankrupt, you'll probably get money from Social Security and perhaps from a traditional defined-benefit pension provided by your employer. To get an estimate of how much your pension will be worth, ask your benefits office. If you haven't received a mailing detailing your projected Social Security benefit, request a copy of your Personal Earnings and Benefit Estimate Statement from 800-772-1213 or on the Internet at www.ssa.gov.

Step Two: Set the Right Goal

No matter how far you are from retirement, you know that the alternative to work is no longer napping on the veranda. Back in the days when it was, financial advisers routinely said you could retire comfortably on 70% of your working income—figuring, perhaps, that you were 30% dead.

Today, however, the Bureau of Labor Statistics says that the more money you live on while you're employed, the more you're likely to spend when you retire. Bureau researchers found that retirees with household income of $70,000 or more spend as much in retirement as they did when they worked.

Certain expenses, of course, are likely to drop. Carrying a mortgage or paying for your kids' education—or for babysitters—should be behind you. Also, you'll avoid the expenses of commuting and of dressing for success in clothes that require dry cleaning.

These tax-favored plans can help your money grow faster:

- **401(k)**
  Eligible: Employees with typically one year of service at companies that offer the plan
  Maximum annual savings: $10,000 or plan limit
  Contributions tax-deferred? Yes

- **403(b)**
  Eligible: Employees of nonprofits like schools and hospitals
  Maximum annual savings: $10,000 or plan limit
  Contributions tax-deferred? Yes

- **Keogh**
  Eligible: Self-employed individuals
  Maximum annual savings: 25% of net income or $30,000
  Contributions tax-deferred? Yes

- **SEP-IRA**
  Eligible: Self-employed individuals
  Maximum annual savings: 15% of net income or $24,000
  Contributions tax-deferred? Yes

- **Simple IRA**
  Eligible: Self-employed individuals
  Maximum annual savings: $6,000 plus match of 3% of income
  Contributions tax-deferred? Yes

- **Roth IRA**
  Eligible: Couples earning less than $160,000; singles earning under $110,000
  Maximum annual savings: $2,000 per individual
  Contributions tax-deferred? No

- **Traditional IRA**
  Eligible: Workers not covered by employer plan; married earning less than $61,000 or single earning less than $41,000; or married, one spouse covered by employer, joint income under $160,000
  Maximum annual savings: $2,000 per individual
  Contributions tax-deferred? Yes

- **Nondeductible IRA**
  Eligible: Individual with earned income
  Maximum annual savings: $2,000 per individual
  Contributions tax-deferred? No

Other costs, however, creep up. When you spend more time at home, utility bills climb—as do maintenance costs for wear and tear. Plus, once you're free of the office, you're likely to spend more than ever on entertainment, hobbies and travel.

More dramatically, you'll probably find that health insurance—even basic Medicare and Medigap policies—costs more than you shelled out for your employer's group coverage. And as you age, your unreimbursed medical costs are likely to soar. According to the National Association of Chain Drug Stores, the average American age 65 and older lays out $931 annually on prescription medicines—and 10% of retirees spend more than $1,500 a year.

Obviously, no single formula for planning a retirement budget works for everyone. You may be able to slash current costs by moving from a house to an apartment, by sharing one car with a spouse rather than maintaining two or by canceling life insurance policies (since you no longer have to worry about covering your kids' education or providing an income for your spouse). But maybe you dream of spending your retirement traveling your way around the world. Some folks need less money after retiring; others need more. And financial advisers report that nearly all retirees need to revise their budgets 12 months after they quit work because the day-to-day reality is never quite what they had anticipated.

Assume your spending won't decline. Your best bet in planning is to start by figuring that you'll need the same annual income in retirement that you need today. Of course, as your salary rises over time, so will your ideal retirement income. Therefore, you'll want to repeat this exercise whenever your income takes a sizable jump.

There's one more variable to consider: inflation. In 10 or 20 years your salary today won't have anything like the buying power it has now. While no one can be sure what the inflation rate will be, many planners build an annual rate of 3% into their calculations. (Yes, the rate was higher in the 1970s and 1980s, but in the U.S. it has averaged just 2.6% a year since 1991 and 3% a year for the past 200 years.) That's the figure we use in the worksheet on page 187.

How big a stash will you need to support your current lifestyle when you're no longer earning a salary? For planning purposes, you can set your goal between two target numbers.

Let's call them the ideal and the minimum. The worksheet shows you how to calculate both figures.

The ideal is the amount you'd need to be fairly sure that you won't run out of money no matter how long you live. To accomplish that impressive feat, your stake must be big enough that you consume no more than 4% of it annually. This assumes an annual inflation rate of 3% and an average 7% annual after-tax return (easily achievable with a sensibly diversified sheaf of investments). In effect, you'll be living off your interest, dividends and capital gains, leaving your original retirement stake intact.

If the amount of money you'll need as forecast by this calculation seems impossibly high, don't despair. There's nothing that says you have to make your money last forever. If you gradually draw down your initial retirement stash for your living expenses, you need a much smaller stake—this is the minimum number in the worksheet.

Let's say you want your money to last for 20 years, which is the average life expectancy at age 65. If you keep earning an after-tax return of 7% on your portfolio while you're tapping it, you can spend 9.4% of your initial stake every year. (Thus, if you have $1 million at age 65, you could spend $94,000 a year for the next 20 years.)

The stake you'll need to produce your desired income under this scenario should be much easier to attain, and it still should provide a comfortable retirement—until you're 86. Where you set your goal is up to you, but ideally you should aim to end up somewhere between the 20-year minimum and the ideal.

Step Three: Shape Your Strategy

You know where you are and where you're trying to go. Now all you need to figure out is how to get there. For road maps, look no further than the Internet. Thanks to some easy-to-use online tools, the task of devising a retirement strategy has become much easier.

Now a new generation of computerized calculators aims to refine even further the process of estimating future investment results. These programs rely on Monte Carlo simulations, a mathematical system that runs thousands of simulations of possible stock and bond market performance under different economic conditions. The results then tell you the probability that you'll

How Much Do You Need?

Use this worksheet to estimate how much money you'll need to accumulate for a comfortable retirement.

Take your current annual income. $ _____

Multiply it by the inflation factor from the table at right, according to how many years you have left until retirement. This is the annual pre-tax income you will need in retirement. $ _____

Subtract your annual projected pension income. $ _____

Subtract your expected annual Social Security income. This is your desired annual retirement income. $ _____

Your ideal stake.
Divide your desired retirement income by 0.04. This is the amount you would need to live on your investment earnings indefinitely without depleting your principal at all. $ _____

Your minimum stake.
Divide your desired retirement income by 0.094. This is the amount you'll need if you plan to exhaust your retirement stake over the course of 20 years. $ _____

YEARS TO RETIREMENT	FACTOR
1	1.03
2	1.06
3	1.09
4	1.13
5	1.16
6	1.19
7	1.23
8	1.27
9	1.30
10	1.34
11	1.38
12	1.43
13	1.47
14	1.51
15	1.56
16	1.60
17	1.65
18	1.70
19	1.75
20	1.81
21	1.86
22	1.92
23	1.97
24	2.03
25	2.09
26	2.16
27	2.22
28	2.29
29	2.36
30	2.43

Source: MONEY estimates.

reach your desired income for retirement. These calculators also let you see how changing certain variables—such as how much you're able to sock away each month—can increase or decrease your odds of reaching your goal.

Until recently, these complex programs were available only through financial professionals. But a Web-based offering called

Financial Engines

We took Financial Engines for a spin, using a hypothetical couple typical of MONEY readers. The 40-year-old couple have amassed about $300,000 in their 401(k) accounts. They wish to retire at age 62 with 100% of their inflation-adjusted income, and they tuck away 10% of their $90,000 current income (plus a 6% employer match) toward that goal. Each one also saved $20,000 in a Roth IRA, contributing the annual maximum of $2,000.

The Financial Engines program (www.financialengines.com) tracks the specific investments—stocks, bonds and mutual funds—the couple have in their accounts and adjusts its forecasts to reflect the real-time performance of those holdings. We selected a moderately aggressive portfolio for the couple.

Financial Engines, charting the thousands of possible paths the future could take, figures that the couple have a 36% likelihood of accumulating enough money to yield 100% of their current income in 2021 (adjusted for inflation).

How can they boost their chances? Despite your lack of control over the market's whims, you do have a say in some key factors. Among the changes you can make if your forecast shows you coming up short: how you invest your savings, how much you put away and how soon you retire.

So we went back to Financial Engines to see how a few tweaks would improve our couple's outlook. We found that if they could swallow a little more risk—upping it from 14% over the market average to 20% over—their chance of reaching their goal inches up to 39%. If they boost their 401(k) savings to 12% from 10% (a monthly difference of $150), their odds improve to 42%. And finally, by working for three more years until age 65, their shot at success soars to a very palatable 62%. In fact, extending your working life just a bit can be a remarkable wealth builder, notes C.P.A. Don Chambers of Santa Barbara: "With the double effect of compounding and not withdrawing, the difference can be huge."

The lesson: Don't be discouraged if your ultimate goal seems difficult to reach. By squeezing an extra few dollars of savings each month, investing more aggressively or—if all else fails—postponing your planned retirement date by a year or two, you should be able to get much closer to your financial target.

Financial Engines, created by Nobel prizewinner William F. Sharpe, a professor emeritus of finance at Stanford, now offers the system to regular folks online at www.financialengines.com. It allows you to import your updated portfolio values with just one click. If you're not sure it's worth the effort, read the box above. The quality of the information you can glean is remarkable. One of the program's key benefits is that it suggests alternative strategies to help you reach your retirement goal.

What are the chances that a 40-year-old couple earning $90,000 a year with $340,000 in savings can retire at age 62 with 100% of their income? We used Financial Engines, a Web-based retirement calculator, to find out.

AMOUNT OF ANNUAL SAVINGS:	**$9,000**
INVESTMENT STRATEGY:	**Moderately aggressive**
DESIRED RETIREMENT AGE:	**62**
ODDS OF SUCCESS:	**36%**

IF THEY MAKE SOME ADJUSTMENTS, THEIR CHANCES IMPROVE MARKEDLY:

AMOUNT OF ANNUAL SAVINGS:	**$10,800**
INVESTMENT STRATEGY:	**More aggressive**
DESIRED RETIREMENT AGE:	**65**
ODDS OF SUCCESS:	**62%**

Step Four: Put Your Money to Work

Creating a diversified portfolio is essential, but only stocks can give you the growth you need to stay ahead of inflation and taxes. And while stocks are subject to wild swings, most retirement investors have the time to ride out market downturns and reap the long-term rewards that equities promise. "As a rule of thumb," says Michael Chasnoff of Advanced Capital Strategies in Cincinnati, "anyone investing with retirement as a goal wants at least 60% in stocks."

Aggressive investors should keep an even higher percentage in stocks. But don't ignore the benefits of bonds. Even gung-ho retirement investors should consider keeping at least 10% of their money in bonds. (For tips on how to adjust your mix of stocks and bonds to preserve your wealth as you near retirement, see the box on page 190.)

When it comes to selecting specific investments, building a fully diversified portfolio can be as simple as picking two funds: a broad stock-index fund like Vanguard Total Stock Market

A Portfolio That Ages Gracefully

Investing for retirement is an exercise in long-term planning. But as you near retirement, it seems only logical to shorten your time horizon, right? Wrong. In fact, short-term thinking could end up shortchanging your retirement years. "It's one of the biggest mistakes people make," says Bambi Holzer, a senior vice president at PaineWebber and the author of *Retire Rich*. She notes that retirement can last 20 years or more, "and you certainly don't want 20 years of 5% growth when you could earn significantly more." Holzer suggests that even the most conservative 65-year-old should have at least 40% of his or her portfolio in large and midcap stock funds, with the remaining 60% in bond funds. The most aggressive 65-year-old retiree may want to keep 100% in equities for the first few years of retirement.

Over time, of course, you want to shift the bulk of your portfolio from stocks to bonds. Ridgewood, N.J. financial planner Paul Westbrook says that retirees who have enough pension and Social Security income to leave their investment stake pretty much untouched can be more conservative; those who need to draw on their investments for support, though, should be more aggressive, so that their portfolios keep growing. His suggested asset allocations for people in each situation are shown below.

While you're bulking up on bonds, you also want to be making a shift within your equity stake to more conservative stocks and funds. Put some money into financially solid, dividend-paying stocks. Dividends not only provide a reliable stream of income, but they can act as a safety net in market downturns. And unlike bond payouts, dividends can increase over time, giving you a better shot at keeping up with inflation.

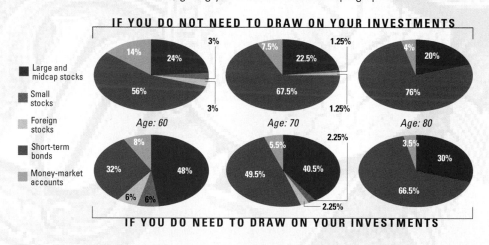

Index and a bond fund like Vanguard Total Bond Market Index. (For more on bonds, see Chapter 4.)

In fact, index funds are ideal for retirement investing. These vehicles—which track benchmark stock and bond indexes and thus produce returns remarkably close to those markets—boast two key attractions: rock-bottom cost and management consistency. When you're dealing with a long time horizon, even fractionally higher fees can end up taking a big bite out of your ultimate returns. In addition, mutual funds that mechanically follow an index veer little if at all in their investment strategies. You'll never have to fret that your hot manager has bolted for another firm or that the fund will change its stripes. (For more on mutual funds, see Chapter 3.)

If you would rather choose actively managed funds, you'll still want to keep the bulk of your assets in broadly diversified funds that hold large and midcap stocks. But refining your portfolio with funds that specialize in small stocks, real estate companies or foreign shares gives you a shot at higher returns with fewer ups and downs along the way. "By mixing a variety of asset classes in your portfolio, you can further minimize the probability of making one large error," says William Droms, a finance professor at Georgetown University's McDonough School of Business.

Step Five: Withdraw Wisely

You've reached your goal and are ready to reap the rewards. Now you'll begin cashing in your investments instead of cashing a paycheck. But you still need a strategy. Keep the following guidelines in mind, and you'll be able to trim your tax bill and make the most of your stash.

Tap your taxable accounts first. You already know that you'll get the most bang for your invested buck if you can leave money to grow in your tax-deferred accounts. But if you leave your IRAs intact as long as possible and draw down your outside funds, you're also setting yourself up to maximize your estate. That's because when you leave your heirs your tax-deferred accounts, they'll be able to take withdrawals based on their own life expectancies and possibly stretch out the deferral for another generation. One caveat: The rules governing inherited IRAs are devilishly complex, so consult a tax adviser.

Get a special break on company stock. If you have a hefty chunk of company stock in your 401(k), here's a nifty way to cut your tax bill. If you keep the stock in your account, you'll

Basket Case

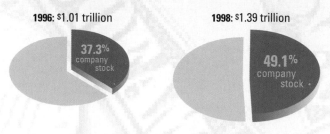

So much for worrying about too many eggs: Company stock accounts for a growing share of the assets in large 401(k) plans.

1996: $1.01 trillion

37.3% company stock

1998: $1.39 trillion

49.1% company stock

Sources: Profit Sharing/ 401(k) Council of America; Cerulli Associates.

pay regular income taxes on it as you withdraw money over time. But before you take your first distribution (or before you roll the money into an IRA), you can elect to withdraw some or all of your stock separately. You'll be taxed not on the full value of the stock, but only on the cost basis, which is what the shares were worth when they went into your account (your employer can tell you the exact amount). When you sell the stock, you'll owe capital-gains taxes (currently no more than 20%) only on your profits.

Say you're in the 31% federal tax bracket, you have $90,000 in company stock in your 401(k) and your cost basis is $10,000. If you leave the stock in the plan and withdraw it over time, you'll pay 31% in taxes, or $27,900. But if you take the stock separately, you'll pay 31% on the $10,000 cost basis, or $3,100. If you then sell the stock, you'll owe 20% capital-gains tax on the remaining $80,000, for a total bill of $19,100. (Of course, once you take the stock you do not need to sell it right away; you can hold it as long as you like, paying capital-gains taxes on your profit when you sell.) Note, however, that most people have too much of their wealth tied up in company stock. Most planners suggest the ideal amount is 10%. But more and more employees are instead increasing their holdings of company stock, as the chart above illustrates).

Minimize your mandatory distributions. After you turn age 70$\frac{1}{2}$, you'll have to start taking distributions from your IRA and 401(k) accounts. The Internal Revenue Service rules that

Retirement Resources

These websites can help you plot your strategy.

- **www.directadvice.com**
  Online retirement planner lets you plug in goals and assets; then it customizes a printable savings and investment plan. **Cost: $75 a year**

- **www.financenter.com**
  Dozens of calculators figure expenses after retirement, the effects of inflation and more. **Free**

- **www.financialengines.com**
  Tells you the probability of reaching your goals. For a fee, recommends specific funds. **Free/$14.95 for three months**

- **www.moneycentral.com**
  Calculators forecast savings, income, Social Security and more. Articles on topics like wills. **Free**

- **www.money.com**
  Site offers easy-to-use portfolio tracker, helpful stock and fund screeners and handy retirement planning tools. **Free**

- **www.morningstar.com**
  Portfolio-planning feature lets you input your current holdings, then tells you how much you have in stocks, bonds and cash—and tracks day-to-day value. **Free**

- **www.personalwealth.com**
  Standard & Poor's site creates a plan including suggested asset allocations. For a fee, it recommends funds and stocks based on S&P research. **Free/$9.95 a month**

- **www.quicken.com/retirement**
  Retirement Planner feature predicts your income in retirement, and whether your savings and investments will help you meet your goal. Information on retirement issues like taxes. **Free**

dictate when and how you'll need to take your money are complicated (there's a shocker); the decisions you make will have a big impact on your heirs. Your goal: Keep money growing in tax-deferred accounts as long as possible. You must begin taking distributions on April 1 of the year after you turn $70^1/_2$. The amount will be based on the time period and method you choose. You can choose one of three time periods (based on IRS tables): your life expectancy, a combination of your and your spouse's life expectancies, or your and a nonspouse beneficiary's. Clearly, if your distributions are based on your life expectancy combined with that of someone younger than you, the mandatory amount will be less—leaving more of your money to continue growing tax deferred.

Once you've decided on the time period, you'll need to determine which distribution method is best for you. "This is where people are really clueless," says Lisa Osofsky, a partner at MR Weiser & Co. in New York City. You'll have two main choices: recalculation and term certain.

Recalculation allows you to determine your life expectancy (or yours and that of your spouse) each year until your death. Under recalculation, your distributions will be smaller, leaving more money in your accounts to grow tax deferred. The **term-certain** method basically means that all calculations are based on whatever your life expectancy (or yours and that of any beneficiary) is when you turn $70^1/_2$. Under term-certain, you must take larger distributions. And if you live beyond that life expectancy, you'll have emptied your account. But term-certain has one key advantage: If you die before your IRS-determined life expectancy, your heirs continue receiving your distributions over the set time period, rather than all at once, thereby reducing their tax bills. If your beneficiary is someone other than your spouse, he or she will have more options for withdrawing your money under term-certain.

CHAPTER 11

Smart Moves for Your 401(k)

*H*ave you taken a look lately at your 401(k) retirement plan? Well, look closer. It's probably no longer the sleepy three-fund offering you signed up for. Driven by new technology, savvy administrators and activist employees, major 401(k) plans have upgraded more frequently than Microsoft Windows. The typical offering today sports at least 10 investment options and often includes such formerly exotic fare as lower-cost institutional funds, higher-risk sector funds and self-directed brokerage accounts. Participants also are getting cutting-edge Internet services, including personal financial advice.

Recognize that along with the expanded choices and whizbang technology comes greater responsibility. To make the most of the new 401(k) plans, you have to work harder. That means sorting through broader and sometimes more complex menus of mutual funds, mastering the new software programs and regularly rebalancing your account. Unfortunately, too many employees haven't even maximized their old plans—some 80% haven't rebalanced since they first signed up, studies show. But here's an incentive: A few necessary tweaks to your account, such as switching to lower-cost funds, can boost your nest egg by hundreds of thousands of dollars by the time you retire. (See the "Savings Grace" chart on the opposite page.)

What to Do Now

Max out on your 401(k) contributions. Be sure to save the maximum amount of pre-tax dollars allowed in your 401(k) plan, which is as much as $10,500 in 2000 (depending on your company's plan.) At the very least, put in enough to get a

Seemingly small differences in costs can add up—big-time—inside your 401(k) plan. How big? Try almost $300,000 over 30 years. That's how much extra money is accumulated within a 401(k) that uses a passively managed index fund with a 0.28% annual fee vs. an actively managed retail mutual fund with a 1.22% fee. (We assumed that the plan participant had a $70,000 salary, contributed 10% annually to the plan, got a 50% employer match on the first 6% of salary and saw average annual returns of 10%.) Actively managed institutional funds, which increasingly are being offered in 401(k) plans, also boast a smaller average fee (0.83%) than retail funds do. That too can mean a big difference: nearly $120,000 over 30 years.

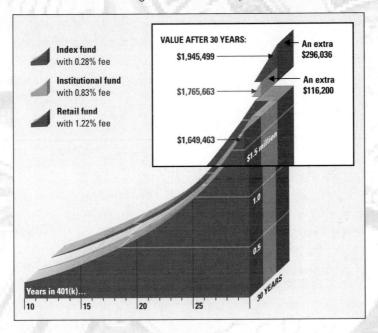

Note: Expenses are the averages for large-cap equity funds.
Sources: Bryan Pendleton Swats & McAllister, Cerulli Associates.

full matching contribution from your employer. If you're changing jobs, ask how quickly you can start contributing. And make sure that you roll over your existing account to your new employer's plan or another tax-deferred account. (More on rollovers later in this chapter.)

Before you choose specific investments, think about asset mix. Although your total portfolio may include a variety of assets, your most important 401(k) investing decision is simple and straightforward: How much do you want to invest in stocks and how much in bonds?

If you are 45 years old or younger, your best bet may be to keep some 85% to 100% of your long-term investments in equities, financial pros say. But be realistic about your risk tolerance. After all, the next market downturn might be steeper and longer than you anticipate. That said, there's no point in stashing your contributions in a money-market fund either. Only equities will provide the growth you need.

Although the temptation may be to run to the relative safety of bonds once you celebrate your 45th birthday, hold off. Financial pros like PaineWebber's Bambi Holzer recommend that even conservative 65-year-old retirees should keep at least 40% or more of their holdings in large and midcap stock funds.

Once you have set your broad asset allocations, diversify your holdings in each category, assuming all the choices are available in your plan. Experts suggest this standard mix of equity funds: 50% in large-company stocks; 25% in small-company stocks; and 25% in foreign stocks. In the fixed-income portion of your portfolio, you may want to include short- and intermediate-term bond funds.

Slash your fees with institutional funds. Many larger plans are switching to institutional funds that once were available only to pension funds and other big investors. In many cases, these funds are run by the same people who manage your retail fund—like the generic version of a brand-name product. Institutional funds on average charge fees that are 30% to 50% less than those of their retail counterparts, since they don't have to pay mass-marketing costs.

You may not know whether you have institutional funds in your 401(k), since many plans still do not advertise that fact. Check with your benefits manager or plan provider. If your plan has these funds, you might consider using them for the bulk of your 401(k) money. But you'll want to remember this caveat: Although institutional funds are generally less expensive than the brand-name funds, there are exceptions. Index funds, even those of the retail variety, can be just as cheap, if not cheaper. And a few lower-cost fund families, such as Vanguard and TIAA-CREF, run actively managed retail funds with expense ratios that rival those of institutional funds. Be sure to compare the costs—and performance—of your plan's various offerings.

Don't keep it all in the family. The typical 401(k) once offered only funds from a single company. But as plans have grown, most employees have a wider range of choices. Today, 70% of large and mid-size companies offer funds from two or more families, up from just 40% two years ago. Spreading your money among funds from different companies can reduce your risk. That's because in some groups, such as Janus and Fidelity, the leading funds often hold many of the same stocks. Besides, no single family excels in all investing styles.

Make the best of the funds offered in your plan. To size up the funds in your plan, compare each one with the performance of its benchmark over the past three years. Standard & Poor's 500 index, for example, is appropriate for gauging the returns of large-cap stock funds. Small-cap funds should be compared with the Russell 2000 index or the averages for their fund category. Ideally, your funds should rank consistently in the top half of their group. (For more on fund-researching strategies, see Chapter 3.)

If you invest in institutional funds, you'll have to rely on your company to provide timely performance data. Most large-company plans make plenty of information available, but in some cases you may need to quiz your benefits officer or the plan provider.

What if one of your funds underperforms and your 401(k) plan doesn't offer any other choices in that category? Your next best strategy is to switch into the funds with better performance and change your investments outside of your plan—where you have unlimited choices—to maintain your portfolio mix.

Invest for the best possible gain, not to save on taxes in retirement. Some financial experts proclaim that to get the highest after-tax returns, investors should put their stocks in taxable accounts (where they are subject only to the capital-gains tax) and their bonds in tax-deferred accounts. Not true. That's because the tax-deferred buildup of equities should more than offset the higher tax rates on stock withdrawals later on.

Don't let your money fly out the brokerage window. About 10% of large company plans offer self-directed brokerage accounts, which allow employees to invest in nearly any stock or mutual fund. Ted Benna, the pension consultant who designed the first 401(k) plan, predicts that wide-open choices will soon be the norm.

Words of caution: If you have a brokerage window, use it with care. Retirement money is best invested for the long haul. Therefore, speculative purchases should be made only with funds you can afford to lose. And even if you're not a frequent trader, using a brokerage window may be more expensive than you realize. For one thing, the funds in your plan may have cut-rate expenses because they're subsidized by your employer, while you'll have to pay full price for funds purchased through a window. Plus, you'll probably have to pay annual fees anywhere from $50 a year to more than $150, plus transaction costs.

Play the company stock game, but hedge your bets.
It's a natural instinct to load up on employer stock. After all, you like the company enough to work for it. Still, most financial advisers say that employer stock should not exceed 10% of your portfolio. That's because your company's stock could plummet, taking your nest egg—and perhaps your job—along with it. Still, you may be sitting on a pile of employer stock simply because you receive it as a matching contribution. If so, try to hedge your risk by putting the rest of your 401(k) in complementary investments.

Do routine maintenance to prevent allocation drift.
Basically, you need to keep an eye on your overall stock and bond mix, says Bill Urban, portfolio manager at investment firm Bingham Osborn & Scarborough. It's that stock-bond mix that will have the biggest influence on your risk and return. If that allocation shifts by as much as 4% to 5%, it's time for you to move it back into line.

You should also monitor your suballocations within your stock and bond holdings—paying attention to how much you have in large-cap funds, small-stock funds and the like. But the farther down the allocation ladder you go, the more you can afford to let the percentages move, since the risk-return benefits of rejiggering are smaller. In most cases, says Urban, you can let your money ride until suballocations are off by 8% or so. When you reach that point, you can lock in the gains on your winners and reinvest the cash. And that provides a painless, low-risk way to maximize your return.

For most plans, reallocating funds is as easy as a phone call or a click of the mouse. No excuses. And since the transfers take place within the confines of your plan, you don't have to worry about being out of the market while your money moves from one account to another. But remember, rebalancing doesn't mean fiddling constantly with your account or attempting to time the market by moving money around to chase the hottest sectors.

The Rollover Dilemma

Are you ready for your 401(k) rollover? No matter what your age, it's coming sooner than you think. Thanks to the long-term bull market, you may be rolling over what could be a six-figure or even seven-figure sum from your 401(k)—probably the biggest pile of money you'll ever handle.

For those whose culture-defining moment was when Kurt Cobain got together with Courtney Love, you also have a rollover in your future. After all, whenever you change jobs, you'll likely get a lump sum that, managed wisely, can be a VIP pass to your retirement security.

While almost 50 million boomers will begin rolling over their retirement plans during the next 20 years, few are prepared for what may be the most important financial decision they'll ever make. Ideally, a lump-sum distribution should be funneled into either an IRA or another employer's plan, where you invest it to last a lifetime. But it doesn't often happen that way. Unfortunately, most employees are ill equipped to handle rollover distributions. How much could a mistake cost you? Oh, more than half your nest egg, once you add up the unnecessary taxes, penalties and opportunity costs.

Don't count on much rollover guidance from your company, however. Too bad, because the rollover decision is much more complicated than it may seem. Plus, your moves should fit into a comprehensive retirement planning and tax strategy. To help sort out all of your options, you may want to work with a financial adviser, especially if you have a big bundle or are hoping to retire soon. Even if you hire a pro, though, you still need to understand the basics for managing a rollover during three critical life stages:

Stage 1: Changing Jobs You've heard this before, but it's worth repeating: Don't cash out your lump sum and spend it. Seems pretty obvious, right? Yet too many workers break that basic rule. A recent survey by benefits firm Hewitt Associates

Rollover Tips

■ **Don't touch:** Cashing out, rather than rolling over, costs you a 10% penalty, income tax charges and years of potential growth.

■ **Be direct:** Have the money directly transferred to the new 401(k) or IRA. If the check is made out to you, you risk losing big-time on various taxes and IRS penalties.

■ **With 401(k)s:** You can more easily tap your money when retiring early (55 to 59$^1/_2$). And assets are protected from lawsuits.

■ **With IRAs:** There usually are far more investment options. The rules for beneficiaries can be more flexible. So can the schedules for withdrawing your money.

---

found that 57% of 401(k) plan participants who are changing jobs choose a cash payment rather than a rollover. Of those with balances under $5,000—mostly younger employees—nearly 80% take the moolah and run. "People look at the money as a big windfall, so they spend it," says Hewitt consultant Mike McCarthy. But cashing out carries a price. You'll owe income taxes plus a 10% penalty if you're under age 59$^1/_2$, and you'll lose the opportunity for future tax-deferred growth.

So let's assume you don't cash out. When deciding what to do with your 401(k), you basically have three choices. You can keep it in your company plan (assuming your balance is more than $5,000); move it to your new 401(k) plan (if its rules allow); or roll it over into an IRA. The right strategy for you will depend on your specific plans and retirement goals, but you'll almost always want to consider these issues:

■ **Keeping the money where it is.** If you like the investments in your previous plan or don't want to go through the trouble of choosing new ones, there's little downside to staying put. It also may make sense to stick with the plan if you've made a significant amount of after-tax contributions. Why? You can't roll over dollars that have already been taxed (although you can roll over the earnings on those contributions).

■ **Moving the money to your new 401(k).** This makes sense if your new plan has more or better options, or lower fees, than your previous one. Other advantages of 401(k)s: Old plan or new, a 401(k) can be helpful if you'll ever need to borrow against the assets during an emergency. You can't do that with an IRA. Also consider a 401(k) if your job involves a high risk of lawsuits or if you fear bankruptcy: Company plans are federally regulated, so they're exempt from creditors; IRA assets, by contrast, are subject to state law, which may not protect them from creditors.

■ **Choosing an IRA**. With all the benefits of 401(k)s, why would you opt for an IRA rollover? There are several reasons. First, an IRA lets you select virtually any investment option. It also provides more flexibility in choosing your beneficiary and (if you are retiring early) taking distributions. Finally, today's good 401(k) plan might morph into tomorrow's bad one, especially if your old company merges or goes through a bout of cost cutting. In fact, most financial advisers prefer IRA rollovers to 401(k)s for their clients.

Keep these two points in mind when you make any rollover:

1. Be sure to do a direct, or trustee-to-trustee, transfer to the financial institution that will hold your IRA or manages your new 401(k). If your old employer ends up writing a check in your name, 20% of the money will be withheld for taxes; therefore, in order to roll over the full amount, you will have to come up with the extra 20% yourself. If you do receive a check directly, you will have just 60 days to make the transfer. If you miss the deadline, the IRS will deem the amount a withdrawal and will impose an additional 10% penalty tax.

2. If you're rolling over into an IRA, the money must go into a regular IRA. You can convert later to a Roth, if you wish to take advantage of its post-retirement tax benefits.

Stage 2: Approaching Retirement The clock is ticking: It's time to decide what to do with your retirement plan money—keep it where it is or make the final rollover that will serve you throughout your retirement. You first need to determine when you will start making withdrawals.

Before making any rollover choice, check the rules of your company plan—details can vary widely from company to company. And consider these key rollover options for pre-retirees:

■ **An early withdrawal from your 401(k).** If you have a sizable 401(k) but little money in your taxable accounts, you may want to stick with your company plan. That's because at many companies you can retire between 55 and 59$^1/_2$ and make regular withdrawals from your 401(k) without paying a penalty. (Your distribution schedule can continue if you later return to the work world—or even rejoin the same employer.) Of course, once you turn 59$^1/_2$ at any company, you're free to take out your 401(k) money at will without penalty if you're retired. But how you take advantage of the 401(k)'s early-withdrawal opening depends on your particular plan's policies. In most cases, you can choose only among the regular retirement withdrawal schedules set by the plan or take a lump-sum distribution. Simply pulling out your money may, in fact, end up being the best choice, since it offers the greatest flexibility. You could set aside what you need to spend in the next few years—taking the income tax hit—and roll over the rest tax deferred into an IRA.

■ **Turning your IRA into a 401(k).** This could be an intriguing option if you have little in a 401(k) but a lot in an IRA rollover. Moving that IRA money into a 401(k)—if the plan rules allow such a switch—will let you tap into your nest egg while avoiding the more restrictive early-withdrawal schedule of IRAs, which we note below.

■ **Know your retirement plan's limitations.** If you're older than 59$^1/_2$ and retiring, there's little reason to stick with your 401(k). Many company savings plans simply aren't that accommodating to retirees, and some plans force workers to take out all their money by the official retirement age, typically 65. If you don't make prior arrangements, such as a direct rollover into an IRA, you could be automatically mailed a check for the distribution—minus the 20% withholding tax.

If you really need to make withdrawals from your nest egg before age 59$^1/_2$, think twice about an IRA rollover. Generally, the only way to avoid paying an early-withdrawal penalty on an IRA is by taking periodic payments based on your life expectancy or the joint life expectancy of you and your beneficiary. The younger you are, the smaller your income stream will be. Plus, once you start taking withdrawals, you must continue for at least five years or until you turn 59$^1/_2$, whichever is later.

Rollover Resources

■ **Taking Your Money Out: IRAs, 401(k)s and Other Retirement Plans**
by Twila Slesnick and John C. Suttle (Nolo, $21.95); not exactly light reading but an excellent starting point

■ **You're Retired, Now What? Money Skills for a Comfortable Retirement**
by Ronald M. Yolles and Murray Yolles (John Wiley & Sons, $14.95); useful stuff from father (an estate and tax attorney) and son (an attorney and financial adviser)

■ **www.irajunction.com**
A fledgling site offered by mPower, which also runs another top investor website called 401kafe.com

■ **www.irahelp.com**
Sponsored by C.P.A. and IRA newsletter publisher Ed Slott, the chief attraction is a forum where he'll help answer your IRA questions.

■ **www.quicken.com/retirement**
A comprehensive though cluttered website that offers the lowdown on various IRAs and rollovers, along with links to expert advice and planning tools

■ **www.onmoney.com**
This sleek site is backed by online broker Ameritrade, but it seeks to offer independent financial-planning advice.

Stage 3: In Retirement. Okay, you're no longer working. Time to chill out. Your chief task these days is managing your rollover and other retirement accounts. If you haven't already rolled out of your former company's 401(k) plan, consider doing so now, since IRAs generally offer the widest investment options for keeping your portfolio on track, as well as the best alternatives for distributions and estate planning. Here's what you need to consider:

■ **Stay with stocks.** If you have a hefty nest egg, you will need to be well diversified among stocks, funds and other assets. Clearly, an IRA rollover to a good brokerage firm or other money-management outfit offers more choice than the typical 401(k) plan. But even though you may be changing your account, don't assume you all of a sudden need to make major changes in your asset allocation. "There are several stages of retirement," notes Ronald Yolles, a financial adviser in Southfield,

Mich. "And in the early stages, you usually need as much growth as you did when you were working."

■ **Update your beneficiaries.** If you wish to pass money on to your heirs, IRAs are the more flexible choice. For example, nearly all 401(k) plans require that your spouse be listed as the primary beneficiary of your account, unless he or she signs a waiver. That makes it more difficult to pass money to your children or other heirs. By contrast, major brokerage and mutual fund companies generally offer plenty of beneficiary options on IRAs. (If yours doesn't, attach a customized form that spells out your wishes—or move your money to a firm that offers more flexibility.) Always double-check your beneficiary forms, and update if necessary. To pass your IRAs to desired heirs, the people must be specifically named on the forms—stating your wishes in your will does not override the account documents.

■ **Watch your withdrawals.** When it comes to mandatory withdrawals, IRAs rule, since they offer more options than company plans do for setting withdrawal schedules. Bear in mind, though, that by April 1 of the year following the year you turn 70—we told you these rules can get thick!—you must begin withdrawing the required minimum distributions from your tax-deferred accounts, be they IRAs or 401(k)s.

After all these details, there's just one other thing about rollovers to note: If you've got a sizable pile, consider getting expert advice. Few things grab the attention of a money manager more than a big, fat IRA rollover walking through the door. You're certainly more likely to get better advice on investing and estate planning than if you keep the money in your company plan. Of course, you needn't rush to an expensive adviser. Depending on your financial needs, you can select from a growing variety of lower-cost resources, ranging from books to online advice to one-shot financial planning (see "Rollover Resources" on page 205 for some suggestions). One new self-help option, for example, is T. Rowe Price's Retirement Income Manager service (800-566-5611). For a cost of $500, it helps analyze your portfolio to determine how much you can safely spend without running out of money.

CHAPTER 12

Saving for College

*T*he good news: College tuition costs are rising less steeply than they were only a few years ago. The bad news: Tuition continues to rise faster than the Consumer Price Index. Bottom line: Paying for college has become a little easier—but not much easier.

There is at least one other development—besides the long-running bull market—to cheer parents struggling to save for their children's college education. New 529 college savings plans are now cropping up around the country. The plans—named for a section in the tax code—allow families to have tax-deferred savings for college. Although not for everyone, they can be very helpful for many families.

Nonetheless, college expenses remain daunting: To put a newborn through four years of Ivy League schooling, you would, in theory, need to save thousands every year.

So here's some unconventional advice: Don't try to do it, especially if it would derail your retirement savings plans. After all, for many families there will be some financial aid available for college, even if it comes in the form of loans—but no one is going to finance your retirement. That's why many financial advisers suggest you treat saving for college like saving for a down payment on a house. You can't expect to pay the whole bill up front, but anything you can put away now reduces the need to borrow later.

Rising Tuition Costs

Over the past decade, higher education costs have risen dramatically; by 2017, one year at a private college may total upwards of $56,000.

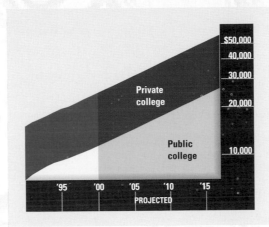

Notes: Figures based on four-year colleges; costs include tuition, books, supplies, room, board, transportation and miscellaneous items.
Sources: The College Board; T. Rowe Price projections.

Assuming you have a number of years to save (see the box on page 213 if you don't), here's your game plan.

Moves That Can Pay Off

Take a look at custodial accounts. You might think that putting money in an account in your child's name is a smart move. You'd be right—but only up to a certain point. Under the Gifts to Minors laws, you can pass along up to $10,000 a year to your child free of taxes (two parents can give $20,000). And that money can be invested in anything from bank accounts to stocks and bonds to mutual funds.

The benefit: The first $700 a year that the account earns in investment income is tax-free, and the next $700 a year is taxed at the child's rate. But that's where the breaks peter out. Any amount above $1,400 a year is whacked at the parents' top rate, as high as 39.6%, until the child turns 14. At that point, the entire amount is taxed at the child's rate.

As your child gets older, your college savings portfolio will need to evolve—that means fewer stocks, more bonds and cash. Here are three asset-allocation models worth following:

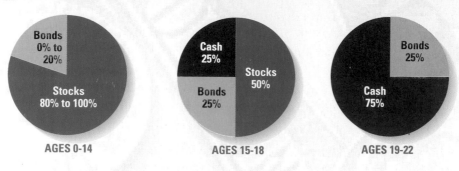

AGES 0-14
Bonds 0% to 20%
Stocks 80% to 100%

AGES 15-18
Cash 25%
Stocks 50%
Bonds 25%

AGES 19-22
Bonds 25%
Cash 75%

Source: College Money, Marlton, N.J.

Moreover, putting money in a custodial account can cost more in aid (including loans) than you save on taxes. The formulas for determining aid require a child to contribute as much as 35% of his or her assets per year, while parents are expected to pay up to 5.6% of theirs. That means a sizable custodial account will limit the aid you receive much more than, say, a fund in your name. In addition, there's a risk that by putting the money in your child's name, you give up control. If you need to draw on those funds for some financial emergency, you won't be able to unless it's for your child's direct benefit. And once the child turns 18 (or 21 in some states), there's little to prevent him or her from using the dough to go to Belize instead of Brown.

So here's a reasonable compromise: Put a limited amount into a custodial account, just enough to qualify for the tax break. If you're certain you won't get aid (and you're confident that your child is college-bound), Kal Chany, author of *Paying for College*, suggests this: Invest in growth stocks, which appreciate in value but pay small dividends. When the student turns 14, sell the stock and take the capital gain, which is taxed at the child's rate. That's around the time you should start to shift to bonds anyway.

Consider a 529 savings plan. A modest custodial account will get you only so far, of course. That's why other specialized plans should come into the picture. Although they're called retirement accounts, Education IRAs are really special educational savings accounts. You do not get a deduction for the money you put away but, just as with the Roth IRA, money saved in an Education IRA can be withdrawn tax-free, as long as it is used for higher education expenses (tuition, books, room, board and the like). Problem is, you can save only a paltry $500 a year per child—barely enough to make a dent in college costs. Another consideration: If you contribute to an Education IRA, you cannot put money in a 529 plan in that same year for the same beneficiary.

For those reasons, you should probably steer toward the latter. State-sponsored 529 college savings plans allow families to save tax deferred for college until the money is withdrawn, at which point it's taxed at the child's rate. By 2001, 32 states will have launched some type of 529 savings plan. Already 529s hold some $7.2 billion spread among 1.2 million accounts.

First, some background. There are actually two varieties of 529 plans. The older version is the prepaid tuition plan, which allows you to lock in the future tuition of selected state colleges at today's rates. But with tuition inflation now averaging 4% (3% for public schools), that's a low rate of return. The newer variety of 529 is the college savings plan, which gives you more options.

These savings plans can be a boon for investors in top tax brackets who have young children and do not expect to qualify for financial aid—they're the ones who can benefit most from the tax-deferred growth. The money can be used to pay the costs of any college, regardless of where you live or where your child wants to attend school. Unlike Education IRAs, there are no income limits for participation in 529 savings plans, and you can put away anything from $2,000 (Iowa) to $100,000 or more per child (New York and others), either in lump sums or through automatic deductions. Your money is placed in a mix of funds based on the age of your child—typically, the allocation is most aggressive for newborns and becomes more conservative as college draws closer. For all savers, the money will grow tax deferred until withdrawal, when it is taxed at the beneficiary's tax rate; for a child, that's usually 15%. (Many states also exempt the earnings on their own plans, and a few even allow a tax deduction on the money you invest if you do so in-state.) And unlike custodial accounts, 529 plans remain in the control of the parents.

Where to go for up-to-date online information

■ **www.collegesavings.org**
The official 529 plan site, sponsored by the state treasurers' association, where you can find links to plans in your state

■ **www.savingforcollege.com**
Run by 529 plan expert Joseph Hurley, this site provides regular updates on college savings plans. You can find details about each plan's strengths and weaknesses, as well as a lively message board.

■ **www.finaid.org**
At this one-stop shop for college planning, you can find everything from aid-eligibility calculators to scholarship searches to detailed explanations of student loans.

■ **www.collegeboard.org**
The purveyors of the dreaded SATs can help with the financial aid process. Their site offers calculators, scholarship searches and useful facts.

■ **www.fastweb.com**
Best known for its searchable database of 400,000 scholarships, this site also provides general financial aid info—including calculators—as well as tips on admission.

If you don't like your in-state plan, some 17 savings plans are available to out-of-state residents, and many are run by well-known investment firms. Among the better performers: Maine (Merrill Lynch), Massachusetts and New Hampshire (both Fidelity). Of course, you'll need to weigh your choice against any potential state tax breaks that you may receive for staying in-state, as well as the plan's fees and withdrawal rules. (For links to these plans, log on to www.collegesavings.org.)

In the meantime, keep in mind that 529s have plenty of flaws. For starters, if you prefer to manage your own investments, you may find 529s too limited. You must submit to the asset allocation of the state—and that's often a conservative ratio of bonds and stocks. If you should become dissatisfied with the plan's performance or if you move to a different state, it can be tough, if not impossible, to shift money into another plan without paying taxes and penalties, notes C.P.A. Joseph Hurley, a 529 plan expert in Pittsford, N.Y. Another potential liability: 529

If You're Starting Late...

So your child is almost ready for college but your finances aren't? Don't panic—and don't raid your retirement accounts. Instead, consider other options. Perhaps your child can qualify for aid, or maybe there are generous grandparents in the picture. You also have plenty of loan choices. Here's how to make the most of your prospects.

■ **Size up your aid eligibility.** Even if your child is still a freshman or sophomore in high school, you should get an early estimate of your financial aid eligibility; for Web-based calculators, see our list of Internet resources on the opposite page. One key point: The base income year (the one colleges use to make their financial aid decisions) is the tax year before college begins—that is, Jan. 1 of the child's junior year of high school to Dec. 31 of the student's senior year. So if you act fast, you may be able to qualify for more aid. Paying off consumer debt, for example, which is not considered in financial needs analysis, will reduce your assets and boost your aid prospects. Also consider such moves as accelerating bonuses or taking capital losses. For more tips, pick up a copy of *Paying for College* by Kal Chany.

■ **Aim for merit aid.** College financial aid packages are increasingly based on the student's merit, not parental income, and at many schools, even a B student can be highly sought after. That's why it's crucial to identify schools where your teen is likely to be in demand. Not only will that help maximize your chances of financial assistance, but you may be able to leverage competing offers. A good source on admissions strategies: *Discounts and Deals at the Nation's 360 Best Colleges* by Bruce Hammond. Or consider hiring an independent college adviser to guide you through the process. (For referrals, call 800-808-4322.)

■ **Explore your loan options.** In the end, you can always borrow. One good deal may be tapping into your home equity. Interest on home-equity loans is generally tax deductible; rates recently averaged 9.93%. You can also turn to federal PLUS loans that let parents borrow up to the full cost of college (current rate: 8.99%). There are no income limits, but you must begin repaying PLUS loans 60 days after you receive the funds. One other option: education loans offered by private lenders, which allow parents to defer repayment until the student graduates.

savings are currently treated as a parental asset, "but these plans are so new that financial aid directors don't know what to make of them," says Kal Chany. "As families start accumulating more money in them, aid directors will want a bigger piece."

One final consideration: When you withdraw the money from your 529 plan, be sure to have additional funds set aside. You can't use 529 assets to pay Uncle Sam without triggering taxes and penalties; that's because tax payments are not a qualified higher education expense. Bear in mind that you will also pay taxes—at your rate—if your child ends up not going to college.

Hedge your bets with stocks and funds. If you choose a custodial account and a 529 plan, you can round out your strategy—and maximize your chances for high returns—by putting additional money in a well-diversified portfolio. And for active investors who want to remain in full control, setting up your own portfolio may be the sole (and preferred) plan of attack. In either instance, the best way to save is the automatic savings plan, which regularly funnels money from your bank account into the fund of your choice. If you're feeling squeezed, start out by saving a small amount—say, $100 a month. Then up the ante as your salary grows.

If your children are still young, at least 80% of your portfolio should be invested in stocks, which have the best shot at out-pacing college costs. (For more details on asset allocation, see the charts on page 210.) You can minimize taxes by focusing on growth stocks that pay little or no dividends, or funds that own such stocks, notes Ray Loewe, president of College Money, a financial planning firm in Marlton, N.J. The truly tax-averse can focus on index funds, which by their nature register few taxable gains, or so-called tax-efficient funds that specifically seek to off-set taxable gains with losses.

A stock investing strategy is working for P.J. and Jeff Broadfoot of Van Buren, Ark. The couple have about $130,000 in college funds set aside for their four children, ages 13, 11, 8 and 6. "We're investing mainly in growth stocks, such as Cisco, IBM and Wal-Mart, as well as funds like Janus," says Jeff, who works for the U.S. Department of Agriculture. But the couple are careful to keep saving in their own retirement plans as well. Says P.J., a veterinarian: "If they want to go somewhere besides a state school, they're going to need to win scholarships."

Then again, with the help of a good strategy—and just the right mix of stocks and funds—you never know.

CHAPTER 13

You Might Need a Financial Planner

W e've tried to fill this book with helpful advice, but for some people a book—or a library full of books—is not enough. For a variety of different reasons, millions of people turn to financial planners for help, often with very positive results.

Studies show that mapping out your long-term financial goals in a well-thought-out written plan can make a dramatic difference in your overall net worth. In fact, a 1997 survey conducted by the Consumer Federation of America and NationsBank found that people with an annual income of $20,000 to $100,000 who had a financial plan (developed by themselves or a pro) had double the savings of others in that income bracket who didn't; people with income over $100,000 and a financial plan had 60% higher savings than their planless peers.

If you can't imagine how you'll be able to juggle competing financial needs, if you feel you're never able to save enough or if you sense your portfolio isn't appropriately diversified, you might need a pro to overhaul your financial life. If you think you need one, don't feel bad. Most people, even some dedicated do-it-yourselfers, do. Well-off individuals who live their whole lives without ever speaking to a financial planner may be making a grievous error of omission. Even if you don't need a full-scale financial plan, you might benefit from a checkup with a planner to make sure your investments are on track.

Deciding to make the call. After 32 years of marriage to her high school sweetheart, Susi Pozzo called it quits a few years ago. Emotional turmoil soon gave way to financial terror as the 54-year-old mother of two realized just how little she knew about money. "I panicked," recalls the Los Angeles part-time landscape designer. "I knew nothing. I wanted a crash course."

Pozzo knew she wouldn't get the kind of financial planning and investment advice she needed from her broker—she thought he was just too condescending—so she found someone who looked and sounded more like herself: Esther M. Berger, a Beverly Hills-based planner. The result: Pozzo feels in control of her nest egg because she has someone who will answer her questions and address her concerns without making her feel dumb for asking.

Like Pozzo, many people tap financial planners only after a turning point in their lives: a divorce, the death of a spouse, an unexpected inheritance. Others simply crave the comfort that comes from working with a trained professional.

Picking the Right Financial Coach

Wanted: a partnership. It's crucial to find an adviser with whom you feel comfortable. Ask yourself if your adviser is listening to your concerns and helping you develop a strategy based on your life goals. Does that person understand your biggest financial issues, your strategies and your tolerance for various levels of risk? A good adviser should be able to help steer you through all things financial, including retirement and asset allocation, tax strategies, insurance and estate planning.

Several hundred thousand people call themselves financial planners, but not all of them are knowledgeable or reputable. To make the cut as a certified financial planner, or C.F.P., a planner must have three years' experience, pass an exam and have a clean regulatory record.

Choosing a good financial planner isn't so simple. A good starting point is our test on the four Cs—comfort, clarity, cost and competence—in the box on the next page.

For a more detailed list of queries, check out the brochure "10 Questions to Ask When Choosing a Financial Planner" from the Certified Financial Planner Board of Standards (www.cfp-board.org).

If you can get a referral to a financial pro from a friend or relative, do so. If not, don't be shy about peppering your potential planner with questions or even requesting a sample plan for a past client. It's not the least bit rude to want to know more about the adviser you're intending to trust with your financial future.

Choosing a Planner

Before signing on with any financial adviser, ask yourself how he or she ranks on four Cs: comfort, clarity, cost and competence.

■ **Comfort.** You really need to feel comfortable talking about your finances and goals with your adviser. If you can't bring yourself to broach a personal topic—such as a recent divorce or worries over a child's inheritance—find someone else.

■ **Clarity.** To get good advice, you need to understand what your adviser is saying. Is he or she talking over your head? Acting condescendingly? Is the advice crystal clear—and does it fit with your own financial goals?

■ **Cost.** Some financial planners get commissions on the products they sell you, while others work on a fee-only basis. You'll want to find out—well before hiring someone—exactly what the cost of the service will be and how it fits in your budget.

■ **Competence.** The real bottom line is this: Comfort means nothing if your adviser steers you wrong. Is he or she a certified financial planner? Ask for references, and then call three clients, to determine how satisfied people are with the advice they've gotten.

You may, in fact, want to go one step further and ask to see a copy of your planner's regulatory Form ADV. Investment advisers who've registered with the Securities and Exchange Commission are required to file this wide-ranging background report and supply it to prospective clients on request. In it you will find the person's professional and regulatory histories as well as his or her specialties and fee structures. After all, you not only want to feel comfortable with your adviser, you need to make sure that she is going to give you good advice as well.

What kind of planner? In recent years, the lines between different types of practitioners—planners, brokers, insurance salespeople and accountants—have blurred as each has encroached on the other's turf. This is only natural in an era in which bankers have morphed into financial services salespeople and financial services concerns into mortgage brokers. Yet even if you're willing to hire hybrids, say a Certified Public Accountant who will also act as your financial planner, it's important to evaluate them separately on each discipline. Among your choices are:

Although personal referrals are ideal, industry associations can be helpful.

The Financial Planners Association (800-322-4237; www.fpanet.org) provides lists of advisers in your area. All members are C.F.P.s.

For fee-only planners, you can call the National Association of Personal Financial Advisers (888-333-6659; www.napfa.com).

For C.P.A.s with a specialty in financial planning, call the American Institute of Certified Public Accountants (888-999-9256; http://www.cpapfs.org).

■ **Traditional planners.** They focus on all aspects of your financial life, not merely investments. Planners get paid in various ways. Some receive commissions from insurance and mutual fund companies, which can create a minefield of conflicts of interest. Others work on a fee-only basis, either charging by the hour or imposing an annual fee (often 1%) on the assets they oversee, which can prove expensive if you have only basic financial questions. Whatever the method of payment, you will want someone who clearly states his or her charges up front and suggests products and services that help you more than they'll help the planner.

■ **Brokerages, mutual fund companies, insurance firms.** If what you're really looking for is investing advice, a broker or a mutual fund rep may be just fine. However, their expertise on broader planning issues depends largely on their training. In fact, 25% of the American Express Financial Advisors and 65% of the financial planners at the Vanguard Group are C.F.P.s.

Naturally, some consumer advocates question whether the primary objective of many financial pros-turned-planners is to construct an overall plan for clients or to recommend investments that generate hefty commissions or fees. "Some of these so-called advisers are simply changing the way they portray themselves without changing the way they do business," complains Barbara Roper, director of investor protection for the Consumer Federation of America.

■ **Accountants.** Certified accountants are also migrating to financial planning as the prevalence and popularity of tax software packages such as Turbotax continue to erode their income. A C.P.A./planner with expertise in investing and insurance can be especially helpful for business owners or individuals with complicated taxes or uneven cash flow. With the proper training, "the transition can be a natural fit," contends Peggy Ruhlin, a C.P.A. in Columbus, Ohio who has been a planner for nearly 20 years. "But many C.P.A.s mistakenly assume that buying the right software is all the training they require."

■ **Wealth managers.** More traditional planners and financial services firms are now positioning themselves as "wealth managers" who go beyond recommending investments. They either run clients' money directly or match them with private money managers, in exchange for a percentage of clients' assets or net worth. That's perfect for folks who don't have the time, patience or expertise to manage their own portfolios.

"Managing investments is very profitable," says Roy Diliberto, president-elect of the International Association of Financial Planners. "However, developing financial plans and helping clients walk through the financial minefields of life is the most important part of the process, even though it's labor-intensive and not a big moneymaker."

■ **Specialized planners.** Increasingly, advisers are developing planning specialties. Some focus on helping corporate executives manage stock options and retirement plan assets, for instance, while others concentrate on divorced or widowed women. One hot target: people who come into "sudden wealth" because they sold a business, received an inheritance or cashed in stock options.

The 2000 FORTUNE 500 Directory

In an era obsessed with pint-sized enterprises rich in potential and little else, the FORTUNE 500 remains the ultimate yardstick of real corporate achievement. Yes, dotcom devotees and biotech boosters may gab about the future of their pet investments, but there's no debating the shadow that FORTUNE 500 companies cast over America's corporate landscape. The businesses on the 2000 FORTUNE 500 employed about 22 million people in 1999, more than 10% of the U.S. work force. They amassed $410 billion in profits, nearly 47% of the nation's total. And they generated $6.3 trillion in revenues, more than the combined '98 GDPs of Japan and Germany.

In a sense, the 500 represents the bedrock of American business, and every list is like a core sample of the year's corporate geology: Each contains traces of the economy that produced it. The 500 has always been a blend of companies that seem perpetually to tower over the rest (General Motors, Exxon and more than 100 others that were on the list in 1955 remain there today) and companies that stay for a while before fading away or succumbing to the competition. In 1999 alone, mergers pushed Ameritech, Bankers Trust and Mobil—to name just a few—out of the running. Throughout its history, the 500 has recorded each of these tales with considerable nuance and unflinching realism.

Nicholas Stein

RANK 1999	1998	COMPANY	REVENUES		PROFITS		
			$ millions	% change from 1998	$ millions	Rank	% change from 1998
1	1	**GENERAL MOTORS** Detroit	189,058.0[1]	17.2	6,002.0	12	103.0
2	3	**WAL-MART STORES** Bentonville, Ark.[2]	166,809.0	19.8	5,377.0	15	21.4
3	4	**EXXON MOBIL** Irving, Texas[3]	163,881.0[E]	62.7	7,910.0	4	24.2
4	2	**FORD MOTOR** Dearborn, Mich.[4]	162,558.0	12.6	7,237.0	11	(67.2)
5	5	**GENERAL ELECTRIC** Fairfield, Conn.	111,630.0	11.1	10,717.0	1	15.3
6	6	**INTL. BUSINESS MACHINES** Armonk, N.Y.	87,548.0	7.2	7,712.0	7	21.9
7	7	**CITIGROUP** New York	82,005.0	7.3	9,867.0	2	69.9
8	10	**AT&T** New York	62,391.0	16.4	3,428.0	30	(46.4)
9	8	**PHILIP MORRIS** New York	61,751.0[E]	6.8	7,675.0	9	42.9
10	9	**BOEING** Seattle	57,993.0	3.3	2,309.0	43	106.2
11	11	**BANK OF AMERICA CORP.** Charlotte, N.C.[5]	51,392.0	1.2	7,882.0	5	52.6
12	35	**SBC COMMUNICATIONS** San Antonio[6]	49,489.0	72.0	8,159.0**	3	102.8
13	13	**HEWLETT-PACKARD** Palo Alto[7]	48,253.0[1]	2.5	3,491.0	27	18.5
14	36	**KROGER** Cincinnati[2,8,9]	45,351.6	—	955.9	114	—
15	14	**STATE FARM INSURANCE COS.** Bloomington, Ill.	44,637.2	0.0	1,034.1	102	(21.6)
16	15	**SEARS ROEBUCK** Hoffman Estates, Ill.	41,071.0	(0.6)	1,453.0	70	38.6
17	22	**AMERICAN INTERNATIONAL GROUP** New York	40,656.1	22.1	5,055.4	16	34.3
18	27	**ENRON** Houston	40,112.0	28.3	893.0[10]	119	27.0
19	18	**TIAA-CREF** New York	39,410.2	9.8	1,024.1	105	21.9
20	28	**COMPAQ COMPUTER** Houston	38,525.0	23.6	569.0	178	—
21	32	**HOME DEPOT** Atlanta[2]	38,434.0	27.2	2,320.0	42	43.7
22	33	**LUCENT TECHNOLOGIES** Murray Hill, N.J.[11,12]	38,303.0	27.1	4,766.0	18	391.3
23	17	**PROCTER & GAMBLE** Cincinnati[13]	38,125.0	2.6	3,763.0	25	(0.4)
24	92	**ALBERTSON'S** Boise[2,14]	37,478.1	134.2	404.1	232	(28.7)
25	80	**MCI WORLDCOM** Clinton, Miss.	37,120.0	110.0	4,013.0	23	—

ASSETS		STOCKHOLDERS' EQUITY		MARKET VALUE 3/14/00		EARNINGS PER SHARE				TOTAL RETURN TO INVESTORS			
							% change from 1998	1989–99 annual growth rate %		1999 %		1989–99 annual rate %	
$ millions	Rank	$ millions	Rank	$ millions	Rank	1999 $		%	Rank	%	Rank	%	Rank
273,921.0	12	20,059.0	20	63,838.5	42	9.18	119.6	3.8	212	26.2	106	11.9	199
70,245.0	52	25,848.0	14	212,666.2	9	1.20	21.2	17.6	51	70.4	30	29.3	31
144,521.0	27	63,466.0	2	268,598.3	5	2.25	(12.8)	5.1	195	12.5	146	16.8	128
276,229.0	11	27,537.0	12	49,471.8	55	5.86	(67.0)	3.6	215	(6.0)	232	18.9	111
405,200.0	5	42,557.0	8	417,175.1	3	3.22	15.0	11.4	102	53.6	55	28.4	35
87,495.0	39	20,511.0	18	193,810.5	10	4.12	25.4	9.8	128	17.6	130	19.3	108
716,900.0	1	49,700.0	5	167,533.1	11	2.83	74.7	24.4	30	69.9	31	35.0	18
169,406.0	23	78,927.0	1	236,704.0	6	N.A.	—	—		—		—	
61,381.0	57	15,305.0	33	46,028.7	61	3.19	45.0	11.6	100	(55.0)	438	9.6	242
36,147.0	90	11,462.0	48	28,722.0	79	2.49	116.5	5.9	185	28.8	97	9.6	239
632,574.0	2	44,432.0	7	71,493.8	36	4.48	54.5	6.8	175	(13.9)	269	11.8	200
83,215.0	44	26,726.0	13	143,028.9	13	2.36	16.3	10.0	126	(7.5)	237	15.9	140
35,297.0	92	18,295.0	22	140,209.0	15	3.34	20.6	14.3	79	67.8	35	26.7	44
16,266.1	167	2,683.4	253	12,047.6	142	1.12	—	—		(37.6)	395	17.7	119
119,143.5	30	45,793.6	6	N.A.		N.A.	—	—		—			
36,954.0	88	6,839.0	93	10,381.7	155	3.81	42.2	(1.2)	268	(26.9)	337	11.3	210
268,238.0	14	33,306.0	9	132,837.7	17	3.23	13.1	11.9	98	40.1	75	24.0	61
33,381.0	94	9,570.0	63	46,643.4	60	1.10	8.9	8.1	155	57.6	49	23.1	73
289,248.0	9	7,025.4	85	N.A.		N.A.	—	—		—		—	
27,277.0	112	14,834.0	34	49,126.0	57	0.34	—	2.8	225	(35.4)	386	26.2	47
17,081.0	158	12,341.0	43	122,934.4	22	1.00	41.5	30.4	15	68.9	32	44.3	13
38,775.0	81	13,584.0	37	214,185.1	8	1.52	316.4	—		36.6	84	—	
32,113.0	96	12,058.0	44	72,693.2	35	2.59	1.2	11.3	105	21.5	121	22.4	79
15,700.9	170	5,701.5	117	10,379.6	156	0.95	(58.7)	2.6	229	(48.6)	427	10.4	225
91,000.0	38	51,000.0	4	122,226.2	23	1.35	—	97.7	1	10.9	153	53.0	9

RANK 1999	1998	COMPANY	REVENUES $ millions	% change from 1998	PROFITS $ millions	Rank	% change from 1998
26	26	**FANNIE MAE** Washington, D.C.	36,968.6	17.4	3,911.9	24	14.4
27	21	**KMART** Troy, Mich.[2]	35,925.0	6.7	403.0	236	(22.2)
28	24	**TEXACO** White Plains, N.Y.	35,690.0[E]	12.6	1,177.0	90	103.6
29	19	**MERRILL LYNCH** New York	34,879.0	(2.7)	2,618.0	37	107.9
30	29	**MORGAN STANLEY DEAN WITTER** New York[15]	33,928.0	9.0	4,791.0	17	46.2
31	23	**CHASE MANHATTAN CORP.** New York	33,710.0	4.1	5,446.0	14	44.0
32	30	**TARGET** Minneapolis[2,16]	33,702.0	8.9	1,144.0	92	22.4
33	25	**BELL ATLANTIC** New York	33,174.0	5.1	4,202.0	19	41.7
34	37	**MERCK** Whitehouse Station, N.J.	32,714.0	21.6	5,890.5	13	12.2
35	38	**CHEVRON** San Francisco	32,676.0[E]	21.9	2,070.0	48	54.6
36	31	**J.C. PENNEY** Plano, Texas[2]	32,510.0	6.0	336.0	259	(43.4)
37	34	**MOTOROLA** Schaumburg, Ill.[17]	30,931.0	5.2	817.0	126	—
38	59	**MCKESSON HBOC** San Francisco[18]	30,382.3	45.7	84.9	408	(45.2)
39	40	**INTEL** Santa Clara, Calif.	29,389.0	11.9	7,314.0	10	20.5
40	48	**SAFEWAY** Pleasanton, Calif.[19]	28,859.9	17.9	970.9	110	20.4
41	55	**INGRAM MICRO** Santa Ana, Calif.	28,068.6	27.4	183.4	342	(25.2)
42	16	**E.I. DU PONT DE NEMOURS** Wilmington, Del.[20,21]	27,892.0[22]	(28.7)	7,690.0	8	71.7
43	51	**JOHNSON & JOHNSON** New Brunswick, N.J.	27,471.0	16.1	4,167.0	20	36.2
44	49	**COSTCO WHOLESALE** Issaquah, Wash.[23,24]	27,456.0	13.1	397.3	238	(13.6)
45	108	**TIME WARNER** New York	27,333.0	—	1,948.0	52	—
46	46	**UNITED PARCEL SERVICE** Atlanta	27,052.0	9.1	883.0	120	(49.3)
47	42	**ALLSTATE** Northbrook, Ill.	26,959.0	4.2	2,720.0	35	(17.4)
48	20	**PRUDENTIAL INS. CO. OF AMERICA** Newark, N.J.	26,618.0	(22.7)	813.0	127	(26.5)
49	61	**AETNA** Hartford	26,452.7	28.4	716.9	142	(15.5)
50	44	**BANK ONE CORP.** Chicago	25,986.0	1.5	3,479.0	28	11.9

ASSETS		STOCKHOLDERS' EQUITY		MARKET VALUE 3/14/00		EARNINGS PER SHARE				TOTAL RETURN TO INVESTORS			
							% change from 1998	1989–99 annual growth rate		1999		1989–99 annual rate	
$ millions	Rank	$ millions	Rank	$ millions	Rank	1999 $		%	Rank	%	Rank	%	Rank
575,167.4	3	17,629.3	24	52,883.6	51	3.72	15.2	16.8	56	(14.3)	270	24.5	58
15,104.0	177	6,304.0	103	4,393.8	264	0.81	(19.8)	0.1	261	(34.3)	380	(2.7)	354
28,972.0	108	12,042.0	45	26,515.5	85	2.14	116.2	(7.3)	303	5.6	174	11.0	217
328,071.0	8	12,802.0	41	37,562.8	67	6.17	105.7	—		26.5	104	31.7	25
366,967.0	7	17,014.0	25	94,889.0	30	4.10	53.8	—		103.1	19	—	
406,105.0	4	23,617.0	15	65,346.5	40	6.27	47.9	—		11.6	149	23.1	74
17,143.0	156	5,862.0	113	27,165.9	83	2.45	23.7	10.6	119	36.2	86	23.5	69
62,614.0	55	15,880.0	31	87,065.1	32	2.65	42.5	6.9	173	16.9	135	13.2	175
35,634.9	91	13,241.6	39	130,865.0	18	2.45	14.0	14.5	73	(7.5)	238	20.6	88
40,668.0	78	17,749.0	23	54,388.0	48	3.14	53.9	24.0	34	7.3	164	14.1	169
20,888.0	140	7,228.0	80	3,613.6	290	1.16	(47.0)	(9.5)	306	(55.5)	439	(1.9)	351
37,327.0	85	16,344.0	28	115,190.4	24	1.31	—	3.2	222	142.6	10	27.0	42
9,081.6	248	2,881.8	240	5,141.9	250	0.31	(80.5)	(12.6)	308	(71.4)	450	12.6	189
43,849.0	68	32,535.0	10	391,816.5	4	2.11	22.3	32.2	12	39.1	78	44.2	14
14,900.3	181	4,085.8	168	18,380.4	105	1.88	18.2	—		(41.3)	406	—	
8,271.9	266	1,966.8	295	2,091.2	356	1.24	(24.4)	—		(62.9)	446	—	
40,777.0	76	12,875.0	40	50,062.7	54	6.99	79.2	14.8	70	26.9	103	15.9	142
29,163.0	107	16,213.0	29	101,099.4	28	2.94	31.8	13.7	82	12.5	147	22.3	80
7,505.0	282	3,532.1	193	19,257.8	101	1.73	(14.8)	(2.8)	284	26.4	105	7.0	288
51,239.0	63	9,713.0	61	112,129.9	25	1.42	—	—		16.8	136	18.3	115
23,043.0	129	12,474.0	42	63,637.2	43	0.77	—	—		—		—	
98,119.0	34	16,601.0	27	14,497.1	125	3.38	(14.2)	—		(36.4)	391	—	
285,094.0	10	19,291.0	21	N.A.		N.A.	—	—		—		—	
112,839.0	32	10,690.4	53	7,232.3	209	4.72	(12.8)	(2.4)	282	(28.3)	348	3.9	320
269,425.0	13	20,090.0	19	28,388.3	80	2.95	13.0	7.9	159	(35.1)	385	10.7	222

RANK 1999	1998	COMPANY	REVENUES $ millions	% change from 1998	PROFITS $ millions	Rank	% change from 1998
51	47	**USX** Pittsburgh	25,610.0[E]	3.5	698.0	145	3.6
52	41	**LOCKHEED MARTIN** Bethesda, Md.	25,530.0	(2.8)	382.0[10]	243	(61.8)
53	39	**METROPOLITAN LIFE INSURANCE** New York[25]	25,426.0	(4.9)	617.0*	163	(54.1)
54	•	**GOLDMAN SACHS GROUP** New York[15]	25,363.0	—	2,708.0	36	—
55	45	**GTE** Irving, Texas	25,336.2	(0.5)	4,032.8*	22	85.7
56	78	**DELL COMPUTER** Round Rock, Texas[2]	25,265.0	38.5	1,666.0	60	14.1
57	43	**UNITED TECHNOLOGIES** Hartford[26]	25,242.0	(1.8)	1,531.0	63	22.0
58	52	**BELLSOUTH** Atlanta	25,224.0	9.1	3,448.0	29	(2.2)
59	93	**CARDINAL HEALTH** Dublin, Ohio[13,27]	25,033.6	57.3	456.3	213	84.7
60	50	**CONAGRA** Omaha[28]	24,594.3	3.2	358.4	250	(41.6)
61	71	**INTERNATIONAL PAPER** Purchase, N.Y.[29]	24,573.0	26.0	183.0	343	(14.1)
62	79	**FREDDIE MAC** McLean, Va.	24,268.0	34.5	2,223.0	45	30.8
63	83	**AUTONATION** Fort Lauderdale[30]	24,206.6[¶]	38.4	282.9	288	(43.4)
64	112	**BERKSHIRE HATHAWAY** Omaha	24,028.0	73.7	1,557.0	61	(45.0)
65	100	**HONEYWELL INTERNATIONAL** Morristown, N.J.[31,32]	23,735.0	56.9	1,541.0	62	15.8
66	53	**WALT DISNEY** Burbank, Calif.[11]	23,402.0	1.9	1,300.0	82	(29.7)
67	56	**FIRST UNION CORP.** Charlotte, N.C.	22,084.0	2.5	3,223.0	31	11.5
68	62	**WELLS FARGO** San Francisco	21,795.0	6.4	3,747.0	26	92.2
69	81	**DUKE ENERGY** Charlotte, N.C.	21,742.0	23.5	1,507.0**	64	20.4
70	68	**NEW YORK LIFE INSURANCE** New York	21,679.3	9.2	554.8	184	(26.3)
71	73	**AMERICAN EXPRESS** New York	21,278.0	11.2	2,475.0	38	15.6
72	60	**LOEWS** New York	20,952.6[E]	1.2	363.2[10]	246	(21.9)
73	65	**PG&E CORP.** San Francisco	20,820.0	4.4	(73.0)[33]	467	(110.2)
74	•	**CONOCO** Houston[34]	20,817.0[E]	—	744.0	137	—
75	57	**CIGNA** Philadelphia	20,644.0	(3.7)	1,774.0	55	37.3

ASSETS		STOCKHOLDERS' EQUITY		MARKET VALUE 3/14/00		EARNINGS PER SHARE				TOTAL RETURN TO INVESTORS			
							% change from	1989–99 annual growth rate		1999		1989–99 annual rate	
$ millions	Rank	$ millions	Rank	$ millions	Rank	1999 $	1998	%	Rank	%	Rank	%	Rank
22,962.0	131	6,856.0	91	9,571.3	163	N.A.	—	—		—		—	
29,799.0	104	6,361.0	100	6,621.7	221	0.99	(62.4)	59.7	4	(46.9)	426	9.6	240
225,232.0	18	13,690.0	36	N.A.		N.A.	—	—		—		—	
250,491.0	17	10,145.0	56	47,018.3	59	5.57	—	—		—		—	
50,831.8	64	10,826.6	52	63,849.0	41	4.12	83.9	7.1	171	11.6	150	12.3	192
11,471.0	212	5,308.0	129	143,488.6	12	0.61	16.2	71.2	3	39.4	77	97.2	1
24,366.0	120	7,117.0	83	23,697.6	93	3.01	19.2	8.5	151	21.4	122	20.1	96
42,453.0	74	14,815.0	35	84,683.0	33	1.80	1.1	7.1	172	(4.6)	222	17.0	126
8,289.0	265	3,463.0	202	11,421.0	148	1.64	10.8	14.3	78	(36.8)	392	24.3	59
12,146.1	208	2,908.8	238	7,694.4	198	0.75	(43.6)	3.3	221	(25.9)	329	11.5	205
30,268.0	102	10,304.0	55	14,156.3	126	0.44	(37.1)	(19.5)	315	28.4	98	9.8	237
386,684.0	6	11,525.0	47	26,547.2	84	2.96	28.1	18.4	49	(26.1)	331	25.8	49
9,613.0	239	4,601.0	152	2,845.4	320	0.66	(37.7)	—		(37.8)	396	—	
131,416.0	28	57,761.0	3	66,904.7	39	1,025.00	(54.7)	10.1	125	(19.9)	296	20.5	91
23,527.0	126	8,599.0	72	35,781.0	70	1.90	(18.1)	7.9	160	31.8	94	23.6	67
43,679.0	69	20,975.0	17	70,502.3	37	0.62	(30.3)	3.8	211	(1.8)	208	12.8	183
253,024.0	16	16,709.0	26	32,614.4	74	3.33	12.9	10.7	114	(43.3)	416	16.7	130
218,102.0	19	22,131.0	16	51,855.8	52	2.23	90.6	13.5	85	3.2	183	25.2	56
33,409.0	93	9,207.0	66	17,188.6	111	4.07	19.7	4.7	199	(18.6)	290	11.1	214
94,979.2	37	6,397.9	98	N.A.		N.A.	—	—		—		—	
148,517.0	26	10,095.0	57	57,398.7	46	5.42	17.1	7.2	169	63.4	42	21.4	82
69,463.7	53	9,977.7	58	4,277.2	267	3.35	(17.5)	(5.7)	292	(37.4)	394	0.8	344
29,715.0	105	6,886.0	88	8,009.2	192	(0.20)	(110.6)	—		(32.2)	373	5.3	310
16,375.0	166	4,555.0	155	14,069.8	127	1.17	—	—		—		—	
95,333.0	36	6,149.0	110	10,346.3	157	8.99	48.6	14.4	76	5.7	172	19.8	100

RANK 1999	1998	COMPANY	REVENUES $ millions	% change from 1998	PROFITS $ millions	Rank	% change from 1998
76	54	**PEPSICO** Purchase, N.Y.	20,367.0	(8.9)	2,050.0	50	2.9
77	72	**AMR** Fort Worth	20,262.0[1]	5.5	985.0	108	(25.0)
78	77	**BRISTOL-MYERS SQUIBB** New York	20,222.0	10.6	4,167.0	20	32.7
79	64	**SARA LEE** Chicago[13]	20,012.0	0.0	1,191.0	89	—
80	161	**FLEETBOSTON** Boston[35]	20,000.0	100.0	2,038.0	51	33.0
81	88	**SPRINT** Westwood, Kans.	19,930.0	16.3	(935.0)	494	(325.6)
82	70	**RAYTHEON** Lexington, Mass.	19,841.0	1.6	404.0	233	(53.2)
83	74	**COCA-COLA** Atlanta	19,805.0	5.3	2,431.0	40	(31.2)
84	109	**MICROSOFT** Redmond, Wash.[13]	19,747.0	36.3	7,785.0	6	73.4
85	58	**CATERPILLAR** Peoria, Ill.	19,702.0	(6.1)	946.0	115	(37.5)
86	84	**UNITEDHEALTH GROUP** Minnetonka, Minn.[36]	19,562.0	12.7	568.0	180	—
87	63	**XEROX** Stamford, Conn.	19,228.0	(4.0)	1,424.0	71	260.5
88	66	**LEHMAN BROTHERS HOLDINGS** New York[15]	18,989.0	(4.5)	1,132.0	94	53.8
89	75	**DOW CHEMICAL** Midland, Mich.	18,929.0	2.6	1,331.0	79	1.6
90	132	**UTILICORP UNITED** Kansas City, Mo.	18,621.5	48.2	160.5	359	21.4
91	90	**ELECTRONIC DATA SYSTEMS** Plano, Texas	18,534.2	9.7	420.9	229	(43.4)
92	76	**J.P. MORGAN & CO.** New York	18,110.0	(1.7)	2,055.0	49	113.4
93	99	**CVS** Woonsocket, R.I.	18,098.3	18.5	635.1	154	60.2
94	82	**UAL** Elk Grove Township, Ill.	18,027.0	2.7	1,235.0	87	50.4
95	98	**WALGREEN** Deerfield, Ill.[23]	17,838.8	16.5	624.1	159	22.1
96	122	**GEORGIA-PACIFIC** Atlanta[37]	17,796.0	34.6	716.0	143	630.6
97	95	**FEDERATED DEPARTMENT STORES** Cincinnati[2]	17,716.0	15.3	795.0	131	20.1
98	97	**SYSCO** Houston[13]	17,422.8	13.7	362.3	249	22.1
99	86	**SUPERVALU** Eden Prairie, Minn.[38,39]	17,420.5	1.3	191.3	337	(17.1)
100	114	**BERGEN BRUNSWIG** Orange, Calif.[11]	17,244.9	25.7	70.6	416	2,175.1

ASSETS		STOCKHOLDERS' EQUITY		MARKET VALUE 3/14/00		EARNINGS PER SHARE				TOTAL RETURN TO INVESTORS			
							% change from	1989–99 annual growth rate		1999		1989–99 annual rate	
$ millions	Rank	$ millions	Rank	$ millions	Rank	1999 $	1998	%	Rank	%	Rank	%	Rank
17,551.0	155	6,881.0	89	44,671.7	62	1.37	4.6	9.2	141	(12.5)	259	15.4	149
24,200.0	121	6,850.0	92	8,570.4	178	6.26	(16.8)	5.7	188	12.8	145	8.7	260
17,114.0	157	8,645.0	71	94,954.9	29	2.06	32.9	19.1	45	(2.8)	215	20.4	93
10,521.0	229	1,266.0	370	13,048.9	134	1.26	—	11.2	107	(19.8)	295	12.8	184
190,692.0	21	15,307.0	32	23,578.2	95	2.10	(16.7)	2.3	233	(20.0)	297	14.6	158
39,250.0	79	13,560.0	38	109,206.2	26	N.A.	—	—		—		—	
28,110.0	111	10,959.0	51	6,297.8	226	1.19	(53.0)	(5.1)	291	(49.3)	429	6.7	295
21,623.0	134	9,513.0	64	107,242.5	27	0.98	(31.0)	4.8	198	(12.1)	256	21.3	83
37,156.0	86	28,438.0	11	492,462.1	1	1.42	70.1	42.2	8	68.4	33	57.9	5
26,635.0	113	5,465.0	125	12,669.7	136	2.63	(36.0)	7.9	158	4.7	180	14.6	159
10,273.0	231	3,863.0	182	8,367.4	182	3.20	—	34.9	10	23.4	113	33.3	24
28,814.0	109	4,911.0	144	15,444.1	119	1.96	276.9	6.0	184	(61.0)	443	12.7	187
192,244.0	20	6,283.0	105	9,603.5	161	8.15	57.0	—		93.4	23	—	
25,499.0	116	8,323.0	74	21,714.1	97	5.93	3.0	(4.3)	288	51.5	57	10.9	218
7,538.6	281	1,525.4	339	1,522.3	381	1.75	7.4	2.6	230	(16.2)	280	9.1	250
12,428.9	206	4,534.6	157	28,234.0	81	0.85	(43.3)	—		34.8	89	—	
260,898.0	15	11,439.0	49	18,109.1	107	10.39	120.6	—		24.6	111	15.5	146
7,275.4	285	3,679.7	188	12,053.9	141	1.55	58.2	(1.4)	271	(27.1)	339	10.0	234
20,963.0	139	5,151.0	134	2,377.0	342	9.94	45.5	10.3	122	29.9	95	9.7	238
5,906.7	315	3,484.3	196	25,156.1	89	0.62	21.6	14.8	69	0.4	193	27.5	39
15,380.0	174	3,750.0	183	7,884.3	196	4.07	653.7	0.9	251	75.5	26	14.2	168
17,692.0	153	6,552.0	95	7,577.7	200	3.62	22.3	—		16.1	138	—	
4,096.6	372	1,427.2	350	9,351.1	167	1.08	25.6	13.8	81	46.1	64	18.9	112
4,265.9	363	1,305.6	361	1,989.3	361	1.57	(13.7)	5.7	189	(26.7)	336	6.2	301
5,535.4	324	1,495.5	343	638.8	436	0.59	1,866.7	2.7	227	(75.7)	451	3.0	328

RANK 1999	1998	COMPANY	REVENUES $ millions	% change from 1998	PROFITS $ millions	Rank	% change from 1998
101	105	**TEXAS UTILITIES** Dallas	17,118.0	16.2	985.0	108	33.1
102	145	**TECH DATA** Clearwater, Fla.[2]	16,991.8	47.4	127.5	383	(1.1)
103	142	**TRW** Cleveland	16,969.0	42.8	468.8	204	(1.7)
104	94	**FEDEX** Memphis[28,40]	16,773.5	5.7	631.3	155	25.5
105	69	**COLUMBIA/HCA HEALTHCARE** Nashville	16,657.0	(15.4)	657.0	152	73.4
106	96	**ALCOA** Pittsburgh	16,446.4	6.2	1,054.1	101	23.6
107	106	**PFIZER** New York	16,204.0	10.2	3,179.0	32	(5.1)
108	131	**JOHNSON CONTROLS** Glendale, Wis.[11]	16,139.4	28.2	419.6	230	24.3
109	137	**LOWE'S** Wilkesboro, N.C.[2]	15,905.6	29.9	672.8	149	39.5
110	103	**MINNESOTA MINING & MFG.** St. Paul	15,659.0	4.2	1,763.0	56	50.0
111	124	**LIBERTY MUTUAL INSURANCE GROUP** Boston	15,499.0	17.7	501.0	198	30.1
112	110	**DYNEGY** Houston[41]	15,430.0	8.2	151.8	366	40.1
113	107	**NORTHWESTERN MUTUAL LIFE INS.** Milwaukee	15,306.3	4.5	1,336.6	78	65.2
114	147	**RELIANT ENERGY** Houston[42]	15,302.8	33.2	1,482.5*	68	—
115	85	**HALLIBURTON** Dallas	14,898.0	(14.1)	438.0**	222	—
116	111	**DELTA AIR LINES** Atlanta[13]	14,711.0	4.1	1,101.0	98	10.0
117	101	**FLEMING** Oklahoma City	14,645.6	(2.8)	(44.7)	460	—
118	119	**COCA-COLA ENTERPRISES** Atlanta	14,406.0	7.4	59.0	422	(58.5)
119	141	**TOSCO** Stamford, Conn.	14,362.1[E]	19.5	441.7	221	315.9
120	91	**ARCHER DANIELS MIDLAND** Decatur, Ill.[13]	14,283.3	(11.3)	266.0	298	(34.1)
121	118	**EMERSON ELECTRIC** St. Louis[11]	14,269.5	6.1	1,313.6	81	6.9
122	120	**MAY DEPARTMENT STORES** St. Louis[2]	14,224.0	6.0	927.0	118	9.2
123	115	**WINN-DIXIE STORES** Jacksonville[13]	14,136.5	3.8	182.3	344	(8.2)
124	121	**EASTMAN KODAK** Rochester, N.Y.	14,089.0	5.1	1,392.0	76	0.1
125	126	**IBP** Dakota Dunes, S.Dak.	14,075.2	9.5	313.3	270	64.9

ASSETS		STOCKHOLDERS' EQUITY		MARKET VALUE 3/14/00		EARNINGS PER SHARE				TOTAL RETURN TO INVESTORS			
							% change from 1998	1989–99 annual growth rate		1999		1989–99 annual rate	
$ millions	Rank	$ millions	Rank	$ millions	Rank	1999 $		%	Rank	%	Rank	%	Rank
40,729.0	77	8,334.0	73	7,400.3	206	3.53	26.5	(2.3)	280	(19.6)	294	7.4	283
4,123.8	371	1,013.7	396	1,367.3	387	2.34	(5.3)	34.3	11	(32.6)	376	30.2	26
18,266.0	150	2,712.0	251	6,382.1	224	3.80	(0.8)	5.8	186	(4.9)	226	11.0	215
10,648.2	227	4,663.7	150	9,296.7	168	2.10	24.6	9.1	143	(8.2)	242	13.6	174
16,885.0	161	5,617.0	120	11,743.9	145	1.11	88.1	—		25.0	110	—	
17,065.8	159	6,317.7	101	22,524.6	96	2.82	16.5	0.6	254	123.9	15	18.2	116
20,574.0	144	8,887.0	69	127,912.8	20	0.82	(3.5)	17.2	53	(21.5)	303	29.9	29
8,614.2	258	2,270.0	271	4,223.9	271	4.48	23.4	13.4	86	(2.1)	211	16.6	131
9,012.3	251	4,695.5	149	16,205.3	116	1.75	28.7	21.4	38	17.0	134	33.3	23
13,896.0	193	6,289.0	104	31,548.0	75	4.34	50.7	4.5	202	41.1	71	12.7	186
55,259.0	61	6,896.0	87	N.A.		N.A.	—	—		—		—	
6,525.2	305	1,309.5	360	8,899.2	172	0.91	37.9	—		122.9	16	—	
85,982.3	41	5,069.0	138	N.A.		N.A.	—	—		—		—	
26,220.9	115	6,306.3	130	6,020.3	231	5.18	—	12.1	97	(24.6)	322	10.1	231
10,728.0	225	4,287.0	162	16,918.5	112	0.99	—	4.5	201	37.6	80	9.4	243
16,544.0	163	4,448.0	158	6,470.3	223	7.20	13.6	4.4	205	(4.0)	220	4.6	316
3,573.2	395	560.7	451	585.7	438	(1.17)	—	—		(0.4)	198	(7.8)	362
22,730.0	132	2,924.0	236	8,742.3	175	0.13	(62.9)	(0.5)	263	(43.3)	417	14.6	157
6,212.4	311	2,108.3	286	3,921.9	280	32.83	322.4	17.4	52	6.2	168	15.8	143
14,029.9	191	6,240.6	107	5,509.7	240	0.43	(33.6)	(4.0)	286	(24.6)	323	3.3	327
13,623.5	195	6,180.5	109	18,239.6	106	3.00	8.3	8.6	148	(3.1)	216	14.3	164
10,935.0	221	4,077.0	169	8,177.3	185	2.60	13.0	7.9	157	(17.9)	286	11.3	211
3,149.1	404	1,411.1	351	2,311.2	343	11.23	(7.5)	3.9	209	(45.1)	424	6.9	293
14,370.0	187	3,912.0	177	16,762.7	114	4.33	2.1	10.3	123	(5.6)	229	11.0	216
3,713.2	391	1,708.8	318	1,182.6	396	3.36	65.5	24.7	29	(37.9)	397	10.3	227

RANK 1999	1998	COMPANY	REVENUES $ millions	% change from 1998	PROFITS $ millions	Rank	% change from 1998
126	143	**PHILLIPS PETROLEUM** Bartlesville, Okla.	13,852.0[E]	16.9	609.0	167	157.0
127	128	**WASHINGTON MUTUAL** Seattle	13,571.2	6.5	1,817.1	54	22.2
128	125	**NATIONWIDE INSURANCE ENTERPRISE** Columbus, Ohio	13,554.9	3.4	512.8	195	(57.1)
129	117	**AMERICAN HOME PRODUCTS** Madison, N.J.	13,550.2	0.6	(1,227.1)	495	(149.6)
130	102	**HARTFORD FINANCIAL SERVICES** Hartford	13,528.0	(9.9)	862.0	123	(15.1)
131	127	**DANA** Toledo	13,353.0	4.0	513.0	194	(4.0)
132	134	**MCDONALD'S** Oak Brook, Ill.	13,259.3	6.7	1,947.9	53	25.7
133	129	**WASTE MANAGEMENT** Houston[43,44]	13,257.4	—	(201.9)	480	—
134	135	**US WEST** Denver	13,182.0	6.5	1,342.0[10]	77	(11.0)
135	133	**ABBOTT LABORATORIES** Abbott Park, Ill.	13,177.6	5.6	2,445.8	39	4.8
136	123	**ATLANTIC RICHFIELD** Los Angeles	13,176.0[E]	(0.1)	1,422.0	72	214.6
137	139	**PUBLIX SUPER MARKETS** Lakeland, Fla.	13,068.9	8.3	462.4	207	22.2
138	136	**KIMBERLY-CLARK** Irving, Texas	13,006.8	5.8	1,668.1	59	43.1
139	157	**WARNER-LAMBERT** Morris Plains, N.J.	12,928.9	26.6	1,733.2	58	38.2
140	130	**GOODYEAR TIRE & RUBBER** Akron	12,880.6	1.8	241.1	315	(64.7)
141	138	**VIACOM** New York	12,858.8	6.3	334.0*	260	—
142	149	**RITE AID** Camp Hill, Pa.[38]	12,731.9	11.9	143.7	372	(54.6)
143	173	**LEAR** Southfield, Mich.	12,428.0	37.2	257.1	304	122.6
144	116	**FLUOR** Aliso Viejo, Calif.[7]	12,417.4	(8.1)	104.2	394	(55.8)
145	152	**WEYERHAEUSER** Federal Way, Wash.	12,262.0	13.9	527.0[10]	188	79.3
146	192	**CISCO SYSTEMS** San Jose[45]	12,154.0	43.7	2,096.0	47	55.3
147	•	**ASSOCIATES FIRST CAPITAL** Irving, Texas[46]	12,131.2	—	1,490.4	66	—
148	151	**TOYS "R" US** Paramus, N.J.[2]	11,862.0	5.9	279.0	290	—
149	113	**DEERE** Moline, Ill.[7]	11,750.9	(15.0)	239.2	316	(76.6)
150	164	**SUN MICROSYSTEMS** Palo Alto[13]	11,726.3	19.8	1,031.3	103	35.2

ASSETS		STOCKHOLDERS' EQUITY		MARKET VALUE 3/14/00		EARNINGS PER SHARE				TOTAL RETURN TO INVESTORS			
							% change from	1989–99 annual growth rate		1999		1989–99 annual rate	
$ millions	Rank	$ millions	Rank	$ millions	Rank	1999 $	1998	%	Rank	%	Rank	%	Rank
15,201.0	175	4,579.0	153	10,052.1	158	2.39	162.6	10.3	124	13.5	142	10.2	229
186,513.6	22	9,052.7	68	12,539.2	137	3.16	23.4	24.1	32	(30.8)	363	19.7	102
120,101.9	29	9,768.0	60	N.A.		N.A.	—	—		—		—	
23,906.3	122	6,214.7	108	60,387.6	45	(0.94)	(150.8)	—		(29.1)	353	15.1	152
167,051.0	24	5,466.0	124	6,516.0	222	3.79	(11.9)	—		(12.1)	257	—	
11,123.0	217	2,957.0	232	3,568.9	294	3.08	(3.8)	6.6	179	(24.2)	320	9.4	244
21,000.0	138	9,600.0	62	41,297.6	64	1.39	26.4	11.0	109	5.4	175	17.6	121
21,425.0	136	4,553.0	156	8,210.1	183	N.A.	—	—		(63.1)	447	27.1	41
23,216.0	128	1,255.0	372	33,760.8	72	2.63	(12.9)	—		14.9	140	—	
14,471.0	185	7,427.6	79	48,151.0	58	1.57	4.0	12.6	92	(24.7)	326	17.9	117
26,272.0	114	8,686.0	70	25,520.9	87	4.33	209.3	(2.6)	283	37.1	83	9.3	247
4,067.7	376	2,676.1	254	N.A.		2.14	23.0	15.4	62	—		—	
12,815.5	203	5,093.1	137	25,130.7	90	3.09	46.4	8.9	145	22.4	118	17.1	125
11,441.5	213	5,098.3	136	76,614.4	34	1.96	32.4	14.4	75	10.2	157	26.8	43
13,102.6	199	3,617.1	191	3,185.3	304	1.52	(64.7)	(1.6)	274	(42.8)	411	5.1	313
24,486.4	119	11,132.0	50	36,687.9	69	0.45	—	—		63.3	43	—	
10,421.7	230	2,953.7	233	1,618.3	374	0.54	(55.7)	(0.6)	266	(77.1)	452	5.5	306
8,717.6	257	1,465.3	346	1,685.8	368	3.80	123.5	—		(16.9)	282	—	
4,886.1	346	1,581.4	333	2,143.2	351	1.37	(53.9)	0.1	259	10.2	158	3.5	324
18,339.0	149	7,173.0	81	12,256.2	140	2.55	73.5	5.0	196	45.2	66	13.9	172
14,725.0	183	11,678.0	46	453,878.8	2	0.62	47.6	—		130.8	12	—	
82,955.8	45	9,800.5	59	11,831.6	144	2.04	—	—		(34.8)	382	—	
8,503.0	259	3,681.0	187	2,632.7	330	1.14	—	0.4	256	(15.5)	279	(5.0)	358
17,578.2	154	4,094.3	167	8,085.4	189	1.02	(75.5)	(4.9)	290	35.1	88	10.9	219
8,420.4	261	4,811.8	147	137,921.5	16	1.27	31.6	29.6	17	261.8	4	53.3	7

RANK 1999	1998	COMPANY	REVENUES $ millions	REVENUES % change from 1998	PROFITS $ millions	PROFITS Rank	PROFITS % change from 1998
151	150	**ANHEUSER-BUSCH** St. Louis	11,703.7[E]	4.1	1,402.2	75	13.7
152	174	**GAP** San Francisco[2]	11,635.4	28.5	1,127.1	96	36.7
153	148	**SOUTHERN** Atlanta	11,585.0	1.6	1,276.0	84	30.6
154	144	**TEXTRON** Providence	11,579.0	0.3	2,226.0	44	266.1
155	•	**R.J. REYNOLDS TOBACCO** Winston-Salem, N.C.[47]	11,394.0[E]	—	2,343.0*	41	—
156	154	**UNION PACIFIC** Omaha	11,273.0	6.8	810.0	128	—
157	196	**ULTRAMAR DIAMOND SHAMROCK** San Antonio	11,079.2[E]	32.7	173.2	350	—
158	163	**TENET HEALTHCARE** Santa Barbara[28]	10,880.0	10.0	249.0	309	(4.6)
159	162	**CSX** Richmond	10,811.0	9.2	2.0[10]	451	(99.6)
160	182	**CIRCUIT CITY GROUP** Richmond[38]	10,804.4	21.8	142.9	373	37.0
161	184	**FARMLAND INDUSTRIES** Kansas City[23]	10,709.1	22.0	N.A.		—
162	156	**AMERICAN GENERAL** Houston	10,679.0	4.2	1,131.0	95	48.0
163	286	**EL PASO ENERGY** Houston[48]	10,581.0	83.0	(255.0)	484	(213.3)
164	155	**WHIRLPOOL** Benton Harbor, Mich.	10,511.0	1.8	347.0	252	6.8
165	175	**NORTHWEST AIRLINES** Eagan, Minn.	10,276.0	13.6	300.0	278	—
166	176	**OFFICE DEPOT** Delray Beach, Fla.	10,263.3	14.1	257.6	303	10.5
167	187	**MONSANTO** St. Louis	10,126.0	17.1	575.0	174	—
168	165	**HUMANA** Louisville	10,113.0	3.4	(382.0)	490	(396.1)
169	195	**BEST BUY** Eden Prairie, Minn.[38]	10,077.9	20.6	224.4	324	137.6
170	160	**ELI LILLY** Indianapolis	10,002.9	(0.5)	2,721.0	34	29.7
171	167	**PACIFICARE HEALTH SYSTEMS** Santa Ana, Calif.	9,989.1	4.9	278.5	291	37.6
172	159	**GILLETTE** Boston	9,897.0	(1.6)	1,260.0	86	16.6
173	153	**MASS. MUTUAL LIFE INSURANCE** Springfield, Mass.	9,841.0	(7.8)	556.5	183	28.6
174	183	**MANPOWER** Milwaukee	9,770.1	10.8	150.0	370	98.3
175	188	**AMERISOURCE HEALTH** Malvern, Pa.[11]	9,760.1	13.8	67.5	418	33.5

ASSETS		STOCKHOLDERS' EQUITY		MARKET VALUE 3/14/00		EARNINGS PER SHARE				TOTAL RETURN TO INVESTORS			
							% change from	1989–99 annual growth rate		1999		1989–99 annual rate	
$ millions	Rank	$ millions	Rank	$ millions	Rank	1999 $	1998	%	Rank	%	Rank	%	Rank
12,640.4	205	3,921.5	176	25,331.7	88	2.94	16.2	8.2	153	9.6	160	16.6	132
5,188.8	332	2,233.0	274	37,368.8	68	1.26	38.0	28.5	19	23.2	116	38.8	16
38,396.0	84	9,204.0	67	13,690.4	130	1.86	32.9	3.3	220	(14.9)	276	11.6	202
16,393.0	165	4,377.0	159	7,570.6	201	14.48	293.5	25.8	26	2.6	184	23.1	72
14,377.0	186	7,064.0	84	1,808.9	366	21.58	—	—		—		—	
29,888.0	103	8,001.0	76	8,735.8	176	3.22	—	1.4	248	(1.5)	206	8.1	274
4,936.0	343	1,493.3	344	2,019.2	359	2.00	—	—		(1.9)	210	—	
13,771.0	194	3,870.0	180	6,238.7	227	0.79	(6.0)	(2.0)	278	(10.5)	247	3.7	322
20,720.0	143	5,756.0	115	4,713.2	256	0.01	(99.6)	(41.6)	318	(22.2)	306	8.6	266
3,445.3	397	1,905.1	303	8,651.1	177	1.48	31.0	6.9	174	80.8	24	24.0	62
3,257.6	403	917.3	405	N.A.		N.A.	—	—		—		—	
115,447.0	31	6,420.0	97	11,457.3	147	4.40	48.6	8.9	146	(0.6)	202	21.8	81
16,657.0	162	2,947.0	234	8,523.7	179	(1.12)	(160.5)	—		14.0	141	—	
6,826.0	297	1,867.0	305	3,641.2	289	4.56	7.3	5.4	191	20.2	126	9.9	235
10,584.0	228	(52.0)	489	1,437.3	383	3.26	—	—		(13.0)	264	—	
4,276.2	362	1,907.7	302	3,376.8	299	0.69	13.7	26.9	23	(55.5)	440	15.2	151
16,535.0	164	5,349.0	127	26,116.6	86	0.88	—	(1.3)	269	(25.2)	327	15.6	144
4,900.0	344	1,268.0	369	1,110.1	402	(2.28)	(396.1)	—		(54.0)	437	(0.7)	348
2,512.5	437	1,064.1	393	12,741.7	135	1.07	105.8	48.3	7	63.7	41	58.6	4
12,825.2	202	5,013.0	139	62,620.5	44	2.46	31.6	11.9	99	(24.2)	321	17.6	120
4,884.0	347	1,977.7	294	1,987.9	362	6.23	41.6	29.2	18	(27.1)	340	15.3	150
11,786.0	210	3,060.0	223	32,715.8	73	1.14	20.0	12.9	91	(12.8)	262	22.6	78
71,991.0	51	3,411.3	204	N.A.		N.A.	—	—		—		—	
2,718.7	427	650.6	440	2,132.4	352	1.91	105.4	—		50.4	60	—	
2,060.6	453	166.3	478	620.2	437	1.31	26.0	—		(53.3)	434	—	

RANK 1999	1998	COMPANY	REVENUES $ millions	% change from 1998	PROFITS $ millions	Rank	% change from 1998
176	189	**CHS ELECTRONICS** Miami[43,44]	9,737.4	—	(301.2)	487	—
177	169	**LIMITED** Columbus, Ohio[2]	9,723.3	4.0	460.8	208	(77.6)
178	158	**EDISON INTERNATIONAL** Rosemead, Calif.	9,670.0	—	623.0	160	(6.7)
179	185	**HOUSEHOLD INTERNATIONAL** Prospect Heights, Ill.	9,499.1	9.1	1,486.4	67	183.6
180	191	**TEXAS INSTRUMENTS** Dallas	9,468.0	11.9	1,406.0	73	245.5
181	290	**ILLINOIS TOOL WORKS** Glenview, Ill.[49]	9,333.2	65.3	841.1	124	25.0
182	197	**ARROW ELECTRONICS** Melville, N.Y.	9,312.6	11.6	124.2	387	(14.9)
183	170	**H.J. HEINZ** Pittsburgh[50]	9,299.6	1.0	474.3	203	(40.8)
184	393	**UNUMPROVIDENT** Portland, Me.[51]	9,242.5	136.7	(182.9)	477	(172.0)
185	200	**SCHERING-PLOUGH** Madison, N.J.	9,176.0	13.6	2,110.0	46	20.2
186	232	**MARSH & MCLENNAN** New York	9,157.0	27.4	726.0	139	(8.8)
187	177	**COLGATE-PALMOLIVE** New York	9,118.2	1.6	937.3	116	10.5
188	178	**BURLINGTON NORTHERN SANTA FE** Fort Worth	9,100.0	1.8	1,133.0	93	(1.9)
189	210	**PACCAR** Bellevue, Wash.	9,021.0	14.3	583.6	172	40.0
190	180	**NORTHROP GRUMMAN** Los Angeles	8,995.0	1.0	467.0	206	140.7
191	320	**GENERAL DYNAMICS** Falls Church, Va.[52]	8,959.0	80.3	880.0	121	141.8
192	236	**STAPLES** Westborough, Mass.[2]	8,936.8	25.5	315.0	268	69.9
193	203	**DILLARD'S** Little Rock[2]	8,921.0	11.7	164.0	357	21.5
194	205	**GUARDIAN LIFE INS. CO. OF AMERICA** New York	8,861.7	11.1	324.5	263	102.4
195	234	**ORACLE** Redwood Shores, Calif.[28]	8,827.3	23.6	1,289.8	83	58.5
196	208	**TJX** Framingham, Mass.[2]	8,795.3	10.6	521.7	190	23.0
197	166	**NIKE** Beaverton, Ore.[28]	8,776.9	(8.1)	451.4	217	13.0
198	146	**ENTERGY** New Orleans	8,773.2	(23.7)	595.0	169	(24.3)
199	224	**NEBCO EVANS** Greenwich, Conn.[43,44]	8,744.2	—	(246.5)	483	—
200	206	**MARRIOTT INTERNATIONAL** Bethesda, Md.	8,739.0	9.7	400.0	237	2.6

ASSETS		STOCKHOLDERS' EQUITY		MARKET VALUE 3/14/00		EARNINGS PER SHARE				TOTAL RETURN TO INVESTORS			
							% change from 1998	1989–99 annual growth rate		1999		1989–99 annual rate	
$ millions	Rank	$ millions	Rank	$ millions	Rank	1999 $		%	Rank	%	Rank	%	Rank
2,620.6	431	535.3	454	55.8	465	N.A.	—	—		(93.4)	456	—	
4,087.7	374	2,147.1	282	7,175.6	211	2.00	(76.0)	7.6	164	59.6	45	12.1	195
36,229.0	89	5,211.0	132	5,403.4	243	1.79	(2.7)	0.1	262	(2.2)	212	8.9	253
60,749.4	59	6,615.3	94	15,031.7	120	3.07	198.1	11.0	110	(4.5)	221	19.4	106
15,028.0	179	9,255.0	65	127,931.8	19	1.68	229.4	16.0	59	126.3	14	37.7	17
9,060.3	249	4,815.4	146	16,448.4	115	2.76	3.4	13.7	83	17.5	131	21.1	86
4,483.3	358	1,550.5	336	2,957.7	315	1.29	(14.0)	—		(4.9)	225	29.3	30
8,053.6	272	1,803.0	310	11,482.1	146	1.29	(40.0)	1.5	246	(27.6)	343	8.7	262
38,447.5	83	4,982.2	141	2,899.1	318	(0.77)	(142.3)	—		(21.7)	304	12.8	182
9,375.0	244	5,165.0	133	51,520.0	53	1.42	20.3	18.4	48	(22.6)	310	25.6	52
13,021.0	200	4,170.0	166	21,261.9	99	2.62	(12.1)	6.7	178	67.5	36	17.5	122
7,423.1	283	1,833.7	308	24,927.3	91	1.47	12.6	11.5	101	41.6	70	26.1	48
23,700.0	123	8,172.0	75	8,835.5	173	2.43	0.0	8.6	147	(28.1)	345	11.2	212
7,933.0	274	2,110.6	285	3,313.1	300	7.41	39.8	9.5	137	13.1	144	13.9	173
9,285.0	245	3,257.0	209	3,403.9	298	6.69	139.8	—		(24.1)	317	16.0	138
7,774.0	277	3,171.0	213	8,065.7	190	4.36	52.4	9.5	136	(9.2)	243	25.6	53
3,846.1	388	1,828.8	309	8,484.6	180	N.A.	—	—		—		—	
7,918.0	275	2,833.0	244	1,573.5	378	1.55	23.0	0.6	253	(28.4)	350	(1.2)	350
31,696.4	97	4,892.7	145	N.A.		N.A.	—	—		—		—	
7,259.7	286	3,695.3	185	217,257.8	7	0.87	61.1	30.6	14	289.8	3	47.4	11
2,805.0	419	1,119.2	386	4,690.0	257	1.64	29.1	—		(29.2)	355	20.5	92
5,247.7	329	3,334.6	207	7,945.5	194	1.57	16.3	10.9	111	23.3	115	23.6	68
22,985.1	130	7,119.4	82	4,198.1	272	2.25	(25.0)	—		(13.8)	268	6.9	292
1,993.2	457	(492.1)	493	N.A.		N.A.	—	—		—		—	
7,324.0	284	2,908.0	239	6,757.9	216	1.51	3.4	—		9.5	161	—	

RANK 1999	1998	COMPANY	REVENUES $ millions	% change from 1998	PROFITS $ millions	Rank	% change from 1998
201	181	**FOUNDATION HEALTH SYSTEMS** Woodland Hills, Calif.	8,706.2	(2.1)	142.4	374	—
202	211	**NAVISTAR INTERNATIONAL** Chicago[7]	8,647.0	9.7	544.0	186	81.9
203	223	**GATEWAY** San Diego[53]	8,645.6	15.8	427.9	226	23.5
204	171	**ST. PAUL COS.** St. Paul	8,641.0[1]	(5.1)	834.0	125	833.4
205	237	**AFLAC** Columbus, Ga.	8,640.0	21.6	571.0	175	17.3
206	207	**CONTINENTAL AIRLINES** Houston	8,639.0	8.7	455.0	214	18.8
207	194	**BESTFOODS** Englewood Cliffs, N.J.	8,637.0	3.1	717.0	141	14.9
208	186	**US AIRWAYS GROUP** Arlington, Va.	8,595.0	(1.1)	197.0	335	(63.4)
209	217	**BINDLEY WESTERN** Indianapolis	8,509.5	11.6	38.3	433	100.1
210	199	**INGERSOLL-RAND** Woodcliff Lake, N.J.	8,504.6	2.6	591.1	170	16.1
211	240	**SUNOCO** Philadelphia	8,485.0[E]	20.8	97.0	399	(65.4)
212	215	**U.S. BANCORP** Minneapolis	8,435.4	10.1	1,506.5	65	13.5
213	250	**EATON** Cleveland[54]	8,402.0	26.8	617.0	163	76.8
214	306	**SOLECTRON** Milpitas, Calif.[23]	8,391.4	58.7	293.9	284	47.8
215	216	**WILLIAMS** Tulsa	8,364.1[E]	12.0	221.4**	325	73.6
216	212	**CONSECO** Carmel, Ind.	8,339.1	8.1	962.6	112	63.7
217	214	**UNITED SERVICES AUTOMOBILE ASSN.** San Antonio	8,319.1	8.2	765.1	134	(21.9)
218	201	**NATIONAL CITY CORP.** Cleveland	8,293.4	2.8	1,405.5	74	31.3
219	89	**NABISCO GROUP HOLDINGS** Parsippany, N.J.[55]	8,268.0[22]	(51.5)	2,968.0	33	—
220	235	**COASTAL** Houston	8,197.2[E]	15.0	498.9	200	12.3
221	238	**KEYCORP** Cleveland	7,989.0	12.5	1,107.0	97	11.1
222	252	**GENUINE PARTS** Atlanta	7,981.7	20.7	377.6	244	6.1
223	413	**AVISTA** Spokane	7,905.0	114.6	26.0	441	(66.7)
224	204	**BEAR STEARNS** New York[13]	7,882.0	(1.2)	673.0	148	1.9
225	230	**PAINE WEBBER GROUP** New York	7,822.8	7.9	628.6	156	45.0

ASSETS		STOCKHOLDERS' EQUITY		MARKET VALUE 3/14/00		EARNINGS PER SHARE				TOTAL RETURN TO INVESTORS			
							% change from	1989–99 annual growth rate		1999		1989–99 annual rate	
$ millions	Rank	$ millions	Rank	$ millions	Rank	1999 $	1998	%	Rank	%	Rank	%	Rank
3,696.5	393	891.2	406	986.0	409	1.16	—	—		(16.4)	281	—	
6,928.0	294	1,291.0	366	2,254.8	346	8.20	99.5	13.6	84	64.9	38	1.9	337
3,954.7	382	2,017.1	291	19,011.9	102	1.32	21.1	—		181.6	7	—	
38,873.0	80	6,472.0	96	5,016.5	251	3.41	965.6	5.3	192	0.1	194	12.3	194
37,041.0	87	3,868.0	181	9,516.8	164	2.07	17.6	22.7	35	8.2	162	27.2	40
8,223.0	269	1,593.0	331	2,305.9	344	6.20	23.5	—		32.5	92	—	
6,232.0	310	938.0	401	10,608.4	153	2.48	18.7	8.9	144	0.7	192	14.5	162
7,685.0	280	(117.0)	490	1,380.9	386	2.64	(52.9)	—		(38.3)	399	(0.4)	347
1,704.8	465	374.7	470	493.0	440	1.05	66.7	16.4	57	(26.5)	334	16.9	127
8,400.2	262	3,083.0	220	5,770.7	233	3.57	15.9	10.5	121	17.9	129	14.8	155
5,196.0	331	1,506.0	342	2,459.5	338	1.07	(63.7)	1.5	244	(32.6)	375	(0.7)	349
81,530.0	47	7,638.0	77	13,512.9	132	12.06	15.7	—		(31.1)	366	19.5	104
8,437.0	260	2,624.0	259	5,432.6	242	8.36	74.2	10.8	112	5.0	177	12.9	181
4,834.7	349	2,793.1	245	24,595.5	92	1.13	37.0	—		104.7	18	70.4	3
25,288.5	117	5,585.2	122	20,214.8	100	0.50	78.6	9.9	127	(0.5)	200	20.5	90
52,053.9	62	5,830.7	114	3,871.0	282	2.89	63.3	20.8	41	(40.4)	405	27.6	38
30,323.0	101	6,874.7	90	N.A.		N.A.	—	—		—		—	
87,121.5	40	5,727.7	116	10,813.2	151	2.22	37.9	7.4	167	(31.9)	371	14.0	171
11,961.0	209	3,161.0	214	2,836.0	322	9.10	—	—		(43.1)	414	—	
15,123.0	176	3,936.9	175	9,187.4	170	2.30	13.3	9.8	130	1.6	187	9.2	249
83,395.0	43	6,389.0	99	7,039.4	213	2.45	9.9	7.8	162	(28.3)	349	14.3	165
3,929.7	383	2,177.5	280	3,612.0	291	2.11	6.6	6.3	180	(23.2)	314	6.2	300
3,713.5	390	656.8	439	1,067.2	405	0.12	(90.6)	(21.5)	317	(17.5)	283	7.0	290
153,894.3	25	4,955.5	142	4,607.4	260	4.48	2.3	16.8	55	27.7	101	23.8	66
61,612.4	56	2,920.0	237	5,541.9	239	3.56	30.9	27.6	22	1.6	186	25.4	55

RANK 1999	1998	COMPANY	REVENUES $ millions	% change from 1998	PROFITS $ millions	Rank	% change from 1998
226	190	**TRICON GLOBAL RESTAURANTS** Louisville	7,822.0	(7.6)	627.0	157	40.9
227	221	**PPG INDUSTRIES** Pittsburgh	7,757.0	3.3	568.0	180	(29.1)
228	198	**CROWN CORK & SEAL** Philadelphia	7,731.8	(6.8)	181.3	345	72.5
229	294	**VALERO ENERGY** San Antonio	7,691.2[E]	38.8	14.3	446	—
230	209	**PNC FINANCIAL SERVICES GROUP** Pittsburgh[56]	7,666.0	(3.4)	1,264.0	85	13.4
231	253	**COMPUTER SCIENCES** El Segundo, Calif.[18]	7,660.0	16.0	341.2	254	31.0
232	213	**PRINCIPAL FINANCIAL** Des Moines	7,659.2	(0.5)	742.1	138	7.1
233	179	**JOHN HANCOCK FINANCIAL SERVICES** Boston[57]	7,654.7	—	153.2	365	—
234	227	**SUNTRUST BANKS** Atlanta	7,620.2	3.1	1,326.6**	80	36.6
235	255	**OCCIDENTAL PETROLEUM** Los Angeles	7,610.0[E]	15.4	448.0*	219	23.4
236	231	**UNISYS** Blue Bell, Pa.	7,544.6	4.7	510.7	196	32.0
237	172	**CBS** New York	7,510.0	(17.1)	780.0	133	—
238	239	**CONSOLIDATED EDISON** New York	7,491.3	5.6	714.2	144	(2.1)
239	256	**WELLPOINT HEALTH NETWORKS** Thousand Oaks, Calif.	7,485.4	13.9	278.5	291	20.4
240	400	**SMURFIT-STONE CONTAINER** Chicago	7,386.0	94.7	157.0	364	—
241	226	**TYSON FOODS** Springdale, Ark.[11]	7,362.9	(0.7)	230.1	321	816.7
242	249	**AMERICAN STANDARD** Piscataway, N.J.	7,287.2	9.5	138.3	378	—
243	254	**BAXTER INTERNATIONAL** Deerfield, Ill.	7,286.0[¶]	10.4	797.0	130	153.0
244	243	**PHARMACIA & UPJOHN** Peapack, N.J.	7,252.6	7.3	803.3	129	16.3
245	242	**ASHLAND** Covington, Ky.[11]	7,251.0[E]	4.6	290.0	287	42.9
246	229	**FORT JAMES** Deerfield, Ill.	7,157.9	(2.0)	516.5	192	3.8
247	202	**ROCKWELL INTERNATIONAL** Milwaukee[11]	7,151.0	(10.9)	562.0	182	—
248	259	**AON** Chicago	7,070.0	8.9	352.0	251	(34.9)
249	251	**AMERADA HESS** New York	7,039.1[E]	6.4	437.6	223	—
250	246	**KELLOGG** Battle Creek, Mich.	6,984.2	3.3	338.3	257	(32.7)

ASSETS		STOCKHOLDERS' EQUITY		MARKET VALUE 3/14/00		EARNINGS PER SHARE				TOTAL RETURN TO INVESTORS			
							% change from	1989–99 annual growth rate		1999		1989–99 annual rate	
$ millions	Rank	$ millions	Rank	$ millions	Rank	1999 $	1998	%	Rank	%	Rank	%	Rank
3,961.0	381	(560.0)	496	3,928.0	279	3.92	38.0	—		(22.9)	312	—	
8,914.0	254	3,106.0	216	8,005.7	193	3.23	(27.9)	4.4	203	10.3	156	15.4	147
11,503.0	211	2,849.0	242	1,702.7	367	1.36	91.5	1.3	250	(24.7)	324	3.4	325
2,979.3	410	1,084.8	392	1,576.9	376	0.25	—	—		(5.0)	227	—	
75,413.0	48	5,946.0	111	10,811.7	152	4.15	15.3	7.6	163	(15.0)	278	13.0	180
5,007.7	341	2,399.9	266	13,229.8	133	2.11	28.7	14.5	74	47.3	63	25.7	51
82,086.3	46	5,552.9	123	N.A.		N.A.	—	—		—		—	
84,455.7	42	4,791.1	148	4,581.6	261	N.A.	—	—		—		—	
95,390.0	35	7,626.9	78	14,666.0	124	4.13	35.9	12.2	96	(8.2)	241	22.6	77
14,125.0	189	3,523.0	194	6,323.6	225	1.24	25.3	1.9	241	34.8	90	2.3	331
5,889.7	317	1,953.3	297	8,114.0	188	1.59	50.0	—		(7.3)	236	8.7	263
33,100.0	95	16,100.0	30	42,275.3	63	1.08	—	(10.2)	307	94.9	22	8.0	277
15,531.5	172	5,624.6	119	5,906.5	232	3.13	3.0	2.3	234	(31.4)	367	8.4	267
4,593.2	354	1,312.7	359	3,807.2	285	4.10	24.6	—		(24.2)	319	—	
9,859.0	233	1,847.0	307	2,943.0	316	0.71	—	—		54.9	52	—	
5,082.7	340	2,128.0	284	2,110.1	354	1.00	809.1	6.8	176	(23.0)	313	7.3	285
4,686.0	353	(496.5)	495	2,560.0	333	1.90	—	—		27.4	102	—	
9,644.0	237	3,348.0	206	15,688.6	118	2.70	147.7	6.1	183	(0.5)	201	14.5	161
10,698.0	226	5,595.0	121	27,435.8	82	1.49	13.7	8.6	149	(18.9)	291	8.8	258
6,424.0	307	2,200.0	277	2,196.0	349	3.89	47.9	9.6	133	(29.9)	357	1.0	342
7,258.2	287	1,127.3	385	3,945.6	278	2.35	4.0	(2.0)	277	(30.2)	360	2.7	330
6,704.0	300	2,637.0	257	7,275.9	208	2.90	—	0.1	260	21.0	124	14.4	163
21,132.0	137	3,051.0	224	5,570.2	238	1.33	(35.9)	2.4	231	10.6	155	15.9	141
7,727.7	278	3,038.2	225	5,259.2	248	4.85	—	(1.9)	276	15.3	139	2.7	329
4,808.7	350	813.2	418	9,579.9	162	0.83	(32.5)	(1.5)	272	(7.2)	235	8.7	261

			REVENUES		PROFITS		
RANK 1999	1998	COMPANY	$ millions	% change from 1998	$ millions	Rank	% change from 1998
251	285	**BANK OF NEW YORK CO.** New York	6,966.0	20.2	1,739.0	57	45.9
252	268	**BOISE CASCADE** Boise	6,952.7	12.8	199.8	333	—
253	264	**AMERICAN ELECTRIC POWER** Columbus, Ohio	6,915.7	9.0	520.2	191	(3.0)
254	233	**UNICOM** Chicago	6,848.0	(4.2)	570.0	176	11.7
255	270	**LINCOLN NATIONAL** Philadelphia	6,803.7	11.8	460.4	209	(9.7)
256	244	**SEAGATE TECHNOLOGY** Scotts Valley, Calif.[13]	6,802.0	(0.2)	1,176.0	91	—
257	263	**CHUBB** Warren, N.J.	6,729.6	6.0	621.1	161	(12.1)
258	262	**ARAMARK** Philadelphia[11]	6,718.4	5.3	150.2	369	16.2
259	260	**SAFECO** Seattle	6,717.1	4.1	252.2	307	(28.3)
260	386	**EMC** Hopkinton, Mass.[58]	6,715.6	69.0	1,010.6	107	27.4
261	245	**SCI SYSTEMS** Huntsville, Ala.[13]	6,710.8	(1.4)	137.8	379	(5.0)
262	266	**CUMMINS ENGINE** Columbus, Ind.	6,639.0	6.0	160.0	361	—
263	274	**PUBLIC SERVICE ENTERPRISE GROUP** Newark, N.J.	6,497.0	9.5	(81.0)	468	(112.6)
264	349	**FEDERAL-MOGUL** Southfield, Mich.	6,487.5	45.2	243.2	314	352.9
265	310	**MBNA** Wilmington, Del.	6,470.1	24.5	1,024.4	104	32.0
266	248	**FPL GROUP** Juno Beach, Fla.	6,438.0	(3.3)	697.0	146	5.0
267	•	**CENEX HARVEST STATES** Inver Grove Heights, Minn.[23,59]	6,434.5	—	N.A.		—
268	427	**FIRSTAR CORP.** Milwaukee[60]	6,424.3	83.5	875.3	122	103.5
269	222	**CAMPBELL SOUP** Camden, N.J.[45]	6,424.0	(14.4)	724.0	140	9.7
270	267	**SAKS** Birmingham, Ala.[2]	6,423.8	3.3	189.6	339	—
271	408	**NEWELL RUBBERMAID** Freeport, Ill.	6,413.1	72.4	95.4	401	(75.9)
272	275	**AVNET** Phoenix[13,61]	6,350.0	7.3	174.5	348	15.2
273	307	**COMPUSA** Dallas[13,62]	6,321.4	19.6	(45.7)	461	(245.0)
274	280	**FIRSTENERGY** Akron	6,319.6	7.8	568.3	179	38.3
275	356	**MASCO** Taylor, Mich.	6,307.0	45.2	569.1	177	19.6

ASSETS		STOCKHOLDERS' EQUITY		MARKET VALUE 3/14/00		EARNINGS PER SHARE				TOTAL RETURN TO INVESTORS			
							% change from 1998	1989–99 annual growth rate		1999		1989–99 annual rate	
$ millions	Rank	$ millions	Rank	$ millions	Rank	1999 $		%	Rank	%	Rank	%	Rank
74,621.0	49	5,143.0	135	23,594.3	94	2.27	48.4	54.1	5	1.0	191	27.7	37
5,138.4	336	1,614.1	329	1,575.4	377	3.06	—	(6.8)	300	32.8	91	1.9	338
21,488.0	135	5,006.0	140	5,216.5	249	2.69	(4.3)	(1.9)	275	(27.2)	341	6.7	296
23,406.0	127	5,332.6	128	8,063.7	191	2.61	11.5	(0.8)	267	(9.4)	245	5.4	308
103,095.7	33	4,263.9	163	4,514.5	262	2.30	(8.4)	4.3	206	0.1	195	14.7	156
7,072.0	291	3,563.0	192	14,043.6	128	4.53	—	97.6	2	53.9	54	20.0	97
23,537.0	125	6,271.8	106	7,864.1	197	3.66	(12.6)	4.1	207	(11.6)	253	11.3	209
2,870.5	418	126.6	482	N.A.		1.48	39.6	20.5	42	—		—	
30,572.7	100	4,294.1	161	2,404.8	340	1.90	(24.3)	(2.2)	279	(39.7)	404	6.1	302
7,173.3	288	4,951.8	143	126,271.9	21	0.92	23.5	—		157.1	8	95.3	2
2,322.7	445	1,164.8	380	6,625.4	220	2.01	(5.6)	14.9	67	42.3	69	34.3	21
4,697.0	352	1,429.0	349	1,307.3	393	4.13	—	—		39.5	76	8.9	255
19,015.0	147	3,996.0	173	5,613.3	237	(0.37)	(113.3)	—		(7.9)	239	9.4	245
9,945.2	232	2,075.2	288	1,070.9	403	3.16	229.2	9.6	134	(66.2)	449	2.1	335
30,859.1	98	4,199.4	165	17,990.0	108	1.21	24.7	—		11.0	152	—	
13,441.0	196	5,370.0	126	7,464.1	203	4.07	5.7	2.7	228	(27.7)	344	7.3	286
2,787.7	422	1,117.6	387	N.A.		N.A.	—	—		—		—	
72,787.8	50	6,308.6	102	17,437.9	110	0.87	33.8	14.6	72	(30.9)	365	27.9	36
5,522.0	325	235.0	474	11,954.6	143	1.63	13.2	51.9	6	(28.2)	346	13.0	179
5,090.1	338	2,208.3	275	2,064.6	357	1.30	—	28.0	21	(50.7)	430	16.5	133
6,724.1	298	2,697.0	252	6,099.1	230	0.34	(85.7)	(7.0)	301	(28.2)	347	12.1	198
2,984.7	409	1,397.6	352	2,566.4	332	4.86	27.9	12.4	94	1.4	188	8.7	264
1,465.8	478	376.1	467	N.A.		(0.50)	(251.5)	—		(61.2)	444	—	
18,224.0	151	4,563.9	154	4,146.8	275	2.50	37.4	1.4	247	(26.5)	333	6.6	297
6,634.9	301	3,136.5	215	8,204.9	184	1.28	(7.9)	6.1	182	(10.4)	246	10.0	233

RANK 1999	1998	COMPANY	REVENUES $ millions	% change from 1998	PROFITS $ millions	Rank	% change from 1998
276	311	**ALLTEL** Little Rock	6,302.3	21.3	783.6	132	49.1
277	276	**WACHOVIA CORP.** Winston-Salem, N.C.	6,287.8	6.3	1,011.2	106	15.7
278	278	**ANTHEM INSURANCE** Indianapolis	6,270.1	6.7	44.9	430	(73.9)
279	272	**GENERAL MILLS** Minneapolis[28]	6,246.1	3.5	534.5	187	26.7
280	292	**COMCAST** Philadelphia	6,209.2	11.1	1,065.7	100	9.6
281	298	**U.S. FOODSERVICE** Columbia, Md.[13]	6,198.4	12.6	83.2	410	—
282	304	**UNOCAL** El Segundo, Calif.	6,198.0[E]	15.2	137.0	380	5.4
283	258	**NCR** Dayton	6,196.0	(4.8)	337.0	258	176.2
284	297	**MICROAGE** Tempe, Ariz.[7]	6,149.6	11.4	(169.0)	474	—
285	273	**APPLE COMPUTER** Cupertino, Calif.[11]	6,134.0	3.2	601.0	168	94.5
286	305	**PROGRESSIVE** Mayfield Village, Ohio	6,124.2	15.7	295.2	283	(35.4)
287	314	**CMS ENERGY** Dearborn, Mich.	6,103.0	18.7	277.0	293	(2.8)
288	283	**MELLON FINANCIAL CORP.** Pittsburgh[63]	5,986.0	3.0	963.0	111	10.7
289	279	**CINERGY** Cincinnati	5,937.9	1.0	403.6	235	54.7
290	354	**KINDER MORGAN** Houston[64]	5,927.2	35.1	(241.4)	482	(502.5)
291	277	**R.R. DONNELLEY & SONS** Chicago	5,901.4[¶]	0.0	308.3	273	4.7
292	288	**UNION CARBIDE** Danbury, Conn.	5,870.0	3.7	291.0	285	(27.8)
293	302	**OWENS-ILLINOIS** Toledo	5,786.7	5.2	298.3	279	176.2
294	303	**3COM** Santa Clara, Calif.[28]	5,772.1	6.5	403.9	234	1,236.7
295	333	**SERVICEMASTER** Downers Grove, Ill.	5,703.5	20.7	173.6	349	(8.6)
296	321	**CNF TRANSPORTATION** Palo Alto	5,592.8	13.2	190.5	338	37.1
297	301	**VF** Greensboro, N.C.	5,551.6	1.3	366.2	245	(5.7)
298	328	**AUTOMATIC DATA PROCESSING** Roseland, N.J.[13]	5,540.1	15.5	696.8	147	15.1
299	316	**FIRST DATA** Atlanta	5,539.8	8.3	1,199.7	88	157.6
300	388	**B.F. GOODRICH** Charlotte, N.C.[65]	5,537.5	40.2	169.6	352	(25.1)

ASSETS		STOCKHOLDERS' EQUITY		MARKET VALUE 3/14/00		EARNINGS PER SHARE				TOTAL RETURN TO INVESTORS			
							% change from 1998	1989–99 annual growth rate		1999		1989–99 annual rate	
$ millions	Rank	$ millions	Rank	$ millions	Rank	1999 $		%	Rank	%	Rank	%	Rank
10,774.2	222	4,205.7	164	21,650.0	98	2.47	30.7	7.9	161	40.8	74	19.4	107
67,352.5	54	5,658.5	118	10,910.5	150	4.90	17.2	9.7	131	(20.3)	298	16.4	134
4,953.2	342	1,660.9	325	N.A.		N.A.	—	—		—		—	
4,140.7	368	164.2	479	9,294.7	169	3.40	30.8	3.0	223	(5.5)	228	12.1	196
28,685.6	110	10,341.3	54	28,848.3	78	1.30	7.9	—		72.4	28	25.7	50
2,012.9	455	829.4	417	2,559.6	334	0.86	—	—		(31.6)	370	—	
8,967.0	253	2,184.0	279	6,667.1	219	0.56	3.7	(6.6)	299	17.5	133	3.8	321
4,895.0	346	1,609.0	330	4,225.2	270	3.35	179.2	—		(9.3)	244	—	
786.6	498	132.9	481	70.6	464	(8.22)	—	—		(77.2)	453	(3.2)	355
5,161.0	335	3,104.0	217	18,419.9	104	3.61	71.9	0.2	257	151.1	9	12.1	197
9,704.7	234	2,752.8	747	3,816.1	284	3.96	(35.2)	15.0	65	(56.7)	442	19.7	101
15,462.0	173	2,456.0	264	2,030.7	358	2.42	(7.6)	(4.4)	289	(33.3)	377	0.9	343
47,946.0	66	4,016.0	171	14,017.4	129	1.85	13.8	10.7	116	1.3	189	26.3	46
9,616.9	238	2,653.7	255	3,198.3	303	2.53	53.3	(1.3)	270	(26.0)	330	8.1	275
9,540.3	241	1,665.8	323	3,042.0	308	(3.01)	(427.2)	—		(13.7)	267	10.0	232
3,853.5	387	1,138.3	383	2,403.1	341	2.38	14.4	5.3	194	(41.7)	407	1.8	339
7,957.0	273	2,617.0	260	6,198.6	228	2.13	(26.8)	(6.3)	298	59.8	44	25.2	57
10,756.3	224	2,349.9	268	2,423.0	339	1.78	187.1	—		(18.2)	288	—	
4,495.4	357	3,196.5	212	18,764.8	103	1.09	1,262.5	14.0	80	4.9	178	29.9	28
3,870.2	386	1,205.7	376	3,671.0	288	0.55	(14.1)	7.1	170	(43.0)	413	20.6	89
3,049.0	405	967.9	399	1,420.2	384	3.35	36.7	26.1	25	(7.2)	234	5.4	309
4,014.5	378	2,163.8	281	2,672.7	328	2.99	(3.5)	8.2	152	(34.4)	381	9.4	246
5,824.8	318	4,007.9	172	29,733.7	77	1.10	11.1	13.3	87	35.3	87	25.5	54
17,004.8	160	3,907.7	179	16,886.7	113	2.76	165.4	—		55.0	51	—	
5,165.6	376	1,293.2	365	2,976.4	313	1.53	(49.3)	(7.2)	302	(20.9)	301	7.0	289

RANK 1999	1998	COMPANY	REVENUES $ millions	% change from 1998	PROFITS $ millions	Rank	% change from 1998
301	299	**CENTRAL & SOUTH WEST** Dallas	5,536.6	1.0	454.6	216	3.3
302	291	**IKON OFFICE SOLUTIONS** Malvern, Pa.[11]	5,522.1	(1.9)	33.8	437	—
303	271	**DOMINION RESOURCES** Richmond[66]	5,520.0	(9.3)	296.0*	281	(44.7)
304	315	**GANNETT** Arlington, Va.	5,518.2	7.8	957.9	113	(4.2)
305	331	**MATTEL** El Segundo, Calif.	5,515.0	15.3	(82.4)	469	(124.8)
306	309	**PECO ENERGY** Philadelphia	5,436.8	4.3	582.4	173	13.6
307	296	**SEMPRA ENERGY** San Diego	5,435.0	(1.6)	394.0	239	34.0
308	282	**CENDANT** New York	5,402.0	(7.4)	(39.0)	459	(107.2)
309	312	**RYDER SYSTEM** Miami	5,363.9	3.4	419.6	230	163.7
310	409	**ROHM & HAAS** Philadelphia[67]	5,339.0	43.5	249.0	309	(43.4)
311	327	**STARWOOD HOTELS & RESORTS** White Plains, N.Y.	5,292.0[¶]	9.5	(741.0)	491	(159.0)
312	308	**AVON PRODUCTS** New York	5,289.1	1.5	302.4	275	12.0
313	347	**SCIENCE APPLICATIONS INTL.** San Diego[68,69]	5,280.1	—	612.0	166	—
314	289	**CHAMPION INTERNATIONAL** Stamford, Conn.	5,268.0	(6.8)	232.0	319	208.1
315	335	**COMPUTER ASSOCIATES INTL.** Islandia, N.Y.[18]	5,253.0	11.3	626.0	158	(46.5)
316	351	**NORFOLK SOUTHERN** Norfolk, Va.	5,195.0	17.3	239.0	317	(67.4)
317	343	**MERISEL** El Segundo, Calif.	5,188.7	14.0	(61.2)	463	(430.5)
318	385	**CENTEX** Dallas[18]	5,154.8	29.7	232.0	320	60.2
319	378	**OMNICOM GROUP** New York	5,130.5	25.4	362.9	248	27.3
320	318	**NORDSTROM** Seattle[2]	5,124.2	1.9	202.6	330	(2.0)
321	329	**FORTUNE BRANDS** Lincolnshire, Ill.	5,122.9[E]	6.8	(890.6)	493	(438.5)
322	352	**DOLE FOOD** Westlake Village, Calif.	5,060.6	14.4	48.5	426	301.9
323	319	**OWENS CORNING** Toledo	5,048.0	0.8	270.0	297	—
324	323	**AIR PRODUCTS & CHEMICALS** Allentown, Pa.[11]	5,039.8	2.1	450.5	218	(17.6)
325	415	**CLARK USA** St. Louis	5,005.6[E]	36.5	(23.9)	453	—

ASSETS		STOCKHOLDERS' EQUITY		MARKET VALUE 3/14/00		EARNINGS PER SHARE				TOTAL RETURN TO INVESTORS			
							% change from 1998	1989–99 annual growth rate		1999		1989–99 annual rate	
$ millions	Rank	$ millions	Rank	$ millions	Rank	1999 $		%	Rank	%	Rank	%	Rank
14,125.0	189	3,665.0	189	3,296.0	301	2.14	3.4	2.8	224	(21.4)	302	6.7	294
5,801.3	319	1,460.5	347	882.9	417	0.23	—	(19.3)	314	(19.3)	292	(5.2)	359
17,747.0	152	5,261.0	131	8,372.5	181	1.48	(46.2)	(6.0)	295	(10.8)	249	9.0	251
9,006.4	252	4,629.6	151	17,803.1	109	3.40	(2.9)	10.7	118	28.0	100	16.8	129
5,127.0	337	1,962.7	296	4,163.3	274	(0.21)	(119.1)	—		(43.3)	415	10.2	228
13,119.5	198	1,910.5	301	6,763.7	215	2.89	29.6	2.0	238	(14.6)	273	10.2	230
11,270.0	214	2,986.0	229	4,035.9	277	1.66	33.9	0.5	255	(26.5)	332	4.0	319
15,100.0	178	2,200.0	277	12,453.8	138	(0.05)	(108.2)	—		37.5	81	30.1	27
5,770.4	320	1,204.9	377	1,176.8	398	6.11	182.9	28.4	20	(3.7)	219	5.8	303
11,256.0	215	3,475.0	198	8,170.7	186	1.27	(48.2)	3.7	214	37.8	79	16.3	135
12,923.0	201	3,690.0	186	4,925.0	253	(3.96)	(161.2)	—		6.0	170	2.0	336
2,528.6	435	(406.1)	492	6,754.2	218	1.17	14.7	30.0	16	(24.2)	318	17.4	123
3,882.7	385	1,762.7	313	N.A.		N.A.	—	—		—		—	
8,318.0	264	3,095.0	218	4,732.7	255	2.41	209.0	(6.2)	297	53.6	56	7.9	278
8,070.0	271	2,729.0	250	34,797.8	71	1.11	(46.1)	14.4	77	64.3	40	34.7	20
19,250.0	146	5,932.0	112	4,879.2	254	0.63	(67.4)	(5.9)	294	(33.4)	378	7.4	284
805.8	497	95.2	485	195.7	457	(0.76)	(430.4)	—		(44.7)	420	(14.3)	365
4,334.7	361	1,197.6	379	1,068.2	404	3.75	58.9	19.0	47	(45.0)	423	13.1	176
9,015.0	250	1,550.0	337	14,831.3	123	2.01	19.6	16.1	58	73.9	27	35.0	19
3,265.1[70]	402	1,217.1[70]	375	2,796.5	325	1.46	3.5	7.6	165	(23.3)	315	4.6	317
6,417.1	308	2,738.2	248	3,570.9	293	(5.35)	(459.1)	—		7.2	165	8.2	272
3,037.7	407	531.9	455	757.3	426	0.85	325.0	(6.1)	296	(44.8)	421	(5.0)	357
6,494.0	306	(881.0)	497	825.6	423	4.67	—	1.4	249	(44.9)	422	(2.3)	352
8,235.5	267	2,961.6	230	5,704.0	235	2.09	(15.7)	7.5	166	(14.4)	271	13.1	177
1,533.0	474	(33.1)	488	N.A.		(1.63)	—	—		—		—	

RANK 1999	1998	COMPANY	REVENUES $ millions	% change from 1998	PROFITS $ millions	Rank	% change from 1998
326	322	**SHERWIN-WILLIAMS** Cleveland	5,003.8	1.4	303.9	274	11.4
327	338	**OLSTEN** Melville, N.Y.[43]	4,970.6	—	17.4	444	—
328	336	**PARKER HANNIFIN** Cleveland[13]	4,958.8	7.0	310.5	271	(2.8)
329	265	**BAKER HUGHES** Houston	4,936.5	(21.8)	33.3	438	—
330	284	**QUANTUM** Milpitas, Calif.[18]	4,902.1	(15.6)	(29.5)	455	(117.3)
331	382	**APPLIED MATERIALS** Santa Clara, Calif.[7]	4,859.1	20.2	746.6	136	223.4
332	358	**OFFICEMAX** Shaker Heights, Ohio[2]	4,842.7	11.6	10.0	448	(79.3)
333	353	**LITTON INDUSTRIES** Woodland Hills, Calif.[45]	4,827.5	9.7	120.6	389	(33.5)
334	412	**CORNING** Corning, N.Y.	4,812.5	30.5	515.8	193	30.9
335	281	**REYNOLDS METALS** Richmond	4,796.0	(18.1)	124.0	388	87.9
336	363	**INACOM** Omaha[43,71]	4,786.9	—	(124.2)	471	—
337	•	**AMERICA ONLINE** Dulles, Va.[13]	4,777.0	83.8	762.0	135	728.3
338	364	**GPU** Morristown, N.J.	4,757.1	12.0	459.0	211	27.5
339	371	**SOUTHWEST AIRLINES** Dallas	4,735.6	13.7	474.4	202	9.4
340	368	**DTE ENERGY** Detroit	4,728.0	12.0	483.0	201	9.0
341	325	**QUAKER OATS** Chicago	4,725.2	(2.4)	455.0	214	59.9
342	293	**RALSTON PURINA** St. Louis[11]	4,720.5	(15.4)	505.1	197	(54.3)
343	435	**CHARLES SCHWAB** San Francisco	4,713.2	39.1	588.9	171	69.0
344	369	**CONSOLIDATED STORES** Columbus, Ohio[2]	4,700.2	12.1	96.1	400	(0.7)
345	366	**STATE STREET CORP.** Boston	4,692.0	10.8	619.0	162	42.0
346	287	**VENATOR** New York[2]	4,647.0	(18.4)	48.0[33]	427	—
347	326	**PRAXAIR** Danbury, Conn.	4,639.0	(4.0)	431.0	225	1.4
348	220	**ITT INDUSTRIES** White Plains, N.Y.	4,632.2	(38.4)	232.9	318	(84.8)
349	401	**PPL** Allentown, Pa.[73]	4,590.0	21.2	432.0*	224	—
350	345	**EASTMAN CHEMICAL** Kingsport, Tenn.	4,590.0	2.4	48.0	427	(80.7)

ASSETS		STOCKHOLDERS' EQUITY		MARKET VALUE 3/14/00		EARNINGS PER SHARE					TOTAL RETURN TO INVESTORS			
							% change from 1998	1989–99 annual growth rate				1999		1989–99 annual rate	
$ millions	Rank	$ millions	Rank	$ millions	Rank	1999 $		%	Rank			%	Rank	%	Rank
4,052.1	377	1,698.5	320	3,116.5	307	1.80	14.6	11.1	108			(27.1)	338	11.2	213
2,185.5	449	785.0	422	843.6	422	N.A.	—	—				55.2	50	5.6	304
3,705.9	392	1,853.9	306	3,694.0	287	2.83	(0.7)	9.6	135			59.1	46	19.2	109
7,039.8	292	3,071.1	221	8,825.7	174	0.10	—	(17.2)	311			21.7	120	(0.1)	346
2,483.6	439	1,389.8	353	2,724.7	327	(0.18)	(116.8)	—				—		—	
6,706.5	299	4,336.6	160	68,953.5	38	1.89	209.8	25.7	27			196.8	5	53.2	8
2,275.0	447	1,116.0	388	668.5	434	0.09	(76.9)	—				(55.6)	441	—	
4,199.9	364	1,300.2	362	1,364.5	388	2.58	(32.5)	(3.1)	285			(23.6)	316	11.5	206
6,526.0	304	2,462.7	263	49,233.0	56	1.97	18.0	3.5	217			189.4	6	24.1	60
5,950.0	314	2,146.0	283	3,491.6	297	1.94	106.4	(14.4)	309			49.2	62	6.3	299
1,937.5	459	439.5	457	134.0	462	N.A.	—	—				(50.8)	431	(3.8)	356
5,348.0	328	3,033.0	226	140,899.2	14	0.60	585.7	—				95.6	21	—	
21,718.1	133	3,477.6	197	2,908.1	317	3.66	29.3	3.9	210			(28.8)	351	8.4	268
5,652.1	322	2,835.8	243	9,457.9	165	0.89	8.5	19.0	46			6.7	166	26.4	45
12,316.0	207	3,909.0	178	4,352.1	265	3.33	9.2	2.3	235			(22.5)	309	8.9	254
2,396.2[72]	443	219.8[72]	475	6,112.3	229	3.23	64.0	9.7	132			12.3	148	12.4	191
5,360.8	327	1,257.0	371	6,854.0	214	1.60	(52.7)	—				(12.0)	254	—	
29,299.1	106	2,273.9	270	39,981.9	65	0.70	64.7	41.1	9			36.3	85	56.7	6
2,186.8	448	1,300.1	364	1,357.6	389	0.85	(1.2)	—				(19.5)	293	20.7	87
60,896.0	58	2,652.0	256	10,582.8	154	3.78	42.1	18.2	50			5.0	176	23.9	64
2,515.0	436	1,139.0	382	944.6	413	0.35	—	(18.0)	312			7.7	163	(12.2)	364
7,722.0	279	2,290.0	269	5,348.0	246	2.66	2.3	—				44.6	67	—	
4,537.8	355	1,099.1	389	2,170.4	350	2.53	(81.3)	(9.0)	305			(14.5)	272	15.4	148
11,174.0	216	1,663.0	324	2,658.4	329	2.84	—	3.4	218			(14.9)	277	7.5	280
6,303.0	309	1,759.0	315	2,762.8	326	0.61	(80.5)	—				10.8	154	—	

RANK 1999	1998	COMPANY	REVENUES $ millions	% change from 1998	PROFITS $ millions	Rank	% change from 1998
351	387	**INTERPUBLIC GROUP** New York	4,561.5	14.9	321.9	265	3.9
352	414	**KOHL'S** Menomonee Falls, Wis.[2]	4,557.1	23.8	258.1	302	34.3
353	373	**PACIFIC LIFE INSURANCE** Newport Beach, Calif.	4,548.9	9.5	168.4	353	(10.2)
354	359	**PITNEY BOWES** Stamford, Conn.	4,547.5	4.9	636.2	153	10.4
355	357	**W.W. GRAINGER** Lake Forrest, Ill.	4,533.9	4.4	180.7	346	(24.2)
356	342	**BLACK & DECKER** Towson, Md.	4,520.5	(0.9)	300.3	276	—
357	360	**TRUSERV** Chicago[59]	4,502.3	4.0	N.A.		—
358	247	**SODEXHO MARRIOTT SERVICES** Gaithersburg, Md.[23]	4,502.0	(32.8)	51.0	424	(58.2)
359	443	**SUIZA FOODS** Dallas	4,482.0	35.0	109.7	391	(16.6)
360	403	**NORTHEAST UTILITIES** Berlin, Conn.	4,471.3	18.7	34.2	436	—
361	397	**MERITOR AUTOMOTIVE** Troy, Mich.[11]	4,450.0	16.0	194.0	336	32.0
362	•	**CRESTLINE CAPITAL** Bethesda, Md.[74]	4,447.1	—	39.9	432	—
363	324	**DOVER** New York	4,446.4	(8.8)	929.0	117	145.2
364	241	**CAREMARK RX** Birmingham, Ala.[75]	4,407.8[¶]	(37.1)	(143.4)	472	—
365	370	**ENGELHARD** Iselin, N.J.	4,404.9	5.5	197.5	334	5.5
366	384	**AMERICAN FAMILY INS. GROUP** Madison, Wis.	4,402.0	10.0	281.7	289	611.6
367	•	**MIDAMERICAN ENERGY HOLDINGS** Des Moines[76,77]	4,398.8	64.0	167.2*	355	31.7
368	379	**MAYTAG** Newton, Iowa	4,323.7	6.3	328.5	262	17.1
369	394	**THERMO ELECTRON** Waltham, Mass.	4,303.8[¶]	11.3	(174.6)	476	(196.0)
370	405	**GRAYBAR ELECTRIC** St. Louis	4,299.9	15.2	64.7	420	8.6
371	•	**EXPRESS SCRIPTS** Maryland Heights, Mo.	4,288.1	51.8	150.2	368	252.0
372	•	**AK STEEL HOLDING** Middletown, Ohio[78]	4,284.8	79.0	65.4*	419	(42.9)
373	389	**BRUNSWICK** Lake Forest, Ill.	4,283.8	8.6	37.9	434	(79.7)
374	377	**KELLY SERVICES** Troy, Mich.	4,269.1	4.3	85.1	407	0.5
375	402	**FLOWERS INDUSTRIES** Thomasville, Ga.	4,236.0	12.2	7.3	449	(82.6)

ASSETS		STOCKHOLDERS' EQUITY		MARKET VALUE 3/14/00		EARNINGS PER SHARE				TOTAL RETURN TO INVESTORS			
							% change from 1998	1989–99 annual growth rate		1999			1989–99 annual rate
$ millions	Rank	$ millions	Rank	$ millions	Rank	1999 $		%	Rank	%	Rank	%	Rank
8,727.3	256	1,628.1	327	10,931.0	149	1.11	0.5	12.2	95	45.8	65	28.5	33
2,914.7	414	1,685.5	322	13,592.2	131	1.55	31.4	—		17.5	132	—	
49,336.9	65	1,219.1	374	N.A.		N.A.	—	—		—		—	
8,222.7	270	1,625.6	328	12,407.6	139	12.34	13.6	11.4	104	(25.6)	328	17.8	118
2,564.8	434	1,532.6	338	4,248.9	269	1.92	(21.3)	5.8	187	16.4	137	13.0	178
4,012.7	379	801.1	420	2,812.0	323	3.40	—	20.9	40	(6.0)	231	12.3	193
1,348.1	481	163.0	480	N.A.		N.A.	—	—		—		—	
1,347.0	482	(494.0)	494	675.1	432	0.81	—	—		(52.8)	433	—	
2,658.9	429	584.0	447	1,164.0	400	3.13	(12.6)	—		(22.2)	307	—	
9,688.1	235	2,083.3	287	2,554.5	335	0.26	—	(18.1)	313	29.1	96	5.1	312
2,796.0	420	348.0	472	933.1	414	2.81	31.9	—		(5.9)	230	—	
964.9	493	400.7	464	284.9	453	1.91	—	—		41.0	72	—	
4,131.9	370	2,038.8	290	8,168.5	187	4.41	160.9	22.7	36	25.3	109	19.8	99
770.8	499	(1,281.5)	499	810.6	424	(0.74)	—	—		(3.6)	218	—	
2,904.0	415	764.4	424	1,644.3	370	1.47	14.0	—		(1.1)	205	15.0	153
9,768.6	240	3,401.6	205	N.A.		N.A.	—	—		—		—	
10,766.4	223	994.6	398	2,095.4	355	2.59	28.9	21.0	39	(2.8)	214	10.9	220
2,636.5	430	427.4	459	2,259.1	345	3.66	22.4	11.2	106	(21.8)	305	12.7	185
5,183.3	334	2,014.5	292	3,589.2	292	(1.13)	(205.6)	—		(11.4)	252	5.2	311
1,704.8	464	359.7	471	N.A.		10.82	1.3	17.0	54	—		—	
2,487.3	438	699.5	431	1,311.6	392	4.06	219.7	—		(4.7)	224	—	
5,201.5	330	1,277.8	367	1,021.5	406	0.56	(70.8)	—		(17.7)	284	—	
3,354.8	399	1,300.2	363	1,400.2	385	0.41	(78.2)	—		(8.1)	240	7.4	281
1,033.7	491	582.4	448	860.1	420	2.36	5.8	2.3	236	(18.0)	287	0.3	345
2,892.0	416	531.3	456	1,203.0	395	0.07	(83.7)	(15.5)	310	(31.5)	368	10.4	226

RANK 1999	1998	COMPANY	REVENUES $ millions	% change from 1998	PROFITS $ millions	Rank	% change from 1998
376	445	**HASBRO** Pawtucket, R.I.	4,232.3	28.1	189.0	340	(8.4)
377	422	**BJ'S WHOLESALE CLUB** Natick, Mass.[2]	4,206.2	18.4	111.1	390	77.9
378	334	**OXFORD HEALTH PLANS** Monroe, Conn.	4,197.8	(11.1)	319.9	266	—
379	399	**MUTUAL OF OMAHA INSURANCE** Omaha	4,191.6	9.7	101.1	396	10.7
380	455	**COMDISCO** Rosemont, Ill.[11]	4,159.0	28.2	48.0	427	(68.6)
381	•	**MEDTRONIC** Minneapolis[50]	4,134.1	58.7	468.4	205	2.4
382	330	**TANDY** Fort Worth	4,126.2	(13.8)	297.9	280	386.0
383	372	**NASH FINCH** Edina, Minn.	4,123.2	(0.9)	19.8	443	—
384	362	**LTV** Cleveland	4,120.0	(3.6)	(212.0)	481	—
385	456	**AUTOZONE** Memphis[23]	4,116.4	26.9	244.8	312	7.4
386	355	**FMC** Chicago	4,110.6	(6.1)	212.6	328	99.6
387	423	**SHAW INDUSTRIES** Dalton, Ga.	4,107.7	16.0	228.0	323	1,004.8
388	404	**PITTSTON** Glen Allen, Va.	4,089.2	9.1	34.7	435	(47.5)
389	398	**NIAGARA MOHAWK HOLDINGS** Syracuse, N.Y.[79]	4,084.2	6.7	(35.1)*	458	—
390	411	**WILLAMETTE INDUSTRIES** Portland, Ore.	4,078.0	10.2	260.5	300	192.7
391	383	**HEALTHSOUTH** Birmingham, Ala.	4,072.1	1.6	76.5*	411	64.3
392	484	**GOLDEN STATE BANCORP** San Francisco	4,071.1	34.5	323.2	264	30.4
393	406	**TEMPLE-INLAND** Diboll, Texas	4,063.0	8.6	99.2	397	53.8
394	•	**PROVIDIAN FINANCIAL** San Francisco	4,036.8	91.4	550.3	185	85.6
395	482	**UNITED AUTO GROUP** New York	4,022.5	20.3	27.5	440	—
396	434	**PETER KIEWIT SONS'** Omaha	4,012.6	17.9	164.9	356	21.3
397	374	**NUCOR** Charlotte, N.C.	4,009.3	(3.4)	244.6	313	(7.3)
398	361	**UNIVERSAL** Richmond[13]	4,004.9	(6.6)	127.3	384	(9.9)
399	•	**CLOROX** Oakland[13,80]	4,003.0	46.0	246.0	311	(17.4)
400	•	**ADAMS RESOURCES & ENERGY** Houston	3,995.5	102.4	6.4	450	172.9

ASSETS		STOCKHOLDERS' EQUITY		MARKET VALUE 3/14/00		EARNINGS PER SHARE				TOTAL RETURN TO INVESTORS			
							% change from	1989–99 annual growth rate		1999		1989–99 annual rate	
$ millions	Rank	$ millions	Rank	$ millions	Rank	1999 $	1998	%	Rank	%	Rank	%	Rank
4,463.3	359	1,879.0	304	2,810.3	324	0.93	(7.6)	7.2	168	(20.7)	300	14.1	170
1,073.4	490	577.4	449	2,233.5	348	1.47	79.3	—		57.6	48	—	
1,686.9	467	98.8	484	1,173.4	399	3.26	—	—		(14.7)	275	—	
13,979.0	192	1,507.4	341	N.A.		N.A.	—	—		—		—	
7,807.0	276	1,060.0	394	7,380.8	207	0.30	(67.7)	(5.8)	293	121.9	17	23.2	71
4,870.3	348	3,654.6	190	55,857.8	47	0.79	(17.7)	13.2	88	(1.5)	207	34.2	22
2,142.0	450	830.7	416	7,580.3	199	1.43	429.6	4.6	200	140.2	11	19.4	105
862.4	495	172.7	477	96.4	463	1.74	—	3.7	213	(53.3)	435	(9.2)	363
6,101.0	313	1,489.0	345	306.1	451	(2.15)	—	—		(26.5)	335	—	
3,284.8	401	1,323.8	357	3,117.9	306	1.63	10.1	—		(1.9)	209	—	
3,995.8	380	743.6	426	1,493.5	382	6.57	115.4	5.7	190	2.3	185	5.0	314
2,291.7	446	868.6	408	1,630.5	372	1.62	912.5	15.2	64	(35.7)	388	8.8	257
2,468.6	440	749.6	425	802.6	425	N.A.	—	—		—		—	
12,670.4	204	3,416.1	203	1,962.1	363	(0.19)	—	—		(13.6)	266	2.3	332
4,797.9	351	2,203.7	276	3,800.9	286	2.33	191.3	2.2	237	40.9	73	15.5	145
6,832.3	296	3,206.4	210	1,883.0	364	0.18	63.6	3.6	216	(65.2)	448	6.5	298
57,019.1	60	1,561.8	335	1,589.2	375	2.31	(24.0)	—		3.8	182	—	
16,186.0	168	1,927.0	300	2,467.4	336	1.78	54.8	(0.5)	264	13.3	143	9.0	252
14,340.9	188	1,332.5	356	9,367.5	166	3.78	85.3	—		21.7	119	—	
1,279.0	486	431.0	458	159.1	460	1.04	—	—		(2.7)	213	—	
1,599.5	472	837.5	415	N.A.		4.71	17.2	—		—		—	
3,729.8	389	2,262.2	272	4,177.0	273	2.80	(6.7)	15.2	63	28.0	99	14.5	160
1,823.1	462	539.0	453	422.8	445	3.80	(4.8)	9.1	142	(32.2)	374	7.2	287
4,132.0	369	1,570.0	334	7,072.8	212	1.03	(27.0)	6.3	181	(12.4)	258	20.4	94
293.0	500	36.0	487	49.0	466	1.51	174.5	13.1	89	49.7	61	10.7	223

RANK 1999	1998	COMPANY	REVENUES $ millions	% change from 1998	PROFITS $ millions	Rank	% change from 1998
401	407	**MCGRAW-HILL** New York	3,992.0	7.0	425.8	227	27.8
402	•	**COUNTRYWIDE CREDIT INDUSTRIES** Calabasas, Calif.[38]	3,976.4	59.4	385.4	240	11.7
403	350	**HERSHEY FOODS** Hershey, Pa.	3,970.9	(10.5)	460.3	210	35.0
404	462	**RICHFOOD HOLDINGS** Glen Allen, Va.[50,81]	3,968.2	23.9	73.0	414	33.5
405	•	**CAPITAL ONE FINANCIAL** Falls Church, Va.	3,965.8	52.5	363.1	247	31.9
406	418	**ESTÉE LAUDER** New York[13]	3,961.5	9.5	272.9	296	15.2
407	339	**FOSTER WHEELER** Clinton, N.J.	3,944.1	(14.2)	(143.6)	473	—
408	452	**CABLEVISION SYSTEMS** Bethpage, N.Y.	3,943.0	20.8	(800.6)	492	—
409	440	**QUALCOMM** San Diego[11]	3,937.3	17.6	200.9	331	85.1
410	•	**QWEST COMMUNICATIONS** Denver	3,927.6	75.1	458.5	212	—
411	392	**GENAMERICA** St. Louis[82]	3,919.5	0.1	(174.3)	475	(253.6)
412	346	**BETHLEHEM STEEL** Bethlehem, Pa.	3,914.8	(12.6)	(183.2)	478	(252.5)
413	490	**SHOPKO STORES** Green Bay, Wis.[2]	3,911.9	30.7	102.2	395	83.7
414	449	**DEAN FOODS** Franklin Park, III.[28]	3,894.9	19.1	151.2	367	42.3
415	459	**DOLLAR GENERAL** Goodlesville, Tenn.[2]	3,888.0	20.7	219.4	326	20.5
416	•	**AMES DEPARTMENT STORES** Rocky Hill, Conn.[2]	3,878.5	54.7	17.1	445	(49.4)
417	488	**BB&T CORP.** Winston-Salem, N.C.	3,877.1	28.8	612.8	165	22.1
418	317	**COOPER INDUSTRIES** Houston	3,868.9	(24.1)	331.9	261	(21.5)
419	447	**YORK INTERNATIONAL** York, Pa.	3,866.6	17.6	75.9	412	(44.4)
420	417	**FLORIDA PROGRESS** St. Petersburg	3,845.1	6.2	314.9	269	11.8
421	•	**KAUFMAN & BROAD HOME** Los Angeles[15]	3,836.3	56.6	147.5	371	54.8
422	428	**AUTOLIV** Ogden, Utah	3,812.2	9.3	199.9	332	6.2
423	340	**MEAD** Dayton	3,799.5	(17.0)	208.1	329	73.9
424	439	**CONSTELLATION ENERGY** Baltimore[83]	3,786.2	12.7	273.6*	295	(10.6)
425	•	**AMSOUTH BANCORP.** Birmingham, Ala.[84]	3,780.3	109.0	340.5	255	29.6

ASSETS		STOCKHOLDERS' EQUITY		MARKET VALUE 3/14/00		EARNINGS PER SHARE				TOTAL RETURN TO INVESTORS			
							% change from	1989–99 annual growth rate		1999		1989–99 annual rate	
$ millions	Rank	$ millions	Rank	$ millions	Rank	1999 $	1998	%	Rank	%	Rank	%	Rank
4,088.8	373	1,691.5	321	9,100.5	171	2.14	28.1	24.2	31	23.3	114	19.5	103
15,648.3	171	2,518.9	262	3,030.6	310	3.29	6.5	26.1	24	(49.2)	428	23.8	65
3,346.7	400	1,098.6	390	5,668.2	236	3.26	39.3	13.1	90	(22.3)	308	12.6	188
1,421.1	480	388.7	466	N.A.		1.53	33.0	—		—		—	
13,336.4	197	1,515.6	340	7,512.4	202	1.72	30.3	—		26.0	108	—	
2,746.7	425	924.5	403	9,623.3	160	1.03	15.7	—		18.5	127	—	
3,438.1	398	375.9	469	224.0	456	(3.53)	—	—		(29.0)	352	(5.7)	360
7,130.3	289	(3,067.1)	500	9,905.5	159	(5.12)	—	—		50.6	59	23.3	70
4,535.0	356	2,871.8	241	88,618.7	31	1.24	68.7	—		2,619.4	1	—	
11,058.1	219	7,001.3	86	39,971.3	66	0.60	—	—		72.0	29	—	
23,594.3	124	783.0	423	N.A.		N.A.	—	—		—		—	
5,536.2	323	1,277.1	368	868.1	419	(1.72)	(368.8)	—		0.0	196	(7.1)	361
2,083.3	452	694.5	432	518.6	439	3.57	70.0	—		(30.8)	364	—	
1,911.9	460	716.4	429	908.7	415	3.74	45.5	9.4	138	(0.4)	197	8.4	269
1,450.9	479	925.9	402	5,441.6	241	0.81	19.1	31.3	13	20.9	125	40.8	15
1,975.3	458	635.3	442	477.1	441	0.62	(55.7)	—		6.7	167	—	
43,481.0	70	3,199.2	211	7,409.9	205	1.83	7.0	4.8	197	(30.7)	362	14.2	166
4,143.4	367	1,743.1	317	2,896.6	319	3.50	(5.1)	3.4	219	(12.8)	261	3.5	323
2,874.5	417	731.9	427	745.7	428	1.91	(43.2)	—		(31.6)	369	—	
6,528.2	303	2,008.7	293	4,319.7	266	3.21	10.7	2.8	226	(0.7)	203	11.7	201
2,664.3	428	676.6	436	754.4	427	3.08	32.8	2.4	232	(14.7)	274	8.0	276
3,646.5	394	1,931.0	299	2,588.3	331	1.95	6.0	—		(20.3)	299	—	
5,661.7	321	2,430.8	265	3,026.7	311	1.99	74.6	1.8	242	50.9	58	11.6	204
9,683.8	236	2,993.0	228	4,421.3	263	1.74	(15.5)	(1.5)	273	(0.4)	199	8.8	256
43,406.6	71	2,959.2	231	4,990.0	252	0.86	(40.6)	5.3	193	(34.9)	383	20.0	98

RANK 1999	1998	COMPANY	REVENUES $ millions	% change from 1998	PROFITS $ millions	Rank	% change from 1998
426	436	**LEGGETT & PLATT** Carthage, Mo.	3,779.0	12.1	290.5	286	17.1
427	390	**HARRIS** Melbourne, Fla.[13]	3,775.9¶	(4.1)	53.1*	423	(60.1)
428	395	**SMITHFIELD FOODS** Smithfield, Va.[50]	3,775.0	(2.4)	94.9	402	77.7
429	430	**AVERY DENNISON** Pasadena	3,768.2	8.9	215.4	327	(3.5)
430	487	**MICRON TECHNOLOGY** Boise[23]	3,764.0	25.0	(68.9)	466	—
431	477	**CONECTIV** Wilmington, Del.	3,744.9	21.9	(198.1)	479*	(229.3)
432	•	**PULTE** Bloomfield Hills, Mich.	3,730.3	29.8	178.2	347	74.4
433	416	**SUPERMARKETS GENL. HOLDINGS** Carteret, N.J.[2]	3,698.1	1.2	(31.4)	456	—
434	•	**LYONDELL CHEMICAL** Houston	3,693.0	155.2	(115.0)*	470	(321.2)
435	450	**LONGS DRUG STORES** Walnut Creek, Calif.[2]	3,672.4	12.4	69.0	417	8.9
436	•	**FIFTH THIRD BANCORP** Cincinnati	3,615.0	36.2	668.0	151	40.3
437	466	**USG** Chicago	3,600.0	15.0	421.0	228	26.8
438	500	**BALL** Broomfield, Colo.	3,584.2	23.7	104.2	393	527.7
439	444	**AMEREN** St. Louis	3,523.6	6.2	385.1	241	(0.4)
440	433	**ALLMERICA FINANCIAL** Worcester, Mass.	3,512.2¶	2.3	295.8	282	47.0
441	438	**U.S. INDUSTRIES** Iselin, N.J.[11]	3,506.0	4.3	141.0	376	—
442	481	**FLEETWOOD ENTERPRISES** Riverside, Calif.[50]	3,490.2	14.4	107.1	392	(1.3)
443	489	**BARNES & NOBLE** New York[2]	3,486.0	16.0	124.5	386	34.8
444	391	**ALLEGHENY TECHNOLOGIES** Pittsburgh[85]	3,471.8¶	(11.5)	300.2**	277	24.5
445	442	**HANNAFORD BROS.** Scarborough, Me.	3,462.9	4.2	98.0	398	3.6
446	451	**INTERSTATE BAKERIES** Kansas City, Mo.[28]	3,459.4	5.9	126.2	385	(1.4)
447	448	**DARDEN RESTAURANTS** Orlando[28]	3,458.1	5.2	140.5	377	38.2
448	486	**LEXMARK INTERNATIONAL** Lexington, Ky.	3,452.3	14.3	318.5	267	31.1
449	•	**ARMSTRONG WORLD INDUSTRIES** Lancaster, Pa.	3,443.8	25.4	14.3	446	—
450	485	**WESCO INTERNATIONAL** Pittsburgh	3,420.1	13.0	24.6*	442	—

ASSETS		STOCKHOLDERS' EQUITY		MARKET VALUE 3/14/00		EARNINGS PER SHARE				TOTAL RETURN TO INVESTORS			
							% change from 1998	1989–99 annual growth rate %	Rank	1999 %	Rank	1989–99 annual rate %	Rank
$ millions	Rank	$ millions	Rank	$ millions	Rank	1999 $							
2,977.5	411	1,646.2	326	3,285.4	302	1.45	16.9	15.9	60	(1.0)	204	21.2	84
2,958.6	412	1,589.5	332	2,462.4	337	0.67	(59.6)	9.3	139	(12.9)	263	9.6	241
1,771.6	463	542.2	452	740.5	429	2.32	73.1	21.5	37	(29.2)	354	22.9	75
2,592.5	433	809.9	419	5,736.6	234	2.13	(0.9)	8.1	156	64.5	39	19.2	110
6,965.2	293	3,964.1	174	30,131.0	76	(0.26)	—	—		54.5	53	44.9	12
6,138.5	312	1,138.2	384	1,352.8	390	(2.02)	(234.7)	—		(27.6)	342	5.4	307
2,606.0	432	1,093.3	391	681.4	431	4.07	74.7	15.0	66	(18.5)	289	16.0	139
835.0	496	(1,163.0)	498	N.A.		N.A.	—	—		—		—	
9,498.0	242	1,007.0	397	1,322.7	391	(1.10)	(264.2)	—		(24.7)	325	1.7	340
1,270.3	487	702.7	430	651.7	435	1.76	7.3	1.6	243	(30.0)	358	4.2	318
41,589.0	75	4,077.0	169	14,961.7	121	2.15	22.2	14.6	71	4.3	181	28.5	34
2,773.0	423	867.0	409	1,539.1	380	8.39	26.9	—		(6.6)	233	—	
2,732.1	426	690.9	434	874.0	418	3.15	615.9	8.1	154	(12.7)	260	5.5	305
9,177.6	247	3,089.7	219	3,816.3	283	2.81	(0.4)	0.7	252	(17.7)	285	8.2	273
30,769.6	99	2,240.2	273	2,117.2	353	5.33	60.1	—		(3.5)	217	—	
3,028.0	408	920.0	404	962.8	411	1.51	—	—		(22.9)	311	—	
1,531.2	475	586.7	446	471.7	442	2.94	(2.3)	6.7	177	(38.8)	402	8.3	271
2,413.8	442	846.4	412	1,162.8	401	1.75	35.7	—		(51.5)	432	—	
2,750.6	424	1,200.2	378	1,570.1	379	3.13	28.3	(2.3)	281	(42.5)	410	1.1	341
1,330.0	483	727.2	428	2,971.6	314	2.28	3.2	8.5	150	32.3	93	17.1	124
1,680.8	470	603.8	444	957.0	412	1.74	1.8	—		(30.6)	361	—	
1,905.7	461	964.0	400	1,641.8	371	0.99	47.8	—		1.1	190	—	
1,702.6	466	659.1	438	15,951.0	117	2.32	36.5	—		80.1	25	—	
4,164.5	366	679.2	435	671.1	433	0.36	—	(21.2)	316	(42.3)	409	2.2	334
1,028.8	492	117.3	483	375.5	448	0.53	—	—		—		—	

RANK 1999	1998	COMPANY	REVENUES $ millions	% change from 1998	PROFITS $ millions	Rank	% change from 1998
451	468	**BECTON DICKINSON** Franklin Lakes, N.J.[11]	**3,418.4**	**9.7**	**275.7**	294	**16.5**
452	480	**UNITED STATIONERS** Des Plaines, Ill.	**3,393.0**	**10.9**	**83.4**	409	**43.8**
453	476	**REGIONS FINANCIAL** Birmingham, Ala.	**3,391.8**	**10.4**	**525.4**	189	**24.6**
454	295	**LG&E ENERGY** Louisville	**3,390.7**[1]	**(38.7)**	**62.1**	421	**—**
455	460	**COMERICA** Detroit	**3,389.6**	**5.3**	**672.6**	150	**10.8**
456	419	**NEW CENTURY ENERGIES** Denver	**3,375.4**	**(6.5)**	**346.6**	253	**1.4**
457	461	**AID ASSOCIATION FOR LUTHERANS** Appleton, Wis.	**3,366.2**	**4.6**	**255.5**	305	**91.2**
458	453	**HORMEL FOODS** Austin, Minn.[7]	**3,357.8**	**3.0**	**163.4**	358	**17.3**
459	465	**CAROLINA POWER & LIGHT** Raleigh	**3,357.6**	**7.3**	**382.3**	242	**(4.3)**
460	•	**SONIC AUTOMOTIVE** Charlotte, N.C.	**3,350.8**	**108.9**	**44.6**	431	**140.6**
461	493	**SOUTHTRUST CORP.** Birmingham, Ala.	**3,350.0**	**13.8**	**443.2**	220	**20.2**
462	•	**ALLIED WASTE INDUSTRIES** Scottsdale, Ariz.[86]	**3,341.1**	**112.0**	**(288.7)**[10]	486	**—**
463	•	**AMGEN** Thousand Oaks, Calif.	**3,340.1**	**22.9**	**1,096.4**	99	**27.0**
464	381	**AMERICAN FINANCIAL GROUP** Cincinnati	**3,334.5**	**(17.7)**	**141.4**	375	**13.7**
465	•	**AVIS RENT A CAR** Garden City, N.Y.	**3,332.7**	**45.1**	**92.6**	403	**45.8**
466	•	**NEXTEL COMMUNICATIONS** Reston, Va.	**3,326.0**	**80.1**	**(1,338.0)**	496	**—**
467	•	**SERVICE CORP. INTERNATIONAL** Houston	**3,321.8**	**15.5**	**(32.4)**	457	**(109.5)**
468	454	**TRANS WORLD AIRLINES** St. Louis	**3,308.7**	**1.5**	**(353.4)**	489	**—**
469	219	**TENNECO AUTOMOTIVE** Lake Forest, Ill.[87]	**3,279.0**[22]	**(56.9)**	**(63.0)**	464	**(124.7)**
470	478	**SLM HOLDING** Reston, Va.	**3,259.4**	**6.4**	**500.8**	199	**(0.1)**
471	•	**AES** Arlington, Va.	**3,253.0**	**35.7**	**228.0***	322	**(26.7)**
472	•	**HERCULES** Wilmington, Del.	**3,248.0**	**51.4**	**168.0**	354	**1,766.7**
473	•	**USA NETWORKS** New York	**3,235.8**	**22.8**	**(27.6)**	454	**(135.9)**
474	472	**KNIGHT-RIDDER** San Jose	**3,228.2**	**4.1**	**339.9**	256	**(7.1)**
475	469	**YELLOW** Overland Park, Kans.	**3,226.8**	**3.7**	**50.9**	425	**—**

ASSETS		STOCKHOLDERS' EQUITY		MARKET VALUE 3/14/00		EARNINGS PER SHARE				TOTAL RETURN TO INVESTORS			
							% change from	1989–99 annual growth rate		1999		1989–99 annual rate	
$ millions	Rank	$ millions	Rank	$ millions	Rank	1999 $	1998	%	Rank	%	Rank	%	Rank
4,437.0	360	1,768.7	312	7,452.8	204	1.04	15.6	4.4	204	(36.3)	390	14.9	154
1,279.9	485	406.0	462	1,019.8	407	2.37	48.1	19.5	43	9.9	159	23.9	63
42,714.4	73	3,065.1	222	4,274.8	268	12.35	25.0	10.5	120	(35.9)	389	16.1	137
5,188.1[72]	333	1,318.6[72]	358	2,836.7	321	0.48	—	(7.7)	304	(35.0)	384	8.4	270
38,653.3	82	3,474.6	199	5,360.7	244	4.14	11.3	14.9	68	(29.9)	356	20.2	95
8,322.0	263	2,732.7	249	3,005.3	312	3.01	(1.3)	1.5	245	(33.6)	379	8.6	265
20,800.4	142	1,756.1	316	N.A.		N.A.	—	—		—		—	
1,685.6	468	841.1	413	2,015.0	360	2.22	20.0	9.3	140	26.2	107	11.4	207
9,494.0	243	3,472.0	200	4,628.4	259	2.55	(7.3)	2.0	240	(32.0)	372	8.8	259
1,500.0	476	402.6	463	350.2	449	1.27	71.6	—		(43.5)	418	—	
43,262.5	72	2,927.4	235	3,526.0	296	2.63	16.9	12.5	93	4.7	179	22.8	76
14,995.4	180	638.0	441	1,016.2	408	(1.69)	—	—		(62.7)	445	—	
4,077.6	375	3,023.5	227	53,480.2	50	1.02	24.8	—		129.8	13	50.3	10
16,047.6	169	1,340.0	355	1,179.4	397	2.35	17.5	(0.5)	265	(38.1)	398	3.4	326
11,065.8	218	661.7	437	470.8	443	2.61	43.4	—		5.7	173	—	
18,410.0	148	2,574.0	261	53,657.7	49	(4.79)	—	—		336.5	2	—	
14,800.0	182	3,500.0	195	901.9	416	(0.12)	(109.2)	—		(81.3)	454	4.8	315
2,137.2	451	(170.9)	491	146.2	461	(5.58)	—	—		(43.6)	419	—	
2,943.0	413	422.0	460	244.1	454	(1.87)	(124.8)	—		(84.5)	455	(17.8)	366
44,024.8	67	840.9	414	4,638.7	258	3.06	3.7	15.5	61	(10.8)	248	14.2	167
20,880.0	141	2,637.0	257	14,863.8	122	1.16	(31.4)	—		57.8	47	—	
5,896.0	316	863.0	410	1,629.1	373	1.62	1,520.0	—		6.1	169	11.6	203
9,253.2	246	2,769.7	246	6,756.2	217	(0.08)	(137.2)	—		66.8	37	—	
4,192.3	365	1,780.7	311	3,901.0	281	3.49	(6.4)	4.0	208	18.5	128	9.9	236
1,325.6	484	409.4	461	409.0	446	2.02	—	2.0	239	(12.1)	255	(2.6)	353

RANK 1999	1998	COMPANY	REVENUES $ millions	% change from 1998	PROFITS $ millions	Rank	% change from 1998
476	491	**TRIBUNE** Chicago	3,221.9	8.1	1,480.0	69	257.3
477	446	**TIMES MIRROR** Los Angeles	3,215.8	(2.3)	259.1	301	(81.7)
478	498	**DANAHER** Washington, D.C.	3,197.2	9.9	261.6	299	43.0
479	432	**PHOENIX HOME LIFE MUTUAL INS.** Hartford	3,193.0[1]	(7.0)	88.9	406	(28.8)
480	257	**COLUMBIA ENERGY GROUP** Herndon, Va.	3,189.2[22]	(51.3)	249.2	308	(7.4)
481	474	**OWENS & MINOR** Glen Allen, Va.	3,186.4	3.4	28.0	439	38.9
482	467	**ACE HARDWARE** Oak Brook, Ill.[59]	3,181.8	2.0	N.A.		—
483	•	**PLAINS RESOURCES** Houston[43]	3,177.0	—	(50.8)	462	—
484	•	**PARK PLACE ENTERTAINMENT** Las Vegas[88]	3,176.0	—	136.0	382	—
485	•	**INTERIM SERVICES** Fort Lauderdale[89]	3,168.0	67.6	70.8	415	26.9
486	437	**RELIANCE GROUP HOLDINGS** New York	3,153.3	(6.4)	(310.5)	488	(195.1)
487	•	**JONES APPAREL GROUP** Bristol, Pa.[90]	3,150.7	87.0	188.4	341	21.7
488	497	**NISOURCE** Merrillville, Ind.[91]	3,144.6	7.2	160.4	360	(17.3)
489	475	**AIRBORNE FREIGHT** Seattle	3,140.2	2.1	91.2	404	(33.6)
490	495	**NEW YORK TIMES** New York	3,130.6	6.6	310.2	272	11.2
491	•	**D.R. HORTON** Arlington, Texas[11]	3,119.0	44.7	159.8	362	71.2
492	•	**LENNAR** Miami[15]	3,118.5	29.0	172.7	351	19.9
493	479	**PHELPS DODGE** Phoenix[92]	3,114.4	1.7	(257.8)	485	(235.0)
494	•	**ARVIN INDUSTRIES** Columbus, Ind.	3,100.5	24.1	91.1	405	16.2
495	•	**MOHAWK INDUSTRIES** Calhoun, Ga.	3,083.3	16.8	157.2	363	46.1
496	421	**CONSOLIDATED NATURAL GAS** Pittsburgh[93]	3,074.4	(13.5)	136.8	381	(42.7)
497	•	**BUDGET GROUP** Daytona Beach, Fla.	3,072.5[1]	17.4	(64.5)	465	—
498	•	**TESORO PETROLEUM** San Antonio	3,065.7[E]	105.7	75.0	413	—
499	•	**TRANSMONTAIGNE** Denver[13,94]	3,047.1	—	1.9	452	—
500	•	**RELIASTAR FINANCIAL** Minneapolis	3,037.3	5.9	253.6	306	6.7
		TOTALS	6,324,961.9		409,583.6		

ASSETS		STOCKHOLDERS' EQUITY		MARKET VALUE 3/14/00		EARNINGS PER SHARE				TOTAL RETURN TO INVESTORS			
							% change from 1998	1989–99 annual growth rate %	Rank	1999 %	Rank	1989–99 annual rate %	Rank
$ millions	Rank	$ millions	Rank	$ millions	Rank	1999 $							
8,797.7	255	3,469.9	201	7,941.1	195	6.84	354.5	24.1	33	68.3	34	18.6	113
3,897.4	384	399.7	465	5,271.9	247	3.38	(79.0)	—		21.2	123	—	
3,047.1	406	1,708.8	319	5,350.4	245	1.79	35.6	10.8	113	(11.1)	250	29.1	32
20,283.1	145	1,761.3	314	N.A.		N.A.	—	—		—		—	
7,095.9	290	2,064.0	289	4,126.4	276	3.01	(6.2)	—		11.2	151	—	
865.0	494	182.4	476	346.7	450	0.82	46.4	24.9	28	(41.9)	408	10.6	224
1,081.5	489	280.0	473	N.A.		N.A.	—	—		—		—	
1,556.7	473	88.6	486	239.6	455	N.A.	—	—		(11.1)	251	7.7	279
11,000.0	220	3,700.0	184	3,163.1	305	0.44	—	—		96.1	20	—	
2,438.9	441	1,159.3	381	1,645.4	369	1.27	3.3	—		5.9	171	—	
14,615.5	184	1,018.3	395	387.6	44/	(2.72)	(200.0)	—		(46.1)	425	7.4	282
2,792.0	421	1,241.0	373	3,033.8	309	1.60	8.8	—		22.9	117	—	
6,835.2	295	1,353.5	354	1,854.3	365	1.27	(20.1)	9.8	129	(38.8)	401	11.3	208
1,643.3	471	858.2	411	858.1	421	1.85	(32.0)	10.7	115	(38.6)	400	10.8	221
3,495.8	396	1,448.7	348	7,229.0	210	1.73	19.3	0.2	258	43.2	68	16.2	136
2,361.8	444	797.6	421	702.9	430	2.50	60.3	—		(39.5)	403	—	
2,057.6	454	881.5	407	977.3	410	2.74	10.0	11.4	103	(35.5)	387	21.1	85
8,229.0	268	3,276.8	208	3,556.3	295	(4.19)	(228.5)	—		37.3	82	12.5	190
2,000.0	456	594.3	445	452.5	444	3.72	15.2	19.4	44	(30.1)	359	9.3	248
1,682.9	469	692.5	433	1,229.6	394	2.61	40.3	—		(37.3)	393	—	
6,535.2	302	2,376.3	267	N.A.		1.42	(43.0)	(4.3)	287	24.2	112	6.9	291
5,083.0	339	568.0	450	176.7	458	(1.77)	—	—		(42.9)	412	—	
1,486.5	477	623.1	443	301.7	452	1.92	—	—		(4.6)	223	2.3	333
1,095.5	488	376.1	468	174.0	459	(0.01)	—	—		(53.7)	436	—	
24,926.9	118	1,945.7	298	2,249.7	347	2.85	11.3	10.7	117	(13.5)	265	18.5	114
,026,616.7		2,502,934.4		10,597,750.3									

Definitions and Explanations

■ **REVENUES** All companies on the list must publish financial data and must report part or all of their figures to a government agency. Private companies and cooperatives that produce a 10-K are, therefore, included; subsidiaries of foreign companies incorporated in the U.S. are excluded. Revenues are as reported, including revenues from discontinued operations when they are published on a consolidated basis (except when the divested company's revenues equal 50% or more of the surviving company's revenues on an annualized basis). The revenues for commercial banks and savings institutions are interest and noninterest revenues. Such figures for insurance companies include premium and annuity income, investment income and capital gains or losses, but exclude deposits. Revenue figures for all companies include consolidated subsidiaries and exclude excise taxes. Data shown are for the fiscal year ended on or before Jan. 31, 2000. All figures are for the year ended Dec. 31, 1999, unless otherwise noted.

■ **PROFITS** Profits are shown after taxes, after extraordinary credits or charges if any appear on the income statement and after cumulative effects of accounting changes. Figures in parentheses indicate a loss. Profit declines over 100% reflect swings from 1998 profits to 1999 losses. Profits for real estate investment trusts are reported but may not be comparable with those of most companies on the list, because REITs are not taxed at the corporate level. Cooperatives provide only net margin figures, which are not comparable with the profit figures in these listings, and therefore N.A. (not available) is shown in that column. Profits for mutual insurance companies are based on statutory accounting.

■ **ASSETS** Assets shown are company's year-end total.

■ **STOCKHOLDERS' EQUITY** Stockholders' equity is the sum of all capital stock, paid-in capital and retained earnings at the company's year-end. Redeemable preferred stock whose redemption is either mandatory or outside the control of the company is excluded. Dividends paid on such stock have been subtracted from the profit figures used in calculating the return on equity.

■ **MARKET VALUE** The figure shown was arrived at by multiplying the number of common shares outstanding by the price per common share as of March 14, 2000. If companies have more than one class of shares outstanding and an equivalency share number is not available, the respective market values for each share class are calculated and combined.

■ **EARNINGS PER SHARE** The figures shown for each company are diluted earnings per share that appear on the income statement. The reporting of diluted EPS began on Dec. 15, 1997, when the Financial Accounting Standards Board began to implement standard 128, requiring companies to change the way they report earnings per share. The 1994 and 1989 figures used for the five-year and ten-year earnings growth calculations, respectively, are primary earnings per share. Per share earnings for 1998, 1994 and 1989 are adjusted for stock splits and stock dividends. They are not restated for mergers, acquisitions or accounting changes (other than FASB 128). Though earnings per share numbers are not marked by footnotes, if a company's profits are footnoted it can be assumed that earnings per share are affected as well. Results are listed as not available (N.A.) if the companies are cooperatives, if the figures were not published or if the stock traded on a limited basis or was not widely held. The five-year and ten-year earnings growth rates are the annual rates, compounded.

■ **TOTAL RETURN TO INVESTORS** Total return to investors includes both price appreciation and dividend yield to an investor in the company's stock. The figures shown assume sales at the end of 1999 of stock owned at the end of 1989, 1994 and 1998, respectively. It has been assumed that any proceeds from cash dividends and stock received in spinoffs were reinvested when they were paid. Returns are adjusted for stock splits, stock dividends, recapitalizations and corporate reorganizations as they occur; however, no effort has been made to reflect the cost of brokerage commissions or of taxes. Results are listed as not available (N.A.) if shares are not publicly traded or are traded on a limited basis. If companies have more than one class of shares outstanding, only the most widely held and actively traded has been considered. Total return percentages shown are the returns received by the hypothetical investor described above. The five-year and ten-year returns are the annual rates, compounded.

Footnotes to the 2000 FORTUNE 500

N.A. Not available.

* Reflects an extraordinary charge of at least 10%.
** Reflects an extraordinary credit of at least 10%.
E Excise taxes have been deducted.
¶ Includes revenues of discontinued operations of at least 10%.

■ 1–9

[1] Includes discontinued operations of Delphi Automotive Systems.
[2] Figures are for fiscal year ended Jan. 31, 2000.
[3] Name changed from Exxon after acquiring Mobil (1998 rank: 12), Nov. 30, 1999
[4] Spun off Associates First Capital (1999 rank: 147), April 7, 1998.
[5] Name changed from BankAmerica Corp., April 28, 1999.
[6] Acquired Ameritech (1998 rank: 87), Oct. 8, 1999.
[7] Figures are for fiscal year ended Oct. 31, 1999.
[8] Acquired Fred Meyer (1998 rank: 104), May 27, 1999.
[9] Changed fiscal year-end from Dec. 31.

■ 10–19

[10] Reflects charge from cumulative effect of change in accounting of at least 10%.
[11] Figures are for fiscal year ended Sept 30, 1999.
[12] Acquired Ascend Communications (1998 rank: 846), June 24, 1999.
[13] Figures are for fiscal year ended June 30, 1999.
[14] Acquired American Stores (1998 rank: 67), June 23, 1999.
[15] Figures are for fiscal year ended Nov. 30, 1999.
[16] Name changed from Dayton Hudson, Jan. 30, 2000.
[17] Acquired General Instrument (1998 rank: 660), Jan. 6, 2000.
[18] Figures are for fiscal year ended March 31, 1999.
[19] Acquired Randall's Food Markets (1999 rank: 558), Sept. 11, 1999.

■ 20–29

[20] Acquired Pioneer Hi-Bred (1998 rank: 713), Oct. 1, 1999.
[21] Spun off Conoco (1999 rank: 74), Aug. 12, 1999.
[22] Excludes revenues from discontinued operations.
[23] Figures are for fiscal year ended Aug. 31, 1999.
[24] Name changed from Costco Cos., Aug. 30, 1999.
[25] Figures do not include GenAmerica (1999 rank: 411), acquired Jan. 6, 2000.
[26] Acquired Sundstrand (1998 rank: 652), June 10, 1999.
[27] Acquired Allegiance Corp. (1998 rank: 341), Feb. 3, 1999.
[28] Figures are for fiscal year ended May 31, 1999.
[29] Acquired Union Camp (1998 rank: 344), April 30, 1999.

■ 30–39

[30] Name changed from Republic Industries, April 6, 1999.
[31] Name changed from AlliedSignal after acquiring Honeywell (1998 rank: 193), Dec. 1, 1999.
[32] Figures do not include Pittway (1999 rank: 824), acquired Feb. 15, 2000.
[33] Reflects credit from cumulative effect of change in accounting of at least 10%.
[34] Spun off from Du Pont (1999 rank: 42), Aug. 12, 1999.
[35] Name changed from Fleet Financial after acquiring BankBoston Corp. (1998 rank: 218), Oct. 1, 1999.

[36] Name changed from United HealthCare, March 6, 2000.
[37] Acquired Unisource Worldwide (1998 rank: 225), July 6, 1999.
[38] Figures are for fiscal year ended Feb. 28, 1999.
[39] Acquired Richfood Holdings (1999 rank: 404), Aug. 31, 1999.

■ 40–49

[40] Name changed from FDX, Jan. 19, 2000.
[41] Figures do not include Illinova (1999 rank: 580), acquired Feb. 2, 2000.
[42] Name changed from Houston Industries, May 5, 1999.
[43] Figures are for the four quarters ended Sept. 30, 1999.
[44] Employee figure in industry listing as of Dec. 31, 1998.
[45] Figures are for fiscal year ended July 31, 1999.
[46] Spun off from Ford Motor (1999 rank: 4), April 7, 1998.
[47] Spun off from Nabisco Group Holdings (1999 rank: 219), June 15, 1999.
[48] Acquired Sonat (1998 rank: 410), Oct. 25, 1999.
[49] Acquired Premark International (1998 rank: 516), Nov. 23, 1999.

■ 50–59

[50] Figures are for fiscal year ended April 30, 1999.
[51] Name changed from Provident Cos. after acquiring Unum (1998 rank: 337), June 30, 1999.
[52] Acquired Gulfstream Aerospace (1998 rank: 568), July 30, 1999.
[53] Name changed from Gateway 2000, June 1, 1999.
[54] Acquired Aeroquip-Vickers (1998 rank: 621), April 9, 1999.
[55] Name changed from RJR Nabisco Holdings Corp. after spinning off R.J. Reynolds Tobacco Holdings (1999 rank: 155), June 15, 1999.
[56] Name changed from PNC Bank Corp., Mar. 7, 2000.
[57] Converted from a mutual to a stock company and changed name from John Hancock Mutual Life, Jan. 27, 2000.
[58] Acquired Data General (1998 rank: 850), Oct. 12, 1999.
[59] Cooperatives provide only net margin figures, which are not comparable with the profit figures on the list.

■ 60–69

[60] Acquired Mercantile Bancorp. (1998 rank: 496), Sept. 17, 1999.
[61] Figures do not include Marshall Industries (1999 rank: 775), acquired Oct. 20, 1999.
[62] Acquired by Gruopo Sanborns (Mexico), March 1, 2000.
[63] Name changed from Mellon Bank Corp., Oct. 19, 1999.
[64] Name changed from KN Energy, Oct. 7, 1999.
[65] Acquired Coltec Industries (1998 rank: 833), July 12, 1999.
[66] Figures do not include Consolidated Natural Gas (1999 rank: 496), acquired Jan. 28, 2000.
[67] Acquired Morton International (1998 rank: 544), June 21, 1999.
[68] Figures are for the four quarters ended Oct. 31, 1999.
[69] Employee figure in industry listing as of Jan. 31, 1999.

■ 70–79

[70] Figure as of Oct. 31, 1999.
[71] Employee figure in industry listing as of Feb. 17, 1999.
[72] Figure as of Sept. 30, 1999.
[73] Name changed from PP&L Resources, Feb. 14, 2000.
[74] Spun off from Host Marriott (1999 rank: 909), Dec. 29, 1999.
[75] Name changed from MedPartners, Sept. 13, 1999.
[76] Name changed from CalEnergy, March 12, 1999.
[77] Became a private company after acquisition by an investor

group including Berkshire Hathaway (1999 rank: 64), March 15, 2000.

[78] Acquired ARMCO (1998 rank: 756), Sept. 30, 1999.

[79] Name changed from Niagara Mohawk Power, March 18, 1999.

■ 80–89

[80] Acquired First Brands Corp. (1998 rank 965), Jan. 29, 1999.

[81] Acquired by Supervalu (1999 rank: 99), Aug. 31, 1999.

[82] Acquired by Metropolitan Life Insurance Co. (1999 rank; 53), Jan. 6, 2000.

[83] Name changed from Baltimore Gas & Electric, April 16, 1999.

[84] Acquired First American Corp. (1998 rank: 706), Oct. 1, 1999.

[85] Name changed from Allegheny Teledyne, Nov. 30, 1999.

[86] Acquired Browning-Ferris Industries (1998 rank: 332), Aug. 2, 1999.

[87] Name changed from Tenneco Inc., Nov. 4, 1999, after spinning off Pactiv (1999 rank: 514).

[88] Spun off from Hilton Hotels (1999 rank: 644), Dec. 31, 1998.

[89] Acquired Norrell (1998 rank: 872), July 2, 1999.

■ 90–94

[90] Acquired Nine West Group (1998 rank: 679), June 18, 1999.

[91] Name changed from Nipsco Industries, April 14, 1999.

[92] Acquired Cyprus Amax (1998 rank: 547), Oct. 16, 1999.

[93] Acquired by Dominion Resources (1999 rank: 303), Jan. 28, 2000.

[94] Changed fiscal year-end from April 30.

UNICOM	254	USG	437	WASHINGTON MUTUAL	127
UNION CARBIDE	292	U.S. INDUSTRIES	441	WASTE MANAGEMENT	133
UNION PACIFIC	156	US WEST	134	WELLPOINT HEALTH NTWKS.	239
UNISYS	236	USX	51	WELLS FARGO	68
UNITED AUTO GROUP	395	UTILICORP UNITED	90	WESCO INTERNATIONAL	450
UNITEDHEALTH GROUP	86			WEYERHAEUSER	145
UNITED PARCEL SERVICE	46	**V**		WHIRLPOOL	164
UNITED STATIONERS	452	VALERO ENERGY CORP.	229	WILLAMETTE INDUSTRIES	390
UNITED TECHNOLOGIES	57	VENATOR	346	WILLIAMS	215
UNIVERSAL	398	VF	297	WINN-DIXIE STORES	123
UNOCAL	282	VIACOM	141		
UNUMPROVIDENT	184			**X**	
USAA	217	**W**		XEROX	87
US AIRWAYS GROUP	208	WACHOVIA CORP.	277		
USA NETWORKS	473	WALGREEN	95	**Y**	
U.S. BANCORP	212	WAL-MART STORES	2	YELLOW	475
U.S. FOODSERVICE	281	WARNER-LAMBERT	139	YORK INTERNATIONAL	419